What Causes Blue Moods?

If you suffer from periodic bouts of depressed moods, you are in the company of *many other women!* The causes of blue moods are not always readily apparent to those who suffer from them, but the reasons most frequently cited in a nationwide survey of 1,000 women were:

- Too many demands on my time
- Feeling tired
- Feeling drained by the needs of others
- Worrying about the future
- Feeling angry
- Feeling misunderstood
- Having problems at work
- Feeling bad about myself
- Feeling lonely
- Having problems with my family
- Having problems with a man
- Feeling sexually frustrated

Wouldn't you like to gain control of your depressed moods so that they become less frequent, briefer in duration, and less disruptive to your life? That is exactly what *GETTING UP WHEN YOU'RE FEELING DOWN* will help you to do!

———————

"Upbeat . . . addressed in particular to women who attempt to excel in every sphere."

—*Publishers Weekly*

"Upbeat . . . *GETTING UP WHEN YOU'RE FEELING DOWN* puts women back in control, offering them both the method and the motivation for feeling good about themselves and their lives."

—*Beverly Hills Today*

GETTING UP WHEN YOU'RE FEELING DOWN

A Woman's Guide to Overcoming and Preventing Depression

Harriet B. Braiker, Ph.D.

POCKET BOOKS

New York   London   Toronto   Sydney   Tokyo

POCKET BOOKS, a division of Simon & Schuster Inc.
1230 Avenue of the Americas, New York, NY 10020

Published by arrangement with G. P. Putnam's Sons
Library of Congress Catalog and Card Number: 88-11484

ISBN 0-671-68327-6

First Pocket Books printing January 1990

10 9 8 7 6 5 4 3 2 1

POCKET and colophon are registered trademarks
of Simon & Schuster Inc.

Printed in the U.S.A.

For my husband,
Steven,
antidepressant extraordinaire

Special thanks are owed to many people who have taught, believed in, and supported me over the years.

To my patients, first, whose efforts and success reconfirm daily my abiding faith in the human spirit to conquer adversity and psychological pain. I am indebted to them for their trust and commitment to me. I am deeply grateful to my dear friend and esteemed colleague Dr. Kay Jamison, for her assistance on this project and for helping me to understand the suffering that is Depression. Dr. Harvey Sternbach has been an ongoing source of information and support with respect both to this project and to his capable and conscientious psychiatric care of our shared patients.

I am grateful to Kathryn Cordes and to No Nonsense Fashions, Inc., for their interest and corporate support of the Gallup survey on women's attitude and experiences with blue moods, the results of which are detailed herein. And to my assistant and secretary, Frederick McSpadden, without whose dedication and skills this manuscript would not have materialized, I express my appreciation.

I also wish to thank Christine Schillig, my editor, for her belief in this project from the beginning, as well as my agent, Sterling Lord, for his continued help. Deepest thanks are owed to Julia Kagen and Anne Mollegen Smith of *Working Woman* for their consistent support.

And to my mother and father I extend my love and perpetual gratitude. You have never let me down.

Contents

Contents

Introduction

◆

Every woman I know occasionally feels down or blue. During these periods, her self-esteem takes a dive, her energy plummets, and her characteristic enthusiasm for living retreats into mental hibernation. Everyday molehills turn into insurmountable mountains as her patience strains and her ability to cope with things or people that bother her is lowered.

Sometimes she can explain—to herself or to others—why she feels so low; other times, though, the reasons elude her, as the depressed mood seems to arise from some black hole within, over which she senses she has little or no control. Either way, her depression feels unpleasant, inconvenient, and unacceptable. She may feel guilty for being down when so many people need and depend on her, and she may berate herself for failing to live up to her own high expectations. This guilt and self-blame, in turn, only serve to drag her mood down even lower.

"I'm so depressed," she might say, "I feel so miserable. I hate myself when I'm like this, but I can't help it."

She wishes she could do something to get herself up when she is feeling so down, but she doesn't know how, nor does she even believe that it's possible.

If you can relate to any of these feelings and thoughts, then I have written this book to help you.

As a psychologist, I concern myself with the kinds of problems that people encounter as they go about the business of living, rather than deal with mental or emotional illness. *Getting Up When You're Feeling Down* is *not* about how to deal with major clinical Depression—a severe emotional illness, often life-threatening in proportion, that affects only 10 to 15 percent of women. I respectfully leave the treatment of such major mood disturbances to my colleagues in the field of psychiatric medicine.

What I am concerned about are the milder forms of depression—the blues—that affect nearly all women. While periodic low moods or the blues do not qualify as a serious emotional illness, I know that the problem is a serious one to you.

My purpose in writing this book is to help you to accept and acknowledge that your periodic low moods are not abnormal but, rather, occasional parts of your everyday life. But I also want to show you the key to beating the blues and reversing depression. By learning and practicing the Triple A Program for mood management, you will gain a better sense of control over the fluctuations in your emotional ups and downs and you will overcome ways of thinking and behaving that are sabotaging your potential to fully enjoy life.

In short, this is an up book about a down subject.

Ultimately, I want to teach you the skills you need to help yourself. You *can* reverse the downward spiral of depression and replace toxic, negative emotions with a positive, productive belief in yourself.

Once you learn the simple three-step program outlined in the pages that follow, you will no longer be the passive victim of your own blue moods.

You *can* get up when you're feeling down.

GETTING UP WHEN YOU'RE FEELING DOWN

PART ONE

Understanding Your Blue Moods

1

◆

Why Women Need This Book Now

◆

Natural forces within us are the true healers of disease.
                                                    —HIPPOCRATES

You have a lot to lose if you don't learn better control over your blue moods and negative emotions.

In the first place, being out of control of your negative emotions can insidiously spread and contaminate your total self-concept and world view. Unless you learn to contain and reverse those negative feelings, your self-confidence will flag, your self-esteem will founder, and before you know it you'll likely be on your way to some dangerous self-fulfilling prophecies.

But self-fulfilling prophecies are only part of the cost of not learning better mood control. Once you let depression in the door, with no plan for reversing the downward spiral, you invite in a host of other troubles as well.

While proper management of blue moods can limit their frequency, duration, and intensity, mismanagement can make a bad situation far worse. It is possible, for example, to deepen a blue mood into a more serious, protracted depressive episode by engaging in ruminative self-blame that

3

blurs the line between your distorted, negative thinking and your perception of reality. Unhappiness, then, can gradually come to dominate your whole outlook, until chronic low-grade depression becomes a way of life.

Most women who believe that they have little or no control over their depressed moods make no secret of their low feelings either. While they may not make a public pronouncement, their mood colors their attitude and behavior at work, alters their relationships with friends, husbands or boyfriends, and often exacts a costly toll by affecting their appearance as well. This can make women more vulnerable to exploitation, manipulation, and even explicit discrimination during times when better emotional control is required or desired. However unfair, displays of moodiness and emotionality in the office or workplace are far more damaging to women than to men.

When a man at the office loses control or shows evidence of a bad mood or ill-temper, for example, he may raise his voice, become angry, or perhaps hypercritical of subordinates. This display may not be appreciated or admired, but it likely will be tolerated and not used against him when promotion time comes along. On the other hand, when a woman similarly loses control and evidences negative emotions or depression, she typically is labeled as "overly emotional," "unstable," "too moody to handle crises or stress," or "simply not top-management material."

When women at work show the irritability that accompanies low mood swings, someone inevitably asks in whispered tones, "Is she on her period, or what?" When a man is grouchy, the whispers warn others to "steer clear and keep a low profile," but no reference is made to his changing testosterone levels.

In short, when women lose control of their moods, they lose power.

The most blatant symbol of loss of emotional control is crying. And those tears we spill in all the wrong places and in response to a wide gamut of emotions—from sadness to gladness, from anger to anxiety—do us no good at all. All too often, crying reinforces the worst stereotypes about women's essential weakness, vulnerability to stress, and unbridled emotionality.

In personal relationships, loss of emotional control or overindulgence in moodiness and depression also can have negative consequences for women. Depressed moods can exert a tyrannical control not only over your own behavior, but also over those with whom you live and love. You may find yourself being unreasonably demanding and dependent as your mood makes you overly needy of comfort and reassurance that even a devoted partner may not be able to provide. Or your depression may lead you to withdraw coldly, feeling isolated, defensive, and misunderstood.

Moreover, allowing your mind to be flooded with negative emotions—in particular, panic and helplessness—is downright dangerous to your health, and I mean physical health, not just emotional well-being. A new field of medicine called psychoneuroimmunology studies the effects of emotional states on immune status—the body's abilities to ward off illness and heal itself from diseases as serious as cancer or even AIDS. While this research is still in its infancy, the data show a consistent relationship between the maintenance of positive emotions—such as optimism, hope, faith, love, and happiness—and the strength of the body's immune response. Conversely, negative emotions—like helplessness, anger, depression, pessimism, hopelessness, and sadness—are related to greater vulnerability to illness and inability to mount a successful immune defense.

What this intriguing research suggests is that you have your good health to lose if you allow negative moods and emotions to take over. If you are well, negative moods and depression can make you more vulnerable to illness; if you are ill, responding with feelings of helplessness, panic, anger, and depression—however understandable and justifiable such feelings may be—will only serve to obstruct the healing process and make you even sicker.

I like to think of the blues—and you should, too—as a temporary mental state of "unwellness" tantamount to being physically out of shape and run-down. In this sense, staying "psychologically fit" by learning the techniques to coun-

5

teract depression and reverse low moods is good medicine for both mind and body.

Learning effective mood management is protective to your health in another way as well. Abdicating responsibility for controlling depression or low moods predisposes women to unnecessary and undesirable dependency on prescription medications, illicit drugs, and alcohol. Mood-altering drugs, including alcohol, are designed to do exactly that: change, preferably lift, your mood. Too often, in the absence of effective techniques to help themselves out of a downward mood spiral, women turn to a drink or drugs as a quick way up. In reality, though, it's a fast way down.

Just like the incline of a terrifying and terrible roller-coaster ride, when the "high" turns downward, as it inevitably does, the drop can be a dramatic crash. And the quicker the high, the steeper the fall. The drug- or alcohol-induced depression that results becomes the occasion for yet another drink, pill, or snort in order to get up again.

While self-medication may be temporarily successful in lifting your spirits, the longer-term consequences of resorting to chemical means of managing or responding to down moods can become truly disastrous. Besides the dangers of self-medication with alcohol, cocaine, or other illicit drugs, the woman who does not accept primary responsibility for managing her own low moods can become prey to another, more subtle, but nevertheless dangerous form of chemical and interpersonal dependency on one or both of two largely over-prescribed groups of drugs: tricyclic antidepressants and minor tranquilizers. ("Tricyclic" refers to the basic three-ring chemical structure of the compounds.)

The tricyclic antidepressants are marketed under 10 or more different brand names. Some of the most common and frequently prescribed medications include Elavil, Pamelor, Tofranil, Sinequan, and Norpramine.

To be sure, when the tricyclic antidepressants are prescribed *appropriately,* they can be therapeutically effective in the treatment of psychiatrically diagnosed Depressive illness (capital D denotes major clinical Depression, a subject we will explore in some depth in Chapter 3). Even when

6

correctly administered for moderate to severe Depression, though, definite improvement occurs in only about 65 to 70 percent of patients. It also should be noted that tricyclics can have quite counterproductive and even harmful effects if the patient's mood problem is *bipolar*—meaning that she suffers from manic-depressive illness or severe up-and-down mood swings.

In general, maximum benefit from the tricyclics occurs after four to six weeks of consistent use, and then only if the dosage prescribed has been sufficiently potent to have therapeutic value and has been taken on a daily basis. Most patients experience some unpleasant side effects from the drugs, including dry mouth, sedation or drowsiness, blurred vision, light-headedness, constipation, and weight gain.

After about a month, if the medication is effective, a Depressed patient who has been suffering from characteristic slowness of thought and fatigue will begin to feel more energized. Her sleeping difficulties will abate somewhat, and some of her more troubling morbid thoughts and obsessive negative thinking may become less intractable.

Patients who are treated successfully with antidepressants often say that the drug provides a kind of "chemical floor," meaning that they feel protected against sinking to their previously felt depths of desperation and despair. They may feel less anxious and better able to concentrate. In this regard, antidepressants can be helpful in making patients more responsive to traditional psychotherapy in which they then are encouraged to address some of the life issues behind their depression and learn better coping skills for handling their mood problems more effectively.

Tricyclic antidepressants do not specifically induce euphoria or any kind of high. Nor do they make you invincible or invulnerable to low moods. The mood-altering effect is far more subtle and, frankly, not much fun. Nobody I know feels "great" on antidepressants. But if the choice is between medication and deep, potentially suicidal Depression, the drugs are preferred. While antidepressants are not physiologically addictive, they never should be stopped abruptly because withdrawal effects do occur. Withdrawal from the medication should be gradual and carefully monitored by a psychiatrist.

A second group of drugs that have received far more publicity because of their abuse potential and their dangerous—even lethal—interaction with only moderate amounts of alcohol are the minor tranquilizers such as Valium, Centrax, Xanax, Librium, and Ativan. Unfortunately, doctors seem all too willing to prescribe this chemical solution even to women who may complain only of mild nervousness, everyday anxiety, or even slight edginess and occasional difficulty falling asleep.

In addition to the dangerous interaction with alcohol and other drugs, the minor tranquilizers are addictive, cause sufficient sedation to make driving a car dangerous, and can even have "paradoxical," or reverse, effects in some patients. Paradoxical effects raise anxiety levels so dramatically that patients often mistakenly increase their dosage believing that their nerves are getting worse instead of recognizing that the drug, in effect, is boomeranging on them.

It is imperative to emphasize that any medication prescribed for psychiatric conditions does not take the place of or alleviate the need for psychotherapy. At best, antidepressants and tranquilizers are only an adjunct to therapy.

The problem that I encounter over and over again in my clinical practice is that far too many women are taking antidepressants and only when the drugs are neither psychiatrically indicated nor appropriately monitored. Many women, for example, are prescribed Elavil or other similar brands by their internists or gynecologists because they have a little trouble sleeping or feel somewhat, though not seriously, depressed or anxious. These prescriptions are issued without a referral to a psychiatrist and an adequate evaluation for Depression. Some women get a prescription for an antidepressant and take it as they would an aspirin for an ache or pain—whenever they feel a little low or down. This use of antidepressants is neither appropriate nor effective.

The point is that many doctors are overprescribing tricyclics and tranquilizers very much like placebos, or as if the solution to blue moods were contained in a pill bottle. Even many psychiatrists, better equipped to diagnose and treat Depression, prescribe antidepressants and then monitor *only* the medication and its side effects without providing adequate psychotherapeutic support.

The message that women get from these overprescription and misprescription practices is that they can and should rely on a pill to manage their moods and, by extension, on the doctors who prescribe their medication. The doctors themselves also are responding to a message that is thrust at them repeatedly every time they read a medical journal or are visited by a sales representative from a drug company. Almost every piece of print advertising and promotional marketing material put out by drug companies who manufacture antidepressants and tranquilizers portrays a *woman* as the patient who needs the drug. So doctors are programmed to see women patients as "needing" antidepressants and anti-anxiety drugs.

The bottom line here is that if you don't accept the ultimate responsibility to manage your low moods on your own, you too may become psychologically dependent on chemical antidepressants and/or tranquilizers and on the doctor who prescribes them.

One final word of caution on medication: If your expectations of what antidepressants can and cannot do are unrealistic, you might misjudge their effectiveness even when the drugs are working.

A patient of mine who had suffered from a major clinical Depression for more than two years before coming to see me appeared for her appointment after about a month of missed sessions. Her absence from psychotherapy coincidentally came right after I had referred her to a psychiatrist colleague for an evaluation for medication. The doctor prescribed Norpramine and informed me, on the basis of his follow-up after two weeks, that the woman's sleep problems and anxiety attacks were improving. He also urged her to return to psychotherapy.

When the patient showed up in my office, she had a different story about the medication. "I guess it just isn't really working," she began, "although at first I was encouraged because I wasn't waking up panicked in the middle of the night. But last weekend my boyfriend and I had a fight and I got upset and depressed."

When I inquired why she doubted that the Norpramine was working she replied, "Well, I thought it was supposed to make me invincible—you know, completely invulnerable to any more depressions. And it didn't. So now I'm not sure whether to keep taking it or not."

Of course, this woman's expectations of what an anti-depressant was supposed to do were not only unrealistically high, but implied that any role she herself might play in psychologically coping and managing her responses to difficult situations would become irrelevant.

Nothing could be further from the truth. In fact, getting your own attitudes straight about just how important your role is in mood management is our next subject.

2

◆

The Seven Mindsets for Managing Your Moods

◆

Happiness, or misery, is in the mind. It is the mind that lives.

—WILLIAM CORBETT

The first thing I have to do is give you a basic attitude adjustment in the way you think about your low moods.

Most women find the very idea of mood management to be not only foreign but even somewhat magical-sounding or just plain too good to be true. This is because the way women think about their low moods is conditioned by a set of beliefs and attitudes that run almost completely counter to the notion of self-control and, therefore, predetermine a stance of helplessness, passivity, and ineffectiveness when it comes to managing depression and negative emotions.

In this chapter, we will uncover together the errors or misconceptions in your thinking that are operating to sabotage your efforts to overcome depressed moods, and I will provide you with the corrective replacement beliefs that are conducive to gaining better control of your emotional life. In a word, I want to create the receptive and proper *mindsets* with which you should read the rest of this book and thereby get the greatest benefit out of the techniques and methods you will learn.

After we accomplish this critical first step of "mental rewiring"—unplugging counterproductive attitudes and beliefs and connecting you to the right set of empowering thoughts—you will be ready to accept and absorb some basic facts about negative moods and depression, some new concepts relevant to mood management and mastery, and some key motivational principles for overcoming the blues.

Mental Rewiring for Achieving Proper Mindsets

The beliefs and attitudes we need to attack and change are those that close off your alternatives leading to mental entrapment in your own low moods. It is useful for this purpose to envision your present mindsets about mood control as a mental maze in which counterproductive, sabotaging thoughts are like dead ends, and corrective, mood-mastering thoughts are like the open pathways that lead to the right solution.

Mindset Change One

The most frequent "wrong turn" you make in your head about low moods is that you can't help yourself or that you can't help "it"—your depressed state. This implies that you see yourself as powerless and helpless.

Helplessness is the great catch-22 of depression and low moods because the very core symptom of depressed moods *is* the sensation of helplessness. But if you respond to your symptom as though it were fact and you behave helplessly by giving in or giving up, you will only dig yourself a deeper hole.

As soon as you accept the belief that you can't help it if you're depressed, you've reached a dead end. There is nowhere to go from here. You have no alternatives. Of course you feel depressed. Who wouldn't? You are dooming yourself with a self-imposed, erroneous belief in your own helplessness.

You not only *can* help yourself out of a low mood, you *must*.

To reach the solution through the mental maze, you must take the correct turn and choose to believe that you *can* change the way you feel. (Don't worry at this point about the fact that you may not know *how* to reverse depression or what exactly to do. You will learn what you need to know later. For now, just work on changing this mindset.)

I want to be very clear at this early stage that I am not promising you sunny skies and happy days for the rest of your life. I am not saying that you have or will have *total* control over the way you feel nor that you can abolish all negative emotions and down moods from your psychological repertoire. That would be dishonest and, frankly, undesirable. Without some lows, you really can't fully appreciate the highs.

What I am promising is that you can achieve *more* control over your negative moods than you probably think. You will be able to reduce the intensity and duration of low moods. You will be more resilient to the flattening effects of depressing episodes or periods in your life.

The mental rewiring to achieve the proper mindset is as follows:

UNPLUG THIS THOUGHT
I'm so depressed. I just can't help it.

REWIRE THIS THOUGHT
I'm feeling down but there are things I can do to get my mood in a better place.

Mindset Change Two

The belief that you *can* control your low moods may at first be difficult to embrace because it is inappropriately linked to a second misconception about depression. The erroneous reasoning goes something like this: "If I can control my moods, then I must be bringing on the bad moods myself. I am causing my own depressions and I feel guilty about doing that to myself and to those around me."

The logic admittedly is seductive. Don't we cause things to happen if we can exert some control on them? Not necessarily.

If a person has a genetic predisposition to heart disease, for example, and accepts the responsibility to maintain control over cholesterol levels, exercise, and other dietary and health habits, does it follow that the person is responsible for *causing* the proneness to heart disease in the first place? The answer is no.

The same logic applies to depressed moods. Accepting your role in responding correctly and controlling negative mood states and emotions is *not* equivalent to admitting causal responsibility.

As we will see in later chapters, there are many causes of low moods. Gaining mastery over your moods means that you can learn to reverse negative mood cycles once they begin. It doesn't mean that you can completely control their occurrence in the first place. Early recognition and response in the prevention of depression means that you can play a role in keeping your blue mood from deepening into a seriously debilitating and protracted depression. It doesn't mean that you will be able to prevent mood slumps from ever happening to you again.

The erroneous belief that you must be causing your blue moods leads to unnecessary fits of guilt and self-blame. Maintaining this highly dysfunctional attitude will prevent you from fully accepting your power to master moods effectively. The guilt you feel as a result of erroneously believing that you are the sole cause of your down feelings is another dead end in your mental maze. To reach the open doorway, the following mental rewiring is required:

UNPLUG THIS THOUGHT
I am causing my depressed mood and I feel guilty.

REWIRE THIS THOUGHT
I am feeling down but it's not my fault. Low moods happen to everyone, and I'm fortunate because I know what to do to get myself out of it.

14

Mindset Change Three

The next self-sabotaging belief you may have about your low moods is that you don't really have any right to be depressed. After all, "So many people depend on me," you might say, "I just *can't* get depressed." Or "I don't know what it is that is getting me down, so I have no reason and no right to be unhappy."

Believing that you have no right to be down or depressed is about as meaningful or useful as asserting that you have no right to have a headache or no right to be tired. It is an invalidation of a basic human experience.

Taking this wrong turn in your head is not only a dead end but an exhausting battle as well. Fighting with yourself over whether or not you are entitled to a bout of the blues, a transitory state of unhappiness, or a spell of irritability is futile, depleting, and very likely to lead only to greater feelings of depression. In addition to feeling depressed, you also will feel guilty over the fact that you are down.

Accepting that you are feeling low is not the same thing as giving in to the depression or giving up control. As we shall see in far greater detail later, it is the absolutely necessary mindset for successfully managing your moods. If you don't accept that you have a problem, you are in no position to do anything positive to produce an effective solution.

Feeling down or low is just that: a feeling. It isn't a sign of moral weakness or lack of willpower. It doesn't mean that you want to be that way, or that you like it, or that you are choosing for depression to happen. And there is no commission that sits to determine who has the "right" to low moods and who does not.

Correct this faulty part of your mindset this way:

UNPLUG THIS THOUGHT
I have no right to feel down or depressed.

REWIRE THIS THOUGHT
I feel down and it has nothing to do with logic or "rights." It is just a feeling or low mood and I know what to do to respond.

Mindset Change Four

Next is a form of direct resistance. This is the belief that learning to control your mood will result somehow in coldness, hyperrationality, a loss of spontaneity, and a fundamental compromise in what it means to be an emotionally open, sensitive woman. Wrong.

The erroneous reasoning here is thinking that mood control is the same thing as mood overcontrol. I certainly am not advocating that any woman surrender her emotionality nor her access to and expression of the full range of feelings of which she is capable.

What we're talking about here is *choice*. If you learn effective techniques for controlling and reversing negative emotions and depressive states, you may choose either to indulge in your emotionality or to curtail some of it, depending on time, place, and circumstances. If, on the other hand, you forgo learning any control techniques, you simply will have *no choice*. Your emotions and moods will control you.

You indeed will be an emotional person, but perhaps overly so, or inappropriately so. Your emotionality is likely to reduce your credibility in certain situations and you may wish that you could be different. But without the skills in your psychological armory, you will have nothing with which to fight back the waves of unwanted, overwhelming emotion.

It is unwise to resist the opportunity to learn more effective mood control on the grounds that you don't want to be some kind of emotionless robot. The correction to this wobbly defense is:

UNPLUG THIS THOUGHT
If I control my moods, I'll lose my emotionality and be a cold, unfeeling, less womanly woman.

REWIRE THIS THOUGHT
If I learn to control my moods better, I'll have more choice about where, how, and to whom I express my emotionality and I'll be a more confident, successful woman.

16

Mindset Change Five

The next belief to alter or refine is that low moods and depressions are entirely determined by biochemicals or biochemical imbalances. There is a good deal of very sound evidence that many mood disorders—especially major psychiatric conditions like manic-depressive illness or major Depressive illness—do have clear biological, biochemical causal factors. And, of course, there is scientific evidence regarding the experience of Premenstrual Syndrome (PMS) that traces it to the effects of fluctuating hormone levels.

The fact that biochemical treatments, such as the tricyclic antidepressants mentioned earlier and other pharmaceutical treatments, are widely and successfully used is more evidence for the biological basis of some, or some component of, mood disorders.

The problem is not with the recognition that biochemicals play a role—often predominant or major—in mood swings or changes. Rather, it is with the faulty belief that only biochemicals determine depression and low moods and the logical extrapolation that alterations or corrections to negative mood states must, therefore, seek to change biochemistry through biochemical means.

In other words, if you believe that your low moods are strictly biochemical, you've just made another dead-end turn in the mental maze through which we are working. Because if you want to believe that it's all in the hormones, then you again are abdicating responsibility for mood self-management and control other than reliance on mood-altering or other biochemically balancing medication.

There is an enormously complex and subtle relationship among mood, mind, and medicine. As I said earlier, even in clear-cut cases of biochemically based Depression treated with antidepressants or Lithium, the medicine is only one adjunct to treatment. The patient must still learn psychological skills to cope with her life, her moods, her thoughts, and her feelings if she hopes to gain control.

The correction for the overestimation of biochemical causes in mood and mood control is:

UNPLUG THIS THOUGHT
My moods are entirely determined by biochemicals so I really have no control other than to take medication.

REWIRE THIS THOUGHT
My moods may have some biochemical basis. But I can help control my own biochemical balance by striving for more positive feelings and practicing the techniques of mood management and mastery. This is still true even if the doctor has prescribed medication for me.

Mindset Change Six

The next sabotaging belief to attack is that if you "just have the blues," it's nothing to take seriously. While a blue mood in and of itself is not a serious condition, the tendency to minimize, deny, or trivialize the feelings or problems that the blues represent can be quite serious indeed.

As mentioned previously, the blues might well presage a far more debilitating depressive episode if they are mismanaged. And denial is most definitely a form of psychological mismanagement.

The blues signify a mild state of psychological pain. Pain, whether physical or emotional, should be read as a signal or message that something is wrong and needs attention and correction.

Frequently, one of my patients will begin a therapy session with a version of this kind of denial. "I know this is probably just a dumb thing and it shouldn't be bothering me, but. . . ," or "My husband thinks I'm ridiculous to feel down about this and he's probably right, but. . . ," or "I just have the blues; it's nothing important" are typical examples of the prologue.

My response is always, "If it's a problem for you then it's important to me, so let's talk about it."

However mild, psychological pain still hurts. And the critical point to keep in mind in order to maintain the optimum state of psychological fitness is that *if something hurts you, it matters.*

18

This warning not to ignore the signal that something is hurting or bothering you is particularly critical when the pain arises from an interpersonal relationship. Many people try to avoid conflicts with their spouse or partner by burying hurt feelings or ruffled feathers on the rationalization that the issue isn't important enough to warrant even a discussion, let alone an argument. The flaw in this reasoning is that stored up "little" problems almost inevitably explode into major fights where intense, previously repressed resentment and hostility surface and tensions ignite.

Acknowledging that your blue moods are serious enough to merit your attention and proper response is not tantamount to dramatizing relatively minor problems or blowing a mild depressive state up into a full-blown case of Depression. On the contrary, the purpose is to avert bigger problems down the road by dealing with issues that are small enough to handle when they occur, such as spats with spouses or boyfriends.

Unfortunately, my view of the importance of dealing with blue moods is not shared by all professionals. Some therapists, particularly psychiatrists and those who operate exclusively on a narrow, medically based model of illness, tend to dismiss the blues as essentially insignificant because (a) they are part of everyone's experience and (b) they are not a sufficiently serious condition to meet the diagnostic criterion of clinical Depressive illness. But just because everyone gets a common cold or flu on occasion doesn't mean that you shouldn't treat it.

A specific case will illustrate the potential "backfire" effect inherent in minimizing the blues. About a year ago I was invited to be the keynote speaker for a women's health conference sponsored by a hospital in the Midwest. After the keynote address, the women attendees were invited to participate in one of four workshop sessions organized around specific issues relevant to women's health concerns.

One of the workshops was titled "How to Handle Your Blue Days" and was to be conducted by a woman psychiatrist. The room was packed with women eager for some answers to what for them was an easily recognizable topic.

The psychiatrist, however, began her remarks by saying that the organizers of the conference had "assigned" her this topic and that, as far as she was concerned, there simply were "no such things as 'blue days,'" nor did a topic as presumably trivial as "the blues" warrant her time and expertise. She proceeded to lecture to the group on the "more important issue of child development."

Within a few minutes, her audience dwindled to only a handful as the women left in protest. I had occasion to talk to these same women, since they moved from the psychiatrist's workshop to the one that I was conducting.

The very upsetting and disruptive effect that the doctor's firm denial of the reality of "blue days" had on her audience was striking. One woman, for example, remarked, "Now I *really* think there's something wrong with me. I get the blues at least once a month and an expert just said there's no such thing. I guess I must be in worse shape than I realized."

Several other women echoed the sentiment that the psychiatrist's denial left them confused, concerned, and feeling low. "When I left the house this morning I thought I just had the blues and was going to find out how to deal with the problem," a woman told me. "Now I find out that if I have the blues, either I have 'nothing,' so I must be imagining I feel down, or I'm just plain nuts!"

The blues are real, and so is the experience of "blue days." The corrective rewiring for your mindset is:

UNPLUG THIS THOUGHT
I just have the blues and it's nothing to even bother with or take seriously.

REWIRE THIS THOUGHT
I have the blues and I need to find out what's bothering me and respond in positive ways that will help the negative feelings go away.

Mindset Change Seven

The one final stumbling block to clearing your mental maze is fear. Specifically, it is the fear of failure that may be keeping you from trying to manage your moods and overcome your depressions.

The key here is to understand that mood management does not mean that you have to be able to manage your moods *perfectly*. As we will see later, depression operates to decrease self-esteem and self-confidence and to increase your tendency to make negative predictions about your own abilities. Consequently, especially when you are in a low or depressed mood, you may feel quite reluctant to take on the challenge that I am posing to you now.

I want you to accept responsibility for becoming more self-aware and accepting of your low moods, for responding in positive, constructive ways designed to keep your moods contained in terms of their negative intensity and duration, and for trying to repair your mood and reverse the downward cycle to an upward direction.

Now you may be reluctant to accept this challenge because of the fear that you might fail. Then, you erroneously reason, you'll feel more desperate and scared because you will realize how inadequate you really are and how bad your depression might be because you can't make it go away completely.

You must overcome this self-sabotaging fear. The only failure that is possible is if you fail even to try to help yourself. If you try, you *will* be at least partially successful—and gaining partial control over some negative emotions and behaviors is a 100 percent improvement over no control at all. I emphatically am not telling you that you must be able to exert *total* control of your emotions, nor that you have to be able to make your blue, depressed moods go away entirely or immediately.

Let me also reassure you that the techniques you will learn in this book do work. I have taught patients and students to use these techniques for mood management and mastery successfully for many years. And many of these same patients who have come to develop considerable proficiency in

21

mood management began with lots of fear that they wouldn't be able to succeed in helping themselves.

Nevertheless, they proceeded in spite of their fears. Subsequently, having gained enough perspective on their mood problems, these patients could see that their fears and lack of self-confidence were only reflections or symptoms of their underlying mood problems in the first place.

You also need to put your fears aside. The program will work and you will succeed in learning the techniques and applying them effectively in your own life. If you listen to your fears, you'll hit the last dead end in the maze and stay trapped in your low mood and self-doubts. Forge ahead and rewire your mindset this way:

UNPLUG THIS THOUGHT
I'm afraid I won't be able to help myself by learning to reverse my low moods.

REWIRE THIS THOUGHT
I'm afraid that I won't be able to help myself reverse depression, but my fear is only a symptom of the problem. The real failure would be not to even try.

Now I've given you the ammunition to blast away at the self-sabotaging beliefs that will keep you stuck as a passive victim of your depressed blue moods. Go back over this chapter and reread the mental rewiring portions. Visualize yourself actually unplugging the old beliefs or attitudes and plugging in the new wiring that represents empowering feelings and thoughts.

If you have trouble understanding the logic of why any particular attitude rewiring is necessary, reread the section on changing your mindset that immediately precedes the rewiring instructions. Then try to explain the argument against the old attitude and in favor of the new one to someone else. Psychologically, the effect of verbal argument in favor of a new attitude operates to strengthen your commitment to the new belief.

Ask yourself this question: Are there any other lingering

thoughts or beliefs you personally hold that make you feel that it won't be possible for you to gain control and mastery over your negative moods and emotions? Try to develop logical arguments to dispute these thoughts and replace them with belief statements that emphasize control.

Because *control* is the single most important word in this book. Once you connect with your ability to control the events in your life—including your experiences of depression, blues, and low moods—you will be on the high road to feeling better.

Now that you've got the best, most receptive mindsets for receiving the good news about how to increase your sense of control over your down moods, we are ready to take a closer look at the experience we call depression.

3

◆

The Illness of Depression Versus Feeling Depressed

◆

The worst bondage is exile from peace of mind.

—JEWISH PROVERB

Trying to define the term *depression* is a lot like the old story of the three blind men trying to describe an elephant after feeling three different parts of the animal: the ears, the trunk, and the tail. Three very distinct descriptions followed.

Depression not only means different things to different people, it can mean quite different things to the same person, depending on particular circumstances, feelings, and behaviors.

And while the word *depression* is used frequently by laypersons and mental health professionals alike, it has quite a distinct meaning in the formal, diagnostic clinical sense, which denotes an illness quite apart from what is meant when the average person says, "I'm kind of depressed today."

To distinguish the psychiatric illness from the range of mood states and negative emotions that I have summarized as "feeling down," I will use the word *Depression* with a

24

capital D when we are talking about the *illness;* when we are discussing the *feeling* of being down, having the blues, or experiencing a low mood that does not signify the clinical illness, I will refer to depression with a lower-case d.

Now let's see if we can get a feel for at least some parts of this complex elephant.

Depression with a Capital D

It would be difficult for me to overdramatize or over-emphasize the mental pain, anguish, and suffering that characterizes the illness of Depression. Suffice it to say that Depression is far and away the leading cause of suicide, accounting for an estimated 60 percent of all self-inflicted deaths. And the suffering of Depression's victims is compounded by the attendant torment of the friends and families of those who are afflicted with the illness.

The evidence that Depression is biologically, bio-chemically based is incontrovertible. In this sense, Depression is a physical disorder with profound psychological reflections or symptoms.

The diagnostic criteria of a *major* episode of Depression are laid out quite specifically in the *Diagnostic and Statistical Manual of Mental Disorders—Revised* (the DSM-III-R), used by virtually every practicing psychiatrist and psychologist.[1] The diagnostic criteria for an episode of major Depression are as follows:

At least five of the following symptoms have been present during the same two-week period and represent a change from previous functioning; at least one of the symptoms is either (1) depressed mood or (2) loss of interest or pleasure.

1. depressed mood most of the day, nearly every day, as indicated by either subjective account or observation by others

---

1. American Psychiatric Association, "Criteria for Major Depressive Episode," DSM-III-R (Washington, D.C.: APA, 1987), 222–224. Reprinted with permission.

2. markedly diminished interest or pleasure in all, or almost all, activities most of the day, nearly every day (as indicated by either subjective account or observation by others of apathy most of the time)
3. significant weight loss or weight gain when not dieting (e.g., more than 5% of body weight in a month), or decrease or increase in appetite nearly every day
4. insomnia or hypersomnia (sleeping too much) nearly every day
5. psychomotor agitation or retardation nearly every day (observable by others, not merely subjective feelings of restlessness or being slowed down)
6. fatigue or loss of energy nearly every day.
7. feelings of worthlessness or excessive or inappropriate guilt (which may be delusional) nearly every day (not merely self-reproach or guilt about being sick)
8. diminished ability to think or concentrate, or indecisiveness, nearly every day (either by subjective account or as observed by others)
9. recurrent thoughts of death (not just fear of dying), recurrent suicidal ideation without a specific plan, or a suicide attempt or a specific plan for committing suicide

In addition to these diagnostic criteria, many psychiatrists and psychologists recognize as additional diagnostic indicators the presence of generalized anxiety or panic attacks, phobia, feelings of hopelessness and helplessness, irritability, anger and hostility, social withdrawal; and a range of physical changes or symptoms, including complaints of nausea, constipation, stomach cramps or pains, chest pains, rapid breathing, sweating, coldness, numbness or tingling of the feet or hands, headache, and feelings of pressure in the head, ears, and neck. Sometimes, the Depressed person with such physical syptoms may believe that she has a terrible disease that is destroying her body. To be diagnostically significant, the preceding psychological and physical symptoms must be seen as accompanying the persistent mood disturbance and loss of pleasure that define the core of Depression, and be ruled out as symptoms of another physical or mental illness other than Depression.

Now let's set the sterile, clinical terminology aside and try to understand the experience of Depression from the perspective of a few individuals who have suffered from the illness.

Diane, 35, has endured four major episodes of Depression, ranging from one month to nearly one year in duration, since she was 24. Both Diane's mother and maternal grandmother experienced severe Depression throughout their lives, and her mother's youngest sister took her own life with an overdose of sleeping pills and alcohol at the age of 41.

Diane describes the early stages of a Depressive episode as a "thick, dark fog that descends all around me. I begin to feel that I am dragging around a twenty-pound millstone, and I am totally exhausted. Then the flatness sets in. I lose my ability to laugh or to be interested in much of anything. Food turns me off. I generally drop ten to fifteen pounds within a few weeks without dieting. Sex holds no appeal to me at all, and of course I start to feel enormously guilty about putting my husband through the inevitable sexual denial that I know is in store for him. And I start imagining that he has lovers and will divorce me.

"Eventually, the pain seeps into everything. I don't sleep well. My eyes pop open at about four A.M. and I feel anxious and overwhelmed by an overpowering sense of doom and dread. A lot of times, I can't get out of bed at all, even though I can't really go back to sleep either. The degree of self-loathing—of genuinely despising myself—is hard to explain and painful to experience. I feel like the lowest person alive. And the fact that my husband or friends still like or love me makes me feel even worse instead of better. I feel like a fraud, like a burden to everyone. Then the thoughts of taking my own life or of just disappearing begin. This is when the pain of life really becomes unbearable. . . ."

Sally, 43, describes her experience of Depression this way: "I had a terrible year when I turned forty-two. It was like the universe was stacked against me. In the space of seven months, my husband left me, my father died, and I lost about fifty thousand dollars in some investments.

"Then I started to feel sick. First came chest pains and tremendous headaches. I went to several doctors, all of whom told me it was stress. I started having unbelievable anxiety attacks in the middle of the night. I would wake up and my heart would race, my palms would sweat, and I was convinced that I was dying. The weird thing is that I kind of wanted to die in a way. I felt like I deserved what had happened to me and that a suitable punishment would be to contact some terrible disease and just kick off.

"But the doctors couldn't find anything wrong and suggested I see a shrink which only made me angrier. Then, I really started losing it. I started sleeping away most of every day as a way of avoiding consciousness, hoping I would die quietly in my sleep. When I was up, I literally dragged myself around in slow motion. Because of the lack of exercise, I started gaining weight. I guess I was eating a lot all the time too—not because I enjoyed the food, but because I was trying somehow to fill up the tremendous void at the center of my life.

"I didn't recognize this as an illness until I finally gave in out of desperation and saw a psychiatrist. You can't begin to understand the depths of this thing called Depression unless you've been there. Believe me, it's not like being in a bad mood or feeling sad. You don't even have the energy to cry."

There are less extreme variations of mood disturbances that still meet the diagnostic criteria for Depression but that don't necessarily involve suicidal thoughts or the depths of emotional despair described above.

Ellen, for example, suffers from a relatively less severe form of Depression but one that has nevertheless caused her a considerable degree of emotional discomfort and life disruption.

At age 29, Ellen works as an associate attorney in a prestigious Los Angeles law firm. She has held her position with the firm for five years, having been recruited fresh out of law school. Ellen works in a rather esoteric area of contract law, and her colleagues and the partners in the firm are quite satisfied with her work.

But nobody relates well to Ellen at a personal level, and

her perceived "coldness, aloofness, and lack of social finesse" have been mentioned as reasons for objecting to her possible future promotion to partner.

In fact, she has been Depressed for two years. Ellen is single and quite overweight. She has virtually no social life nor contact with people outside of the office other than her mother. On weekends, Ellen doesn't get out of bed until noon and has little or no enthusiasm for hobbies, athletics, or interest outside of law, though occasionally she reads fiction as "escape junk."

Basically she is cynical about her life and any prospects for change, believing that her lonely existence is deserved since she doesn't really "like people much" and prefers to be alone. Ellen doesn't actively think about suicide; she just views life as a boring, difficult process that is bereft of pleasure or high points but accepts that "that's all there is and it's stupid and useless for me to expect more."

Ellen's experience of Depression is flatter and grayer than the dramatic abyss and black void described by Sally and Diane. Still, Ellen's pain is apparent. Chronic low-grade Depression, like Ellen's, has been recently dubbed Dysthymic Disorder (DD).

These accounts of Depression give you a taste of the deep despair, despondency, and emotional desolation that characterize this severe, life-threatening illness. Depression is often referred to as the "common cold" of mental illness because it is the form of emotional distress most frequently seen by psychiatrists, psychologists, and physicians alike. Obviously, though, the comparison to the common cold fails to acknowledge the severity of the condition.

But while Depression is indeed more widespread than other forms of mental illness, its prevalence should not be overestimated either. Among women, for whom Depression is twice as common as for men, 10 to 15 percent are estimated to be afflicted with the illness at any one point in time. Over the space of a lifetime, somewhere between 20 and 30 percent of all women are expected to experience at least one episode of major Depression. Substantial and disconcerting as these figures are, they still indicate that the great majority of women at any point in time do *not* suffer from Depression; and 70 to 80 percent will thankfully never know first-hand the ravages and emotional pain of the illness in their lifetimes.

While you may recognize your own experience—past or present—in some of these descriptions of Depression, most likely you are part of the fortunate majority of women who don't suffer from Depression *per se,* but rather from milder mood problems, feelings of depression, or the blues. This recognition should come as a relief. I know, however, that the low moods you experience still exact a high enough cost to the quality of your life to be of concern and to motivate you to learn how to get yourself up when you are feeling down.

It is quite possible that you are not sure where you properly fit in between the illness of Depression and the condition or state of feeling depressed. This chapter, and some important self-assessment questionnaires and rating forms in the next chapter, will help you to determine where you fit. First, though, let's compare some of the differences between feeling depressed or having a blue mood and the illness of Depression.

Feeling Depressed

No formal diagnostic criteria exist for depressed mood states as they do for the illness of Depression, since the blues or low moods are *not* illnesses. Essentially, what doctors and therapists use as the differentiating line is that with blue moods or depression you may have a sad mood or reduction of interest, or pleasure in your usual activities, but you do *not* also report a sufficient number of accompanying symptoms, or the persistence of the unpleasant mood and related symptoms for an uninterrupted span of at least two weeks.

In other words, to most doctors, if you are not suffering from "true" Depression, you're "just normally depressed or down."

But as you know, being "just normally depressed" can be a significantly unpleasant and disruptive experience. The blues deserves attention and recognition as a condition to treat even if it isn't a serious form of mental or emotional illness.

For our purposes, let's look at how feeling depressed is different from the illness of major Depression in terms, first, of depth or intensity; second, of duration, pattern, and frequency of occurrence; and third, of breadth of life areas or psychological experiences that become involved or affected.

Illness of Depression	*Blue Mood or Feeling Depressed*
The feelings are extremely intense in terms of emotional pain, depth of despair, sense of hopelessness and helplessness, and damage to essential life energy. In severe cases, the intensity can turn into a deadening flatness and inability to feel anything other than mental pain.	The feelings are characterized by an absence of normal intensity. Typical sensations are of being "muted," "dulled," "suppressed," or having "the blahs." The lack of intensity is noticed and intensity is missed.
Your recollection of any experience of pleasure is distant. It is difficult to remember pleasure or the last time you felt different, happy, or anything other than emotional pain.	You are not far removed from the experience of laughing, making love, or feeling good. You may feel blue at the moment, but you can easily remember the last time you felt better or up.
You sink so low into the abyss of black Depression that the sunlight at the top can barely be recalled, let alone glimpsed. It is hard for you even to imagine experiencing pleasure again or ever enjoying true happiness.	You not only can recall the sunlight, you can generally "see" it—but it's just out of reach. You feel impatient to "shake the blues" and to return to feeling better again.

Illness of Depression	Blue Mood or Feeling Depressed
Symptoms are long lasting—a month or more is not uncommon—and are generally uninterrupted, persistent, and intractable.	Your low mood does not last as long—perhaps a week, a few days, or even less—and is generally punctuated by brighter moments, hours, or even longer periods of respite from the blues.
The dark mood is pervasive, dominating all conscious thought. The bleak and brooding feelings are all-consuming.	The gray, temporary haze of your mood may make concentration somewhat more difficult but is not all-consuming. There are occasional breaks in the bleakness and you feel annoyance with your inability to make the relief last longer.
Depression becomes your way of life, or life itself. You identify with your condition. You *are* Depressed—it is not only how you feel, it is who you *are*.	The depressed feelings seem like time spent away from life at its best or normal living. You sense that you are "off"—not your usual self.
Episodes of the illness occur with less frequency but last much longer than blue moods. Even one episode is sufficient to warrant medication and ongoing psychiatric treatment or psychotherapy.	Blue moods occur more frequently, but are relatively short-lived. The frequency of occurrence and degree of disruption or discomfort determine whether therapy is needed.

Illness of Depression	*Blue Mood or Feeling Depressed*
You have recurrent thoughts of death or suicide and may make plans for how to take your own life. Fantasies about disappearing are common.	You have no serious thoughts of, or plans for, suicide. Occasional impulses to "escape" from life's pressures may be present.
Your self-esteem is crippled or destroyed completely. Predominant feelings and thoughts of unworthiness, tormenting guilt, self-reproach, self-blame, and self-abasement exist.	Your self-esteem is lowered or deflated and self-confidence is reduced. Your low mood and self-esteem interact in subtle circular ways, so that the depressed feelings and thoughts lower self-esteem, and low self-esteem fuels the depressed feelings.
Symptoms often involve loss of appetite, interest in food and consequently of weight. Sometimes weight gain occurs, but food is rarely experienced as very pleasurable. When weight gain occurs, you don't care much how you look. Your essential self-esteem is so thoroughly degraded that you become almost wholly unconcerned with issues of vanity and pride in your appearance.	Overeating and/or overdrinking with accompanying weight gain, remorse, and guilt are common. A depressed mood may trigger binge eating or cravings for sweets, which are enjoyed in the short term as quick "fixes" or relief from the frustration or discomfort of feeling down. Because the core of your self-worth is still intact, you are disappointed, disgusted or bothered if the weight gain is enough to keep you from wearing good clothes. Because vanity

Illness of Depression	Blue Mood or Feeling Depressed
	and pride are still important to you, you may resolve to diet and exercise to "undo" the damage. The overweight itself is often a sufficient cause for the depressed feelings.
Major fatigue and loss of energy generally are present, along with noticeable sluggishness and inactivity. Staying in bed to "escape" pain by sleeping is very common. Despite excessive sleeping, you are still exhausted and mentally depleted because Depression is enervating by nature. Alternatively, fatigue may result from extreme agitation and noticeable restlessness—you can't sit still or stay in one place since you are propelled by anxiety.	Temporary though often frequent feelings of fatigue and low energy are common but may result from too much stress and daily activity. Feeling depressed is especially common in women who feel depleted and exhausted from stress, and may experience the fatigue as a dramatic contrast to their normally high energy levels.
Sleep is disturbed. You may be awakened by panic attacks with a frightening, irrational sense of doom. Rising at four or five A.M. (or earlier) is common, with inability to go back to sleep.	Sleep may be slightly disturbed owing to stress, mental overload, and generally "real" problems. No pervasive panic or sense of doom is present.

Illness of Depression	*Blue Mood or Feeling Depressed*
Symptoms involve loss of interest or pleasure in all, or almost all, usual activities. You lose the ability to derive or desire pleasure as though the illness had attacked and destroyed the connections or "wiring" linked to joys of sensory experiences. Still, emotional pain is profoundly felt.	Your capacity to feel pleasure is not absent, just temporarily inactivated. You feel bored, unmotivated, unenthused and dispassionate about activities that you know are likely to bring pleasure simply because you're "not in the mood" to do them.
Your thought processes like memory, decision making, concentration, and the ability to accurately process and interpret information are severely impaired. You are preoccupied with negative, morbid thoughts and obsessional worry. An illusion that reality is black becomes all-consuming and real to you. You cannot and do not recognize that it is the illness that makes you think that things are as bad as they seem. You believe that you are without value and that your life situation and future are totally grim.	Your thought processes may be slightly to moderately impaired or distorted. But you still retain enough perspective on your own thinking to suspect that you are seeing things in an exaggerated, negatively biased, pessimistic, "out-of-whack" way and you hope that your way is wrong.

◆

These differences between the illness of Depression and the blue mood of feeling depressed are valid for people in general. Now it is time for you to assess yourself in order to bring the concepts down to a personal level.

4

◆

How Black Are Your Blues?

◆

I've got those weary Twentieth Century blues.

—NOEL COWARD

It is vitally important for you to evalutate the nature and severity of your mood problems for several reasons. First and most important, if you find that you score sufficiently high on the two tests that measure the illness of Depression that follow, be sure to seek competent professional help for your problem immediately. Depression is too serious to ignore and, for all the reasons just discussed, too embedded in your fundamental ways of looking at your life situation, your thinking, and both your physical and emotional feelings to tackle all alone.

The best news about Depression is that it is treatable. You can and will be relieved of the debilitating effects of the illness when you get the treatment you need.

Self-help books like this one should be used as an adjunct or addition to (but not a replacement for) professional therapy if you are suffering from the illness of Depression. If, on the other hand, you find that your problem is not Depression, but rather the experience of periodic depressed, blue, or low moods, then seeking professional help can be optional.

37

The program in this book may help to clarify some issues and decisions about changing your life that you may want to make, and seeking the supportive assistance of a good therapist to aid you in that process may well be a good idea. Or you may find the self-help methods for managing and mastering your mood problems sufficiently beneficial to make the help of an outside professional unnecessary.

Beyond the issue of whether or not professional therapy for your problem is necessary or optional, these self-assessment measures will help to get your mood problem in focus now so that we can proceed to the actual program designed to help you. Instead of expending mental energy worrying about what is "really wrong" with you—i.e., whether you are just in a normal depressed mood or have a more serious form of Depressive illness—you will get the necessary answers. And you will have a much clearer sense than before of what you actually mean when you say, "I'm depressed."

Getting the problem into focus also means understanding in what ways your mood needs major repair or perhaps only fine-tuning. As you will see, there is more than one psychological dimension involved in a blue mood. Becoming more aware of your mood problem is an essential part of finding effective solutions for what is hurting you emotionally.

Remember, both the illness of Depression and the blue mood of feeling depressed mean that you are in emotional pain or discomfort. And that means that there are things that you can and should do to help yourself get better.

Let's start by taking a measure of exactly what hurts and determining how black your blues are.

Self-Diagnosis of Depressive Illness

A word of caution at the outset: No self-diagnostic measure of any illness should take the place of a complete physical and psychological assessment by a trained professional. That said, the two measures that follow will help you decide whether you have enough of the important warning signs and symptoms of the illness to make consulting a professional mandatory.

The Braiker
Mood Scale for Women

The questions that follow ask you to rate the frequency of various feelings or experiences that are related to blue moods and Depressive illness. Read each question carefully and base your answer on how much of the time you have had these feelings *during the last three months.*

A. I feel that I am not as happy as most other women.
1. rarely
2. sometimes
3. frequently
4. almost always

B. My sleep is disturbed by panic attacks or feelings of doom that wake me in the middle of the night.
1. rarely
2. sometimes
3. frequently
4. almost always

C. I feel bored, unmotivated, and uninterested in activities that are pleasurable for most people and used to be pleasurable for me.
1. rarely
2. sometimes
3. frequently
4. almost always

D. I seem to function much better at work than I do at either love or play.
1. rarely
2. sometimes
3. frequently
4. almost always

E. I wake up several hours earlier than my normal rising time and am so beset by worries that I can't go back to sleep.
1. rarely
2. sometimes
3. frequently
4. almost always

F. I feel pretty much defeated and pessimistic that my prospects of getting happier in my life will be better in the future.
1. rarely
2. sometimes
3. frequently
4. almost always

G. I feel down on myself, inadequate, unattractive, or unworthy of other people's love.
1. rarely
2. sometimes
3. frequently
4. almost always

H. I feel so low on energy and so fatigued that it seems like I am dragging myself around.
1. rarely
2. sometimes
3. frequently
4. almost always

I. I tend to blame myself when things go wrong in my life and to avoid taking credit or patting myself on the back when things go right.
1. rarely
2. sometimes
3. frequently
4. almost always

J. My unhappiness and worry make it very difficult for me to concentrate and work effectively.

   1. rarely
   2. sometimes
   3. frequently
   4. almost always

K. I vacillate back and forth over deciding on both important and unimportant matters.
   1. rarely
   2. sometimes
   3. frequently
   4. almost always

L. I am harder on myself and more self-critical than I am of other people.
   1. rarely
   2. sometimes
   3. frequently
   4. almost always

M. I am conscious of lots of aches and pains, and worried about the state of my physical health.
   1. rarely
   2. sometimes
   3. frequently
   4. almost always

N. Having sex or making love doesn't seem as interesting or enjoyable to me as it once did.
   1. rarely
   2. sometimes
   3. frequently
   4. almost always

O. I have intense, persistent feelings of hopelessness and despair.
   1. rarely
   2. sometimes
   3. frequently
   4. almost always

P. I feel helpless and out of control of my mood and my life situation.
   1. rarely
   2. sometimes
   3. frequently
   4. almost always

Q. I have very little appetite or interest in food.
   1. rarely
   2. sometimes
   3. frequently
   4. almost always

R. I feel isolated and shunned by most of my friends because of my bad moods.
   1. rarely
   2. sometimes
   3. frequently
   4. almost always

S. I feel like my fate is either to suffer through life or to end my suffering by taking my own life.
   1. rarely
   2. sometimes
   3. frequently
   4. almost always

T. I am so preoccupied by my own troubles and sadness that I have lost interest in most other people.
   1. rarely
   2. sometimes
   3. frequently
   4. almost always

U. I am short-tempered and irritable with myself and just about everyone around me.
   1. rarely
   2. sometimes
   3. frequently
   4. almost always

V. I feel disgusted with the way I look and/or the way I have been acting.
1. rarely
2. sometimes
3. frequently
4. almost always

W. I feel that blue moods and sadness have become pretty much a way of life for me.
1. rarely
2. sometimes
3. frequently
4. almost always

X. I feel disappointed with myself and with the way my life has worked out so far.
1. rarely
2. sometimes
3. frequently
4. almost always

Y. I feel agitated, anxious, and disturbed over the problems I am facing in my life.
1. rarely
2. sometimes
3. frequently
4. almost always

Z. It occurs to me that I can't even remember the last time that I really felt "up" or happy.
1. rarely
2. sometimes
3. frequently
4. almost always

Scoring and Interpreting
the Braiker Mood Scale for Women

To score this test, simply add up the numerical value of your answers. The highest score you can have is 104; the lowest is 26.

If your score falls within the range of 26 to 30, your moods are within the range of up-and-down variations that are considered normal. Using the techniques in this book will help to strengthen your coping skills and keep your moods stabilized.

If your score falls within the range of 31 to 45, you may be suffering from a mild mood disturbance characterized by periodic, recurring bouts of the blues and feelings of depression. In general, though, scores in this range do not indicate the presence of Depressive illness. You may wish to consult a professional for further evaluation and/or psychotherapy. Using the techniques in this book will help to diminish the frequency of your low moods as well as to lessen their duration and intensity.

If your score falls in the range of 46 to 64, your mood disturbance should be considered "borderline" clinical Depression. In other words, you have enough of the warning signs to require further evaluation by a professional. Scores in this borderline range, in particular, may indicate the presence of Dysthymic Disorder (DD), which is a chronic, low-grade Depression that is treatable and for which you should seek help. Using the techniques in this book will be an important adjunct to your psychotherapy and will help you maintain better control over your moods when your formal treatment is terminated.

If your score is within the range of 65 to 80, you have definite indicators of a moderate to severe Depressive mood disorder or episode. Scores in this range also indicate definitive presence of DD or chronic, low-grade Depression. You should seek the help of a professional to further diagnose your condition and help you overcome your emotional pain. The techniques in this book should be used as an additional aid to psychotherapy.

Finally, if your score is higher than 80, you are probably suffering from a severe, acute episode of major Depressive illness and should seek help *immediately*. With effective professional treatment and the techniques in this book, you *will* find relief from what may now seem to be a hopeless state of despair and emotional pain.

No matter what your score, take comfort in the fact that deciding to help yourself reverse your negative emotions is the most positive step you can possibly take at this point.

The Carroll Rating Scale

It is generally a good idea to use more than one diagnostic test to raise your confidence level. Taking a second test is like seeking a second medical opinion. If both tests confirm that your mood reflects the illness of Depression, or if both tests disconfirm the diagnosis and put you in the category of women who get down but who are not clinically Depressed, your confidence in the self-diagnosis process will be increased.

If you are one of the rare individuals whose scores on the two tests are contradictory, then you should seek professional assistance in order to clarify your diagnosis. Sometimes symptoms of Depression mask other physical illnesses that require medical diagnostic expertise and treatment.

The Carroll Rating Scale is designed to measure the severity of your current mood. Complete all of the following statements by circling YES or NO, on the basis of how you have been feeling *during the past few days*.[1]

---

1. B. J. Carroll, M. Feinberg, P. E. Smouse, S. G. Rawson, and J. F. Greden, "The Carroll Rating Scale for Depression. I. Development, Reliability and Validation," *British Journal of Psychiatry*, 138 (1981), 194–200. Reprinted with permission of *British Journal of Psychiatry* and Bernard J. Carroll, M.D., Ph.D.

1. I feel just as energetic as always. YES NO

2. I am losing weight. YES NO

3. I have dropped many of my interests and activities. YES NO

4. Since my illness I have completely lost interest in sex. YES NO

5. I am especially concerned about how my body is functioning. YES NO

6. It must be obvious that I am disturbed and agitated. YES NO

7. I am still able to carry on doing the work I am supposed to do. YES NO

8. I can concentrate easily when reading the papers. YES NO

9. Getting to sleep takes me more than half an hour. YES NO

10. I am restless and fidgety. YES NO

11. I wake up much earlier than I need to in the morning. YES NO

12. Dying is the best solution for me. YES NO

13. I have a lot of trouble with dizzy and faint feelings. YES NO

14. I am being punished for something bad in my past. YES NO

15. My sexual interest is the same as before I got sick. YES NO

16. I am miserable or often feel like crying. YES NO

17. I often wish I were dead. YES NO

18. I am having trouble with indigestion. YES NO

19. I wake up often in the middle of the night.   YES   NO

20. I feel worthless and ashamed about myself.   YES   NO

21. I am so slowed down that I need help with bathing and dressing.   YES   NO

22. I take longer than usual to fall asleep at night.   YES   NO

23. Much of the time I am very afraid but don't know the reason.   YES   NO

24. Things which I regret about my life are bothering me.   YES   NO

25. I get pleasure and satisfaction from what I do.   YES   NO

26. All I need is a good rest to be perfectly well again.   YES   NO

27. My sleep is restless and disturbed.   YES   NO

28. My mind is as fast and alert as always.   YES   NO

29. I feel that life is still worth living.   YES   NO

30. My voice is dull and lifeless.   YES   NO

31. I feel irritable or jittery.   YES   NO

32. I feel in good spirits.   YES   NO

33. My heart sometimes beats faster than usual.   YES   NO

34. I think my case is hopeless.   YES   NO

35. I wake up before my usual time in the morning.   YES   NO

36. I still enjoy meals as much as usual.   YES   NO

37. I have to keep pacing around most of the time.   YES   NO

38. I am terrified and near panic.   YES   NO

39. My body is bad and rotten inside.   YES   NO

40. I got sick because of the bad weather we have been having.   YES   NO

41. My hands shake so much that people can easily notice.   YES   NO

42. I still like to go out and meet people.   YES   NO

43. I think I appear calm on the outside.   YES   NO

44. I think I am as good as anybody else.   YES   NO

45. My trouble is the result of some serious internal disease.   YES   NO

46. I have been thinking about trying to kill myself.   YES   NO

47. I get hardly anything done lately.   YES   NO

48. There is only misery in the future for me.   YES   NO

49. I worry a lot about my bodily symptoms.   YES   NO

50. I have to force myself to eat even a little.   YES   NO

51. I am exhausted much of the time.   YES   NO

52. I can tell that I have lost a lot of weight.   YES   NO

◆

Scoring and Interpreting the Carroll Rating Scale

To score the test, compare your answers with the scoring key below and give yourself one point each time your answer is the *same* as the one on the key.

1. no	14. yes	27. yes	40. yes
2. yes	15. no	28. no	41. yes
3. yes	16. yes	29. no	42. no
4. yes	17. yes	30. yes	43. no
5. yes	18. yes	31. yes	44. no
6. yes	19. yes	32. no	45. yes
7. no	20. yes	33. yes	46. yes
8. no	21. yes	34. yes	47. yes
9. yes	22. yes	35. yes	48. yes
10. yes	23. yes	36. no	49. yes
11. yes	24. yes	37. yes	50. yes
12. yes	25. no	38. yes	51. yes
13. yes	26. yes	39. yes	52. yes

A score greater than 10 on the Carroll Rating Scale indicates some degree of clinical Depression. The higher your numerical score over 10, the more severe your Depression.

Again, remember that clinical Depression may look like some other physical illnesses that also cause fatigue, decreased sexual drive, or weight loss. So a borderline score on this test may not necessarily mean that you definitively are Depressed. What it does mean is that you have enough symptoms to warrant a professional evaluation.

Also, keep in mind that your scores may be elevated if you are going through a particularly stressful transition or event at the moment, such as changing jobs, ending a personal relationship, or grieving over the death of a loved one. These kinds of reactive Depressive symptoms also should be considered serious enough for you to seek professional assistance if they continue for a period of two weeks or more.

Almost every self-help book on Depression stops the self-assessment portion at this stage. You are told to assess whether or not you suffer from true clinical Depression, and then you are encouraged to read on in either event. But the principal focus of most other books is on the more severe condition or illness.

This book is different because the focus is *not* on the illness of Depression. Our main concern is what to do about the moodiness that falls within the "normal" or "mild" range but still feels unpleasant and gets in the way of your feeling as good about yourself and about your life as you might like.

Measures of Blue Moods and Depressed Feelings

What can we measure about mood beyond the diagnosis of Depression? First, there are some general questions about frequency, duration, and causes of your typical bouts of the blues or low moods, and some questions about things you may have tried to get yourself up when you have felt down in the past.

These questions are included—and will be explained in more detail shortly—for two reasons. One is to make you more aware of your experience of low moods, of what causes them, and what helps you to reverse them. Second, by answering the questions that follow you will be able to compare your answers to those given by a sample of 1,000 women surveyed in a nationwide Gallup Poll using the same questions. Those results, presented and discussed in the next chapter, will provide reassurance that you are not alone with your down feelings and that there are ways you can help yourself that have worked for other women like you.

◆

Blue Mood Questionnaire

1. How often do you experience a low mood such as feeling depressed, having the blues, or being down?
1 [   ] Once a week or more
2 [   ] Two or three times a month
3 [   ] Once a month
4 [   ] Less than once a month—several times a year
5 [   ] A few times a year
6 [   ] Never

2. On the average, about how long does a case of the blues or depression generally last?
1 [   ] Less than one day
2 [   ] One or two days
3 [   ] Three days to a week
4 [   ] One to two weeks
5 [   ] Two weeks or longer

3. How well do you think you manage your low moods—keeping them contained in terms of how long they last or how intense or bad they become—and being able to turn them around?
1 [   ] Very well
2 [   ] Fairly well
3 [   ] Not very well
4 [   ] Not at all well

4. People can feel depressed for many reasons. Check how often each of the following is a significant cause or contribution to your feeling low or depressed—very often, fairly often, not very often, or never.

	Very often	Fairly often	Not very often	Never
a. Feeling tired	[ ]	[ ]	[ ]	[ ]
b. Feeling bad about yourself	[ ]	[ ]	[ ]	[ ]
c. Having too many demands on your time	[ ]	[ ]	[ ]	[ ]
d. Feeling drained by the needs of others	[ ]	[ ]	[ ]	[ ]
e. Feeling lonely	[ ]	[ ]	[ ]	[ ]
f. Feeling misunderstood	[ ]	[ ]	[ ]	[ ]
g. Feeling sexually frustrated	[ ]	[ ]	[ ]	[ ]
h. Feeling angry	[ ]	[ ]	[ ]	[ ]
i. Having problems with your husband or boyfriend	[ ]	[ ]	[ ]	[ ]
j. Having problems at work	[ ]	[ ]	[ ]	[ ]
k. Having problems with your family	[ ]	[ ]	[ ]	[ ]
l. Worrying about the future	[ ]	[ ]	[ ]	[ ]

5. Following is a list of things that some people do to make them feel better when they are down. For each one, check whether it has worked very well, fairly well, or not at all well for you personally or if you have never tried that particular activity.

	Very well	Fairly well	Not at all well	Never tried it
a. Exercise	[ ]	[ ]	[ ]	[ ]
b. Talking or thinking about your problems	[ ]	[ ]	[ ]	[ ]
c. Spending time alone	[ ]	[ ]	[ ]	[ ]
d. Sleeping	[ ]	[ ]	[ ]	[ ]
e. Having a drink or drinks	[ ]	[ ]	[ ]	[ ]
f. Watching a funny movie or TV show	[ ]	[ ]	[ ]	[ ]
g. Going shopping	[ ]	[ ]	[ ]	[ ]
h. Analyzing your bad mood— trying to understand why you feel down	[ ]	[ ]	[ ]	[ ]
i. Taking medication	[ ]	[ ]	[ ]	[ ]
j. Distracting yourself by putting your mind on work	[ ]	[ ]	[ ]	[ ]
k. Praying or meditating	[ ]	[ ]	[ ]	[ ]
l. Reading	[ ]	[ ]	[ ]	[ ]
m. Listening to music	[ ]	[ ]	[ ]	[ ]
n. Being held or cuddled	[ ]	[ ]	[ ]	[ ]
o. Making love, having sex	[ ]	[ ]	[ ]	[ ]

53

6. Many women suffer from Type E stress—the stress
   that comes from trying to be everything to everybody. To what extent do you agree or disagree that
   this kind of stress is a problem for you personally?
   1 [　] Agree strongly
   2 [　] Agree somewhat
   3 [　] Disagree somewhat
   4 [　] Disagree strongly
   5 [　] Don't know

◆

Daily Mood
Rating Form and Diary

Knowing how your mood naturally varies according to
your habitual routines, menstrual cycle, days of the week,
and the times of day will be very helpful toward achieving
better mood management.

Use the following form to rate your mood three times each
day. You should rate your mood first thing in the morning,
within an hour of rising; sometime in the midafternoon, generally between three and five P.M.; and again before bedtime,
less than an hour before falling asleep.

The important thing is that you do the rating at the same
times each day so that meaningful comparisons can be made.
Ideally, the ratings should be done for 60 days.

After recording the date and time, you will complete five
simple rating scales. Make general, overall, quick judgments
that reflect how you are feeling at the moment you make the
rating.

The diary portion asks you to note whether any event or
situation occurred to affect your mood since the last rating
period, and any specific techniques or portions of the mood
management program you may have tried or used during the
period since the last rating.

Collecting this kind of data on yourself is an important part
of the self-help program. You will become far more aware of

the variations and rhythms of your mood cycles, which will give you a context for understanding, and not overreacting to, predictable downswings or mood slumps caused by natural fatigue, low energy, hormonal variations, and the like.

Keeping ratings of your moods while you learn the methods for mood management also will be of invaluable aid in measuring your progress and in selecting techniques that work best for you.

Daily Mood Rating Form and Diary

DATE:

TIME:

Right now, I feel (circle one number on each scale):

Down _____ Up
1 2 3 4 5

Tired _____ Energetic
1 2 3 4 5

Bad about myself _____ Good about myself
1 2 3 4 5

Under high
stress _____ Under low stress
1 2 3 4 5

Comfortable _____ Uncomfortable
1 2 3 4 5

Notable events, situations, or people that have affected my mood:

Behaviors, techniques, methods of mood management that I have tried:

Other notes:

Three-Dimensional Evaluation of Low Moods

Most people think of their moods in fairly one-dimensional terms—how "up" or "down" they feel. According to some fascinating research by Dr. Albert Mehrabian of UCLA, however, mood states actually have three separate and independent dimensions: pleasure, activity or alertness, and sense of control.

By completing the evaluation below, you will have information that will allow you to fine-tune or adjust your mood on each dimension in order to bring your feelings as close as possible to the optimal, desirable mood state. The methods for altering your scores on each dimension will be detailed in later chapters.

Think about how you are feeling now. Circle the number between 1 and 9 on each scale below that comes closest to describing the way your mood and feelings are:

---

1. How pleasant or unpleasant does your mood feel?

Extremely   Extremely
unpleasant _____ pleasant
              1 2 3 4 5 6 7 8 9

2. How physically active or aroused and/or how mentally alert do you feel?

Extremely
inactive
and/or   Hyperactive
underalert _____ and/or
              1 2 3 4 5 6 7 8 9 overalert

3. How much in or out of control do you feel?

Totally out   Totally
of control _____ in control
              1 2 3 4 5 6 7 8 9

The optimal, desirable mood state is one in which you feel very to extremely pleasant, moderately active or alert, and mostly, though not totally, in control. In numerical terms, your scale "profile" for an optimal mood state would be a score of 8 to 9 on the first dimension, 4 to 6 on the second, and 7 to 8 on the third. Don't be overly concerned now if your scores are too high or too low. Use your scores as a benchmark and know that we will be discussing how to fine-tune your moods in a later chapter.

The Rosenberg Self-esteem Scale

A final measurement, strongly related to feeling depressed, is the Rosenberg Self-esteem Scale.

On the 10 items below, indicate for each whether you strongly agree, agree, disagree, or strongly disagree with the statement:[2]

	Strongly Agree	Agree	Disagree	Strongly Disagree
1. On the whole I am satisfied with myself.	[ ]	[ ]	[ ]	[ ]
2. At times I think I am no good at all.	[ ]	[ ]	[ ]	[ ]
3. I feel that I have a number of good qualities.	[ ]	[ ]	[ ]	[ ]
4. I am able to do things as well as most other people.	[ ]	[ ]	[ ]	[ ]

2. The scale is reprinted with permission from Morris Rosenberg, Ph.D., and was previously published in Morris Rosenberg, *Conceiving the Self* (New York: Basic Books, 1979).

	Strongly Agree	Agree	Disagree	Strongly Disagree
5. I feel I do not have much to be proud of.	[ ]	[ ]	[ ]	[ ]
6. I certainly feel useless at times.	[ ]	[ ]	[ ]	[ ]
7. I feel that I'm a person of worth, at least on an equal plane with others.	[ ]	[ ]	[ ]	[ ]
8. I wish I could have more respect for myself.	[ ]	[ ]	[ ]	[ ]
9. All in all, I am inclined to feel that I am a failure.	[ ]	[ ]	[ ]	[ ]
10. I take a positive attitude toward myself.	[ ]	[ ]	[ ]	[ ]

◆

The self-esteem scale is scored as follows. For items 1, 3, 4, 7, and 10, give yourself a score of 4 for each time you said "strongly agree," 3 for "agree," 2 for "disagree," and 1 for "strongly disagree"; on items 2, 5, 6, 8, and 9, give yourself a score of 4 for each "strongly disagree," 3 for "disagree," 2 for "agree," and 1 for "strongly agree" answer.

Now total your scores. Scores on the Rosenberg Self-esteem Scale can range from 10 to 40, where lower scores indicate poor or low self-esteem and higher scores, positive or high self-esteem. If your score is lower than 20, you are not feeling good enough about yourself and your negative self-esteem may be a significant causal factor in your blue moods and feelings of depression.

You now have learned a great deal about two very different forms of depressive states or conditions—major, clinical Depressive illness versus milder forms of depressed, blue, and down moods—and about how to categorize and describe your own mood problem.

You've gone beyond didactic learning to a personal assessment of your mood problems. On the basis of the Braiker Mood Scale for Women and the Carroll Rating Scale you may have found that your mood problem is—or may be—Depressive illness. And you have been advised, and I hope are following the recommendation, to seek professional help.

More likely, though, you have discovered that although you may have been worrying about whether you are seriously Depressed, in fact you are not. Instead, your problem is that you have periodic bouts of low moods and down feelings and are about to find out how many other women share your experience.

5

◆

You're Not Alone:
A Depression Survey

◆

*Draw from others the lesson that may profit
yourself.*
                              —PUBLIUS TERENTIUS

Feeling down also can make you feel quite alone. But, as you
will see, if you suffer from periodic bouts of depressed moods
and the blues, you are in the company of a great many other
women. It is a simple fact of human nature that a measure of
comfort comes from just knowing that other people share
some of your problems.

In this chapter you will have the opportunity to compare
your responses to the Blue Mood Questionnaire you just
completed with those given by a sample of 1,000 women
across America. My opportunity to ask this large group of
women about their experiences with depressed moods came
when a leading manufacturer of women's hosiery, No Nonsense Fashions, Inc., engaged my services to design and
analyze a corporate-sponsored nationwide attitude survey of
contemporary working women. The results of the survey that
you are about to read were not released prior to the publica-
tion of this book.

"The No Nonsense Women's Attitude Survey," conducted
by the Gallup Organization in December 1987, surveyed

women ranging in age from 18 to 54, all of whom worked full- or part-time. The 1,000 women surveyed came from all regions of the United States and all socioeconomic and occupational groups; the sample included single, married, divorced, separated, and widowed women, with and without children. The survey design allowed some fascinating comparisons between the attitudes and experiences of working women in traditional families (married with children), married working women without children (called DINKs—for Dual Income, No Kids), single mothers (divorced or separated), and single women who had never been married.

Frequency of Feeling Depressed

The overwhelming majority of women in the survey acknowledged that they do experience low moods. Fully 93 percent reported that, with varying frequency, they "feel depressed, have the blues, or get down." Only 5 percent denied having periodic depressions with 2 percent stating that they simply "didn't know."

Of the total sample, almost half (48 percent) said that they get the blues or feel depressed at least once a month or more often. Fifteen percent reported getting down very frequently—once a week or more often—and another 10 percent estimated that their low moods occur about two to three times a month. Almost a quarter (23 percent) said that they feel depressed once a month.

About an equal portion of the sample stated that their down moods occur less frequently than once a month, with 5 percent indicating that they feel down several times a year and another 41 percent estimating that their depressions are relatively infrequent, occurring only a few times a year.

Single women who had never been married and relatively younger women reported a tendency to get depressed slightly more often than those who were married or those in the over-40 age group. Women whose household incomes exceeded $50,000 were less likely to report frequent bouts of depression (18 percent) compared to those whose household incomes were under $20,000 (32 percent).

The respondents were asked to what extent they felt that Type E stress—defined as the stress that comes from "trying to be everything to everybody"—was a problem for them personally. Across all categories, three out of four women labeled themselves as suffering from Type E stress, with the highest proportion among women in traditional families (80 percent) and the lowest among singles (65 percent). Both DINKs and single mothers were intermediate between the two.

Feeling the stress that comes from trying to be everything to everybody was related to the likelihood of experiencing relatively frequent low moods. Among Type E women, 59 percent had frequent bouts of the blues (more than once a month) as compared with only 27 percent of those who said they did not suffer from Type E stress. And women who reported getting down once a month were also more likely to say they suffered from Type E stress. Those who said they didn't suffer from Type E stress were more likely to state that their depressed moods occurred infrequently.

How Long Do the Blues Last?

Of all the women surveyed, the great majority said that their depressed feelings lasted for a week or less. A very sizable minority (40 percent) said that, on the average, when they get down, their low moods last for only several hours. Most, however, estimated that a typical bout of the blues lasts either one to two days (43 percent) or as long as about a week (9 percent). Only 5 percent of the sample reported having longer-lasting depressions, with only a very small group (2 percent) meeting the criterion for major Depression (a sad or blue mood that lasts for at least two weeks or longer). The latter statistic is not surprising, however, since the estimated prevalence of major Depression among all women is 15 percent and the survey sample included only women who work: consequently it would underrepresent women whose illness is so severe as to make holding even a part-time job impossible.

How Well
Are the Blues Managed?

More than half of the women surveyed indicated that they were able to manage their low moods only "fairly well" in terms of how long their moods last, how intense they become, or how easily they can be turned around to more positive moods. Women over 40 rated themselves as somewhat better mood managers than those in the younger age groups, and women who work at full-time jobs or careers also reported better mood management than those who work only part-time.

Women who rated their effectiveness at managing their depressed moods as very high were less likely to see themselves as Type E women; among the minority who stated that they did not manage their depressed feelings and low moods well at all, more were likely to say they suffered from Type E stress. These findings suggest that mood management and stress management are probably strongly related.

What Causes Blue Moods?

The most frequently cited reasons for getting down given by women in this sample were "having too many demands on my time," "feeling tired," and "being drained by the needs of others"—all of which are defining features of the Type E stress syndrome. The complete list of reasons, rank-ordered by how often respondents said they were a frequent cause of blue moods, is shown below:

◆

**Reasons for Feeling Low or Depressed
(percent saying "frequent")**

Too many demands on my time	66
Feeling tired	53
Feeling drained by needs of others	48
Worrying about the future	41
Feeling angry	36
Feeling misunderstood	29

Having problems at work	27
Feeling bad about myself	26
Feeling lonely	24
Having problems with my family	23
Having problems with a man	20
Feeling sexually frustrated	14

◆

There were some interesting differences between the four main survey groups in terms of how often each saw the reasons as important causes of their depressed moods:

◆

Reasons for Feeling Low or Depressed
(percent saying "frequent")

Reason	Women in Traditional Families	DINKs	Single Mothers	Singles
Too many demands on time	75	60	60	57
Feeling tired	59	49	57	53
Drained by needs of others	55	39	43	44
Worried about the future	35	43	59	52
Feeling angry	38	29	29	40
Feeling misunderstood	31	21	30	36
Problems at work	25	39	26	34
Feeling bad about myself	21	24	26	32
Feeling lonely	13	12	45	29
Problems with family	18	21	24	27
Problems with a man	19	20	15	28
Feeling sexually frustrated	14	9	27	17

◆

What Helps to Lift Low Moods?

Finally, women in the survey were asked about the kinds of things they do to get themselves up when they are feeling down. Seven activities were identified as something that 90 percent of the respondents had tried as a way to get out of a low mood.

- Talking or thinking about your problems
- Analyzing or trying to understand why you feel down
- Spending time alone
- Watching a funny movie or television show
- Going shopping
- Listening to music
- Being held or cuddled

With the exception of going shopping and spending time alone (which were rated as only moderately effective), the same activities were rated as working the best to help respondents get out of their low moods.

Some activities that a majority of respondents rated as working very well in raising their spirits had never even been tried as a remedy by 15 to 20 percent of the sample:

- Exercise
- Reading
- Distracting yourself by putting your mind on work
- Making love or having sex
- Praying or meditating

Although 88 percent said that they tried sleeping when they felt down, it was rated as being among the least effective methods for restoring a better mood. Also rated as least effective methods were taking a drink or drinks (tried by 54 percent), and taking medication (tried by 30 percent).

You Can Get Out in Front of the Pack

It appears from the survey that being prone to depressed feelings and bouts of the blues is a normal part of the experience shared by almost all working women. And I assure you that blue moods are a part of everyday life among what has now become the minority of women who do not work. So you are by no means alone, despite how isolated or unusual your depressed moods might make you feel.

Now that you know that your experience of having the blues or feeling down puts you right smack in the mainstream, wouldn't you like to move ahead of the pack by learning how to better manage your depressed moods so that they become less frequent, briefer in duration, and less disruptive to your life? I hope your answer is yes, because that is precisely what the program you are about to learn is designed to do.

6

◆

Blue Alert

◆

Forewarned, forearmed.

—LATIN PROVERB

Nan, 39, is a social worker for a county agency that administers financial aid to families with dependent children. She lives alone, having divorced her husband two years ago. At the moment there is no special man in Nan's life.

Around five P.M. on a dark, cloudy Friday afternoon, as Nan is straightening up her desk preparing for the weekend, she begins to feel edgy and restless. Gazing out the window at the overcast sky and descending darkness, Nan feels lonely and sorry for herself.

"I've got no place to go and nobody who cares if I come home or not. This is really going to be a miserable weekend," she mumbles.

Her friend and co-worker, Hillary, overhears the lament and invites Nan to join a group from the office that is going out for Mexican food and margaritas. Nan declines on the grounds that she'll "probably be bad company and bring the others down."

On the way home, Nan is particularly impatient and irritable with the traffic and the crowds of "all the people who are eager to get home so they can get ready for a fun weekend."

As she pulls the car into the garage of her apartment building, she mutters, "I hate weekends alone. This is such a drag."

Nan's weekend turns out to be every bit as lonely and boring as she predicted it would be. Since she is "not in the mood for people," she keeps her telephone answering machine on and avoids returning calls, putting them off until Monday. The majority of her weekend is spent doing chores and errands that she finds unpleasant but sufficiently exhausting to enable her to fall asleep before nine P.M. each night.

By Monday morning, when Nan reluctantly awakens to her alarm, the black cloud of depression that has hung over her head all weekend seems to envelop her entire being. She decides to stay home from work on the grounds that "the world is too depressing a place for me to handle today." As she pulls the blankets over her head, she says aloud, "I can't face one more homeless family or abused child." She calls in sick at eight A.M., and by eight-thirty she actually begins to *feel* sick.

Nan inventories her body for signs of aches, pains, and stiffness. "I'm definitely losing it," she thinks aloud. "By next year, when I turn forty, I'll need plastic surgery just to get a date."

This line of thought leads her to a mental review of all of her unhappy relationships with men since her divorce. "Men are the pits," she declares. "I'll never find anyone to love me again. Who would want to wake up to someone who feels like me anyway?"

By noon her blues have darkened. Now she feels guilty and fraudulent for staying home from work. "I'm such a loser," she complains. "I'll probably get fired for this. My boss always looks at me with those hard, contemptuous eyes. Why do people hate me?"

And so it goes for Nan. By nightfall on Monday, she is thoroughly exhausted and in far lower spirits than when she awoke. Her strategy of avoiding life for the day has hopelessly backfired. She has spent an entire day trapped inside her own head, thinking dismal, morbid thoughts and projecting negative expectations about her future. And she takes her misshapen version of reality very seriously.

Nan is a classic example of a woman mismanaging the blues. What she doesn't recognize is that her negative mood is distorting the way she is thinking and processing information. Nan thinks she feels depressed because the world (i.e., men, her boss, herself) is a negative, woeful place; actually the world *seems* negative because Nan is evaluating her life *while* she is mired in the blues. And, by remaining inactive, avoiding people and her normal activities, ruminating, and summoning forth negative memories, Nan all but guarantees that the dark void of her mood will only widen and deepen, leaving her feeling helpless and hopeless.

If Nan had known more about depression and responded differently to the early stages of her low mood on Friday afternoon, she might have prevented the whole downward spiral from happening, or at least slowed its momentum and reduced its intensity. Nan could have fought back against the onslaught of her blues if she had been more aware of what was happening to her and had known what steps to take to ward off the danger. But Nan wasn't prepared for a fight and her depression won an easy victory.

In order for you to successfully defend yourself against an attack of depression, you have to be in battle-ready psychological condition. And now is the time to start your training. Otherwise, you might find yourself as defenseless as Nan, vanquished by the enemy forces of a negative mood.

First, your emotional radar should be sensitive and powerful, able to detect the very earliest signs of a depressed mood approaching so that you can get prepared to respond and defend yourself accordingly. With a well-honed mood-sensing capability, you can respond early enough to effectively deter many depressions from developing altogether.

If the blues can't be aborted completely, as is sometimes the case, you will need to mount your psychological defenses and launch an effective campaign of counterattack behavior. But your defense strategy will require accurate information about where and how the depression will strike.

Negative mood states affect far wider psychological territory than just your feelings or emotions. At a minimum, depression alters and distorts your thought and memory processes, your interpretive and perceptual judgment, as well as your attitudes and behavior toward other people and yourself. But the distorting effects, fortunately, operate in predictable and systematic ways for almost everyone. Awareness of how depression operates will greatly reduce its power. By learning to anticipate how and where the blues will affect you, and interpreting the distortions as reflecting depression rather than reality, you can overcome and reverse its insidious influence.

The United States armed forces operate on the premise that the purpose of the military during peacetime is to stay prepared for war. Psychologically or militarily, preparation reduces uncertainty and vulnerability. Coming from a position of strength and preparedness will eliminate the sense of helplessness you feel when depression threatens to destroy your emotional balance.

Low moods are the enemy; your happiness, psychological well-being, and quality of life are endangered whenever depression rears its ugly head. Once you learn how to "man" your mental and behavioral battle stations and activate a "Blue Alert," you will be ready to do battle with your depressions. And you will emerge victorious.

But before we turn to the battle itself, we must begin by recognizing the signs that the enemy is in the area—with the cues and signals that a depression is about to encroach on your sovereign state of mind.

Emotional Radar: Your Early-Warning System

Late Friday afternoon, Nan was experiencing the early warning signs of her impending depression. But her emotional radar either failed to pick up the signals or failed to properly activate her Blue Alert system.

For years, I have noticed that patients often describe "pre-depression" sensations and feelings. One of my patients, for example, says, "I could feel my mood starting to sink in the early afternoon and by dinnertime the depression really hit me." Another remarks, "As soon as I got off the phone with him, I started feeling angry, frustrated, and confused. And I just knew that sooner or later I'd get overwhelmed with depression." Still another describes the predepression experience this way: "For a few days, I felt very stressed and anxious. I was having disturbing dreams and waking up a lot during the night. This always seems to happen to me right before a bout of the blues sets in and the bottom drops out."

What these statements reveal is something you also may know to be true of your experience with depression: You can *feel* it coming on. You may not have actually described this sense of premonition or verbalized the abstract feelings, but like most people, you can probably tell that something is "off" or wrong with your mood and state of mind *before* you actually label the experience as feeling down or depressed.

This predepression stage has a name, borrowed from the lexicon of medicine, and it is *prodrome*. The word *prodrome* comes from a Greek root meaning "running before" and is defined as the warning symptoms of a disease. So the feelings and sensations that precede the actual onset of a depressed mood are the prodromes of the problem.

If you become sensitive to your own prodromal signals, you will take a major step forward in the mood-management process. This is because depressed moods, like some other medical conditions that produce prodromes, can often be averted if you act promptly and correctly.

Migraine headache sufferers, for example, are taught to recognize the prodrome of their pain. The prodromes of migraine include visual disturbances like flashing lights, swirling images, or extreme light sensitivity. Other signs can be light-headedness followed by a sense of tightening or constriction in the skull, nausea, or in the case of allergic or cluster headaches, swelling and tearing of one or both eyes. If the migraine patient learns to identify these signs as the prodrome of a headache, she or he can take the proper medication immediately, go to sleep, and often successfully abort the acute, intense pain stage altogether.

Knowing the prodromal signs of *your* mood changes will help you control depression in at last three important ways. First, you can respond to the prodromal symptoms directly and by *treating or removing the prodrome,* greatly reducing the probability that the depression will ensue. Second, you can take immediate steps to *counteract the depression* itself. Finally, by recognizing the prodrome, you can alert yourself to the possibility that depression may start to distort your thinking, judgment, feelings, and behavior so that you can *buffer yourself* accordingly against its effect.

Having good emotional radar and an effective early warning system depends on developing the ability to observe yourself—to monitor changes and cues in your moods or reactions and interpret their meaning. By keeping a watchful eye on your moods and being particularly vigilant regarding their prodromes, you will be far less vulnerable to a "surprise attack" where you suddenly feel very down, out of control of your negative emotions.

Recognizing Your Own
Prodrome of Depression

Developing mood-sensing capabilities takes time and practice. Your Daily Mood Rating Form and Diary (from Chapter 4) will be very helpful by revealing the patterns of your mood cycles and the situations, feelings, and time periods associated with downward shifts.

Just knowing about the concept of a prodrome will sensitize you to the signals that are forerunners of your low moods. You can assist or guide your self-observation by asking yourself these questions:

1. Looking back over my experiences with depression and the blues, how do I sense that my mood is dropping?
2. What kinds of feelings seem to lead to or produce down moods in me?
3. What starts to change in my behavior or attitude when a low mood is coming on?

Some of the most common prodromes of depressed moods include anxiety or irritability, stress, exhaustion, and feeling overloaded. Some people report restlessness and/or "spaciness"—a sense of detachment or withdrawal from others. Others point to feeling burdened or weighted down as forerunners of depression.

One of my patients says that she can tell that she is starting to get depressed when her facial expression changes. "I can tell that I've stopped smiling or even looking pleasant. My face feels like it's sagging. I feel older when I'm starting to get down."

Another patient describes her prodrome this way: "Before I know I'm depressed, I just don't like the way I feel. It's like feeling uncomfortable in my own skin. I lose my patience and lots of little things start getting on my nerves. And there's a heaviness or seriousness to my whole appearance. Friends of mine usually know that I'm down before I even recognize it."

You also might find that your friends and family will be helpful in giving you feedback about how they can tell when you are getting into a low mood. Conversely, think about someone that you know very well and how you pick up subtle cues like changes in appearance, vocal inflection and tone, or behavior that signal that he or she is in a bad mood and is feeling down. Then try looking for similar behavioral signs in yourself.

The prodrome for your blue moods may be like those of some of my patients or like your friends'; or it may be largely or completely idiosyncratic. You may discover that you have different kinds of prodromes for different kinds of low moods. The important point is that you get to know yourself and how you feel and behave when a depression is looming.

Tuning in your emotional radar doesn't mean that you should become totally preoccupied with your internal, mental experiences. Nor should you always be sensing or expecting trouble. But you should be aware of danger signs that do pop up on your emotional landscape. And of course you should know what to do about them once the Blue Alert is sounded.

Treating the Prodrome:
The Preemptive Strike

If you become sufficiently sensitized to your prodromal signals, you will have the advantage of making a preemptive strike on your low mood. In other words, you can behave proactively instead of reactively, and hit the depression before it hits you.

Joan, for example, has learned how to prevent most of her depressed moods from ever materializing by treating her prodrome directly. Joan is a teacher in her early 50's with a very active social and professional life. She belongs to a number of professional organizations and community groups, as well as being the principal source of emotional support to family members, friends, foster children, and students whom she privately tutors.

For the most part, Joan is the kind of woman who thrives on staying busy, helping people, and being continually involved in projects and activities. But periodically she starts to feel stressed out and overwhelmed. Joan has learned that when she begins to feel out of control over the demands on her life, and too out of balance with respect to the energy she is putting out for others versus what she is taking in or reserving for herself, depression will be the consequence.

Joan used to experience a short but disruptive episode of depression every few months when she worked herself literally to the point of collapse. Weakened by her exhaustion, she was then flooded with negative emotions and feelings of helplessness and failure.

In therapy, Joan was able to see that she could intervene in this dangerous cycle and not have to wait to react until she was at the point where she had no alternative. Joan's prodrome for depression is Type E stress. Type E stress, Joan learned, can be managed effectively by prioritizing and cutting back on some activities, by saying "no" to some of the people in her life at least some of the time, by delegating some of her detail work on projects to others, and by communicating her needs and asking for others to help, assist, and support her when she tires.

By directly addressing the prodrome of her low mood episodes, Joan is now able to keep her Type E stress under threshold levels so that it no longer escalates into depression and collapse.

Type E stress is an epidemic problem among women today and will be addressed in greater detail in a later chapter. Suffice it to say here that if you recognize tendencies in yourself to try to be everything to everybody and deny your own needs to rest and regenerate your energies, then Type E stress may well be a prodromal condition for your down moods. By adjusting the stress level down, you will likely forestall the appearance of many of your blue episodes. A number of highly effective methods for reducing Type E stress are detailed in another of my books, *The Type E Woman: How to Overcome the Stress of Being Everything to Everybody*.

In an analogous way, other prodromal symptoms can be treated directly and the depression can be headed off at the pass. Instead of waiting for the prodrome to escalate and for the depression to hit you, you can choose instead to take the initiative and to preemptively attack the forerunning problem in order to prevent the depressive consequences.

Exhaustion, for example, requires rest, relaxation, and restorative sleep. Anxiety may be lowered by physical exercise, massage, relaxation methods such as rhythmic breathing, calming visual imagery, or exposure to soothing music or nature sounds.

Feeling overwhelmed by work or overloaded by time pressures can be addressed by learning and applying time-management skills and prioritizing methods. (These techniques and others that work effectively to reduce or eliminate the prodromal symptoms of depression directly will be explained more fully in later chapters.)

Some prodromes, however, cannot be treated directly. Feeling "off," "out of sorts," or "uncomfortable inside your own skin," for example, are less clearly defined, more abstract descriptors of the prodromal stage and are not easily treated in a direct way. Nevertheless, recognition of the prodrome will allow you to act quickly and effectively to counteract the depressed mood itself.

Distraction and Physical Activity: First Lines of Defense

There is an intriguing and important difference between the characteristic ways that women and men handle their depressed moods. The bad news is that what women do is the psychological equivalent of running barefoot into a blizzard with a blossoming head cold, clad only in a T-shirt and jogging shorts. When women get down, they typically respond by slowing down physically, becoming inactive, and focusing their thoughts inward. They begin to ruminate about their down mood, conjuring up negative memories and thoughts and worrying about all their problems. This response only serves to amplify, intensify, and prolong depressed feelings.

According to Dr. Susan Nolen-Hoeksema at the University of Pennsylvania, there are several reasons why rumination and inactivity operate to lengthen the course and deepen the intensity of your depressed moods.[1] First, when you are depressed, a storehouse of negative memories is activated. Counterbalancing positive memories are excluded. Your mind becomes flooded with negative thoughts. In turn, these negative thoughts and memories function to distort your interpretation of current events, so you see them as fitting into a pattern of negative outcomes, failures, and losses. Nan's lonely weekend, for example, is incorporated into her memories of disappointments with men and viewed as part of a never-ending pattern of failure and defeat.

Second, rumination increases your tendency to blame yourself for whatever problems and negative feelings you are having. Because your mental energy and attention are focused inward, the relative salience or "size" of your contribution to undesirable events is blown out of proportion and made to seem larger than it actually may be. Because atten-

---

1. S. Nolen-Hoeksema, "Sex Differences in Unipolar Depression: Evidence and Theory," *Psychological Bulletin*, 101, 2 (1987), 259–282.

tion is not diverted by physical activity or other means of distraction, the negative energy is spent on punitive self-flagellation, self-blame, and calling yourself names, which only lead to apathy, pessimism, and further expectations of failure. In short: You stay depressed.

Third, rumination and inactivity focused on the implications of your depressed mood interfere with your attention, concentration, and motivation to complete work or other projects that are likely to generate rewards. In other words, if you spend a day at your desk unable to complete a report that your boss is waiting for because instead you are ruminating about your depression, you will not generate praise from your boss (which might help to reverse your negative feelings) but will most likely actually reap criticism. Because rumination disrupts effective action-oriented problem solving, your sense of helplessness in the face of your difficulties is only enhanced.

Fourth, becoming inactive reduces or perhaps even stops the production and release of natural antidepressant and painkilling substances—endorphins and enkephalons—that the brain releases during pleasurable experiences and physical activity. So giving in to the inertia and inactivity of depression is biochemically counterproductive.

Finally, if you're like a lot of other women, becoming inactive, holing up in the house, and ruminating over people and things that depress you are often accompanied by excessive eating. If you find yourself turning to food—and especially sweets—as a way to feel better when you're down, you already know all too well that the only thing that's going to go up from excessive eating is your weight, not your mood. Unfortunately, rumination and overeating is a common and dangerous combination that produces a vicious cycle of further depression, self-flagellation, guilt, and eventually more overeating.

That's the bad news for women. The good news is that women can learn something from the way men typically respond to the onset of low moods. Most men, when they feel down, tend to increase their activity level and, specifically, engage in activities that are designed to distract them from thinking about their low moods and problems. Many women, in fact, complain about the way their husbands or boyfriends deal (or fail to deal) with depression. These women view the distracting activities as ways of avoiding or denying the psychological reality and "hiding from problems."

Of course, no one should avoid dealing with *bona fide* life problems and mood disturbances that may be signaled by a bout of the blues. But a transitory mood slump may be a false alarm that should not be invested with too much significance. Real blue moods and depressions are unlikely to vanish completely with physical activity and distraction. On the other hand, many an emotional low or slump that gets overinvested with meaning by a woman who sits inactively ruminating might pass within a few hours if, instead, she engages in some distraction and physical activity.

In fact, research shows that this is one time when the male style of ignoring emotionality or negative moods works to men's advantage. Responding to the prodrome or initial stirrings that a depression may be forthcoming by engaging in physical activity and in distracting activities is the right thing to do. *Distraction and physical activity are your first lines of defense against a prodrome of the blues.*

Once you have identified or recognized the prodrome of a possible bout of the blues, you can act quickly and often effectively to abort the depression entirely. When you sense a prodrome of the blues, immediately try to get your mind focused on something other than your mood for a period of at least 30 minutes to perhaps two hours. Optimally, if time and circumstances permit, engage in physical exercise or activity. A brisk walk right outside your home or office for 20 minutes can have very beneficial effects on your mood.

If, in fact, your prodrome has signaled only a passing rain squall instead of a more serious emotional downpour or storm, your mood may recover spontaneously after a relatively brief period of distraction and physical activity.

However, you may find that your mood is still in a slump even after your trial period of first-line defensive behaviors. This should not be interpreted as meaning that you or the methods have failed. On the contrary, by engaging in the right behaviors instead of the counterproductive instinctive responses of inactivity and rumination, you have succeeded in preventing your mood from getting much worse.

If the prodrome remains and/or the depressed mood continues to develop, you will need to implement the mood-management program described in overview in the next chapter, and elaborated fully throughout the rest of the book.

Before turning to the program, however, it is important to emphasize a final aspect of the Blue Alert mode—alerting yourself to the effects and influences of your depressed mood and its prodrome on your thinking processes, perception, judgment, and behavior.

Seeing the World
Through Gray-Tinted Glasses

Getting yourself into a Blue Alert means readying yourself for an important fight. That battle is to beat back the blues and to reinstate in their place an optimistic attitude and positive state of mind.

But fighting off depression can be a particularly difficult struggle, especially since you will be handicapped by the fact that depression itself alters, distorts, biases, and misrepresents the way the world appears to you in fundamental ways. It is vitally important for you to be able to recognize the ways in which depression dims and diminishes the accuracy of your view of reality; otherwise, you will accept your assessments as valid when they are not.

In the first place, the world you see through the miasma of depession is a darker, bleaker place. But you must know that you are seeing things through the mental equivalent of gray-tinted lenses that distort everything toward the negative. If you don't recognize and try intentionally to compensate for the "graying" effect, you will make basic and serious errors in judgment that will lead you to believe that you are helpless, that you can't feel any better, that there are no good alternatives, or that there is very little hope. Those conclusions reflect the depressed mood itself and not reality.

When your head is congested because of a cold, your senses of taste and smell can become impaired. Yet you are not likely to believe that food, in general, has lost its taste or that roses have lost their fragrance forever. Instead, you correctly attribute the source of the difficulty to your nasty cold. Moreover, you know that when the cold is gone, all of your senses will be fully restored and food will taste and smell delicious once again.

Think of depression as a temporary condition, like a cold, that for a brief time alters your mental, perceptual, and behavioral apparatus, much as a cold impairs your senses. You will need to learn to discount your impaired view of things when you are feeling down in much the same way you discount the absence of fragrance in a rose when you have a stuffy nose.

When you are in a depressed mood, you will tend to be more pessimistic and more willing or able to see the negative, downside of things than when your mood is positive. Given a half-full glass of water, as the old saying goes, you will see the glass as being half empty.

Apparently, one reason the future seems bleak when you're depressed is that your depressed mood makes you think that bad things are more likely to happen. Several research studies demonstrate the negativity bias caused by depression. In one, slides of people, places, and situations that were designed to be inherently ambiguous were presented and subjects were asked to say what each slide was describing. Depressed subjects saw the slides as representing more unpleasant information than did subjects whose moods were neutral. Subjects in positive moods, conversely, interpreted the ambiguous slides as representing more positive information.

Negativity and pessimism creep into the interpersonal perceptions of depressed people as well. Depressed people are far more likely than those in a positive mood to make negative judgments about others and about their own abilities or qualities. They accept the blame for negative outcomes, while attributing the credit for positive outcomes to others. Problems are seen as more complicated by depressed subjects, and such people tend to underestimate the degree of control they do have over outcomes. Depressed people are less able to maintain their self-esteem and will see themselves as helpless to change themselves or their situations.

Depressed thinking is riddled with logical flaws, exaggeration (especially of one's own flaws and the extent one blames oneself), negativity biases, and polarized, extreme, black and white judgments.

These errors amount to the kinds of data-processing "bugs" that lead to the phenomenon known in the computer vernacular as "garbage in, garbage out." The conclusions that such distorted and erroneous reasoning generates perpetuate depression and unhappiness—which brings us full circle, back to Nan.

Nan's self-talk at the opening of this chapter is replete with examples of the kind of flawed thinking that characterizes depressed moods. Chances are you may have overheard some of your own self-talk. Wallowing in verbal self-flagellation, Nan's conclusions and analyses left her mired deeper and deeper in her down feelings, flooded with negative emotions, thoughts, memories and dire predictions.

What all of this adds up to is that depression does some very noticeable things to your head. The problem is that you may be so ensconced in your depressed way of looking at things that you do not notice how negatively biased you have become about yourself, other people, and the future in general.

So dangerous are the implications of naively believing your negative perceptions to be true that a state of Blue Alert is mandatory when you sense the earliest signs of a down mood starting. The Blue Alert mode should activate your internal sensor, keeping you on your toes and healthfully skeptical about trusting yourself to think entirely clearly or objectively when you are down. As long as you are alerted to the effects of depression on how you are looking at life, you immediately will know that nothing is as bad as it appears. That's not really you talking, saying all of those negative things: *That's your depression talking.*

When your depression talks, you should listen, but only to discover what to do to get yourself out of the hole. And doing that is what the next chapter is all about.

7

◆

The Triple A Program for Effective Mood Management

◆

It is not enough for a man to improve his ways; help him to do so.

— THE KORESTER RABBI

Depression, in a word, feels bad, but that's actually good news for you.

This is because pain of any kind—physical or emotional—triggers a natural, instinctive motive to halt the discomfort and restore a more positive, comfortable state. Your built-in psychological defense mechanisms are designed to ward off painful feelings such as depression and anxiety. Left to its own devices, your mind would reflexively fight depressed feelings and reestablish your mental equilibrium.

The catch is that you don't leave your mind's natural defense system to its own devices. This is because—much to your own disadvantage—over the years you have learned many patterns of thought and behavior that prevent the defense system from operating effectively. The program you will learn in this book will remove those obstacles and help you to lubricate the gears of your natural self-protective mechanism for battling blue moods.

In this chapter, I will give you a very brief overview of the mood-management program and the rationale for why and how it works. Then, in the next three parts of the book, I will take you through each of the three vital elements of the program in far greater depth and detail and give you concrete, step-by-step instructions for how to apply the principles and techniques to your own mood problems.

An Overview
of the Triple A Program

There are three basic steps in effective mood management:

Step One: ACCEPT your depressed mood.
Step Two: ATTRIBUTE your depressed mood to its cause.
Step Three: ACT to restore a positive mood.

None of these steps appears problematic or difficult on its face. Indeed, as you learn to remove the self-imposed obstacles and unlearn the damaging thought and behavioral habits that currently block you from effectively accomplishing each step, you will see that the program is simple. But my experience treating women who have trouble managing their moods convinces me that these are the steps over which most women stumble and often fall.

Let's take a quick glimpse at each to understand, first, what it is about the particular psychological process that poses difficulties and, second, why the completion of each step is the quickest, most effective, and most rewarding path to overcoming depression.

Step One:
Accept Your Depressed Mood

Unless you fully accept your negative mood as a problem to be dealt with, you won't be in the right position to develop solutions. Acceptance only begins with acknowledging that you *are* feeling depressed. Beyond the acknowledgment are a host of other issues. You must learn, for example, to give yourself permission to feel depressed without either feeling guilty or giving in to your down mood. Then, you must learn to accept the responsibility to act in ways that will restore more positive feelings, and to accept the reality of situations, people, and circumstances that you cannot change, while meeting the challenge of changing what you can. Finally, you must learn to accept the cyclical, repetitive nature of mood swings, knowing that you can confidently control your next experience of depression without succumbing to undue fears.

Effectively managing your depressed moods requires overcoming many resistance beliefs that block full acceptance. You also must learn to stop counterproductive denial efforts that only dissipate energy and leave you feeling even more depressed and inadequate.

You may believe, for example, that you cannot afford to be down because so many other people depend on you for emotional support, nurturance, or encouragement. Or you may feel that you have no right to be depressed because you "have it all"; conversely, you may block accepting your depressed mood by expending your mental efforts in convoluted arguments with yourself to the effect that you wouldn't be down if you didn't expect so much out of life, and who are you anyway to entertain such high expectations?

It may seem contradictory for me to assert that women can acknowledge their negative emotions relatively easily, but they don't accept their blue moods and depressions in ways that are helpful toward alleviating their problems. My patients, for example, often insist, "Of course I know I'm depressed. That's why I came to see you. I'm down in the dumps a lot of the time and I hate myself for it. I've accepted that I've got a problem."

"No," I answer, "you've only acknowledged that you're down but you haven't given yourself *permission to accept* your low moods without attacking yourself as being hateful and flawed simply because you feel depressed."

Acknowledging that you are feeling down is not the same thing as accepting the problem in all its dimensions.

Step Two: Attribute Your Depressed Mood to Its Causes

There is a long-standing debate in psychology as to whether gaining insight into the reasons behind your emotional problems and symptoms is sufficient or even effective in getting you to change. Despite much insight-oriented talk therapy, research shows that knowing *why* you have a problem generally is not enough to produce a solution. You also have to know what to do to change, how to do it, when to do it, and how to sustain your motivation. And these behavioral directives may or may not pertain to why you developed the problem in the first place.

The hard truth is that seeking insight and understanding into your problems may really be a form of procrastination designed to lure you into thinking that you are doing something when, in fact, you are only thinking instead of acting. As I often say to my patients who have self-destructive habits like overeating, smoking, problem drinking, and the like, "Spending precious time trying to determine *why* you are doing what you do is a costly luxury. You can't afford to indulge yourself in the luxury of spending a year on the couch exploring the depths of your personality trying to understand why you are doing something that is obviously so dangerous to your health. The right questions to ask first are: *How* are you going to stop? *When* are you going to stop? *What* are you going to do to reward yourself and sustain your motivation to change?"

To a considerable extent, the same is true about asking yourself why you feel so down. Very often, the fact that you are unable to figure out why you feel down keeps you stuck in a state of inactive rumination. This kind of "analysis paralysis" serves to make the depression worse. Or if you discover why you are depressed, but realize that there is objectively nothing you can do to change the situation (or that changing the situation would involve such excessive costs as not to warrant change), you might respond by feeling that there is no hope. Then, of course, you would only reinforce the worst and most deceptive symptom of your depressed mood, which is that you are helpless to make things better.

Asking yourself why you feel depressed is risky for yet another reason. There is a perilously fine line between asking "Why?" objectively and crying "Why me?" emotionally. The latter is a line of inquiry or, more accurately, lament to be strictly avoided, as it only amplifies the depression you already feel.

The program for Step Two will show you how to attribute your depressed mood to its actual causes in appropriate and productive ways. You will learn about the cognitive, or thinking, component of depression, including the kinds of errors in interpretation and logic that typify depressive thought patterns. And you will learn how to interrupt destructive ways of talking to yourself about your depressed moods that cause damage to your self-esteem.

One of the biggest mistakes you can make in dealing with your mood problem is to get stuck, unguided, in the mire of causal analysis. Remember, any thinking that you do when you are feeling down will be biased toward the side of negativity and pessimism. Getting bogged down in inward exploration that tilts toward the dark will only cast a wider and wider shadow over your emotional state.

The most important thing you will discover about Step Two is that there is a limit to the amount of time and effort that you can usefully or safely put into the attribution process.

Step Three:
Act to Restore a Positive Mood

You will recall that the key word to keep in mind throughout learning the mood-management program is *control*. Focusing on the fact that you *can* do something to help yourself feel better is, in and of itself, curative of the blues and restorative of a better state of mind and more positive emotions.

The emotional pain that depressed moods produce triggers the impulse or motivation to *do something* to make yourself feel better. But while the impulse may be instinctive, knowing *what* to do to alleviate the pain is not. In fact, as you now know, doing what comes naturally for women—inactivity and rumination—is exactly counterproductive to overcoming depression.

The action regimen that constitutes Step Three of the mood-management program is centered around one basic psychological principle. That principle holds that if your feelings and behavior are incompatible, one or the other will change in order to restore a state of psychological harmony.

When we apply this principle—technically called cognitive dissonance—to the relief of depression, the rule becomes: To restore a positive mood, engage in behaviors that are incompatible with depression. Depression-Incompatible Behaviors, or D.I.B.'s, are the "something" you should do—the action you should take—if you are seeking effective and prompt relief from your emotional discomfort. By engaging in D.I.B.'s while you are feeling depressed, you will induce a state of cognitive dissonance. In other words, your mood of depression will not fit with the fact that you are doing behaviors or engaging in activities that people who are depressed do not typically perform. By sustaining the behaviors *in spite of your low mood*, your mind, which is motivated to resolve the dissonance and reestablish consistency and compatibility between your feelings and actions, will have no alternative but to correct your mood toward the positive in order to make it more consistent with your actions.

Selecting the right kinds of behaviors and activities is critical to the process. In the section of the book devoted to Step Three, you will learn what kinds of actions specifically work best to counteract depression. The action step also will teach you new ways to monitor, evaluate, and reward your own behavior to overcome destructive tendencies that perpetuate and deepen your low moods. You will find out just how critical positive action is to controlling depression and reversing low moods.

Action—and only action—will energize you out of the malaise of your blues. *Waiting* to get in the mood to act is self-sabotaging. Believing that there is nothing you can do to help yourself get up when you are feeling down is not only self-sabotaging but, as you will see, patently false.

Becoming a Mood Mechanic

The Triple A Program will give you both the mental and behavioral tools you need to manage and overcome depression. As you develop your skills in mood management, try to adopt the attitude of a well-trained mechanic who, when necessary, can do repairs as well as protective maintenance work on your own emotional machinery.

When your mood is low and broken, you will have the tools and the skills to fix it; when it is running well and positively, you will know what to do to maintain the desirable good mood. Mood repair, mood protection, and mood maintenance are concepts that will appear repeatedly in the pages ahead.

Talking with
Your Inner Adviser

One of the reasons that blue moods feel so uncomfortable is that they create a state of conflict in your mind. While one part of you is feeling emotional pain, another, healthier part of your mind seeks ways to stop or reduce the discomfort. This conflict means that the fact that depression feels bad is actually good news for you. The bad feelings—provided they don't become overly tense or overwhelming—will automatically trigger your motivation to restore a better, more positive state of mind.

You have to know how to channel that motivation toward efforts that will be effective. And you have to believe in your ability to reverse low moods through proper action. Feeling the pressure to "do something" to stop the depression but simultaneously feeling at a loss as to how to control your moods or skeptical about your ability to do so is what contributes to your sense of helplessness and frustration when you get down.

Once you learn the principles and techniques in the mood-management program, you will know exactly where and how to channel your motivation to change. But it is vitally important that you know how to tap into the positive motivation that flows from the healthier part of your mind. To overcome depression and quiet the internal conflict that it produces, you have to ally your intentions and actions with the part of you that doesn't want to feel depressed.

When I work with a patient in psychotherapy, my comments are always directed to the healthiest part of my patient's personality—to the side of her that genuinely wants to solve her problems and to feel happy again. Now I am talking to the best part of you—the part of you that is reading this book and following the Triple A Program because you *want* to be in better control of your moods and to reduce the amount of time that you spend feeling down and depressed.

Incidentally, there is nothing "schizophrenic" about referring to "parts" of any person's mind or personality. Talking about the parts of your mind is an understandable metaphor for discussing internal psychological conflicts. People commonly use the metaphor conversationally to reflect a state of ambivalence or conflict. "Part of me wants to see him again," a woman might say about a man toward whom she has mixed feelings, "but another part of me knows it would be damaging and foolish if I did." Or in describing her feelings about a stressful job, a woman might say, "A part of me loves the challenge and responsibility of management, but another part of me is tired of the hours and the hassles."

In reflecting on your low moods, you will realize that a part of you gets down, while another part of you hates the depression and is impatient to make the discomfort stop. It is this latter part of you—the best part of you—that we want to put in charge of your mood control efforts.

One way to access your healthiest side is to think of it as a kind of "inner adviser"—a benevolent, nurturant, protective part of your personality that knows what is best for you and will help you to do what is right. Your inner adviser, for example, would not want you to call yourself self-derogating names or encourage you to indulge in self-castigations and derisory remarks aimed at knocking down your self-esteem. Your inner adviser knows that these behaviors are not healthy for you and that they will only cause you to feel greater depression.

When you feel down, then, you will want to engage the motivation, wisdom, and cooperation of your inner adviser. You will need to turn a deaf inner ear to the depressed part of your mind; as you know, listening to your depression will only serve to drag you further down.

As you prepare yourself to learn more about each of the three steps of the Triple A Program, make sure that you are in contact with your inner adviser. The part of you that wants to feel good again will excel at learning the program and will ultimately triumph over your depressed moods.

PART TWO

Acceptance

8

◆

The More You Resist, the More It Persists

◆

It's not what we know that hurts, it's what we know that ain't so.

—WILL ROGERS

Step One of the Triple A Program starts with a paradox: You must accept your depressed mood in order to let go of it. Let me explain this paradox by means of an example.

Roberta believed that she was exhausted and defeated from her ongoing battle with blue moods and depression.

"I'm tired of fighting it," she said, "I know it's not right to be depressed and to get into such bad moods. Bob and I have everything anybody could possibly want. We have our health, we have money, and we have an adorable baby son. Bob is getting fed up with my crummy moods and I don't blame him. Other people look at me and think, 'What does she have to complain about? She's an advertising executive making a lot of money, her husband is a successful doctor. . . . They've got it all,' and I know that people are right."

But Roberta wasn't tired from fighting depression. She was tired from *resisting* the fact that she had low moods at all. When Roberta came to see me in therapy, she was very skeptical about the idea that she could learn to reverse her emotional slumps and restore positive, happy feelings.

"I *know* I should be happy. It really worries me that I'm not happy all the time. I mean, if I can't be happy with all I've got then I must really be hopeless. I feel like an ingrate, like an incredibly selfish, self-centered person for even thinking about myself so much. I'm thoroughly disgusted with myself about all of this. But I just don't think I can get rid of these low moods—I've been trying unsuccessfully for years."

I challenged Roberta on the point that she hadn't been trying in effective ways. I explained that her efforts were failing because she was draining off enormous amounts of productive energy just trying to resist the fact that she occasionally felt depressed. Her motivation to fight off her down moods, I assured her, was appropriate and positive. But, in order to focus the motivation in ways that would successfully combat the depression, she had to stop criticizing and attacking herself.

"Once I started working on accepting my down moods by describing them, and dealing with them in a more objective way, I stopped feeling like such a bad person for getting depressed. I honestly think that most of my feelings were a reaction to getting depressed in the first place, instead of to anything in my life."

Roberta's case illustrates the paradox involved in accepting your depressed mood before you can let go of it. By becoming agitated and critical of herself for feeling down, Roberta actually injected her blue moods with far more energy and power than they otherwise would have had. She elevated her occasional bouts of low moods (Roberta got down about once or twice a month) to the level of condemning statements about her personal character and values.

The underlying, erroneous belief causing Roberta to react so strongly when she started to feel depressed was that "a happy person never has down moods." The illogical reasoning that followed from her badly flawed assumption was that if happy people never have down moods, and she had periods of feeling down, then she must be an unhappy person.

From that point on, Roberta just cascaded along a downward spiral of her own making. She would ask herself, "If I'm not happy, given everything I have in my life, then what is life about anyway?" Since she concluded that her down moods meant she wasn't happy, she began to search for shortcomings in her marriage, or her career, or herself that would account for what was "wrong" in her life causing her to be "so unhappy."

In fact, Roberta was not an unhappy person. After keeping her Daily Mood Ratings for a month, she could see that she indeed felt happy and up most of the time, and that her depressed moods were exceptions to the norm rather than her dominant state of mind.

Once Roberta came to see how her errors in thinking were fueling a depressed reaction to being depressed, she was ready to examine the real causes for her mood slumps—principally feeling stressed, overloaded, and fatigued—and to implement the action techniques that taught her to rest, recharge her psychological batteries, and restore her characteristically positive mood state.

"The best part," Roberta remarked, "is that I no longer worry about getting down. I can accept my slumps as inevitable, given just how full and busy my life is. By going right into the three-step solution at the first sign of the blues, I don't waste any time beating up on myself for feeling low. I think I'm even *entitled* to some down time once in a while."

Roberta was also able to reduce the frequency of her low moods by better management of stress (her prodrome) and to significantly shorten and lower the duration and intensity of her down periods when they did occur.

What Roberta learned—and what you need to clearly understand—is that the more you try to resist accepting depressed moods, the more they will persist. Obviously, I am not saying that you should welcome your blues with open arms and be delighted that you are feeling down and out. Nor am I saying that there are no effective ways to thwart or abort a down mood from taking hold, as you have already learned from the chapter on Blue Alerts.

Resistance, though, is a futile endeavor when it comes to depression. And it is counterproductive. Because what you try to resist is not the down mood itself but rather the reality that the experience is happening to you.

In working with patients over the years, I have heard many variations on the theme of resistance. But I have always seen the same discouraging results. By trying to fight and deny the reality that occasional bouts of the blues and depression occur, you only deplete yourself of energy that could be far better spent on making yourself more resilient to their effects and on actions aimed directly at reversing your mood's downward direction.

To make it through the first step of acceptance, you will have to rid yourself of beliefs and assumptions that are keeping you stuck in the mud of resistance.

Resistance Beliefs

Here are 12 statements that are frequently verbalized by my patients and typical of resistance thinking. See if you can identify elements of your own resistance beliefs in these examples:

1. I can't get depressed because too many people depend on me at home or at work.
2. I have no right to be depressed.
3. I don't want to accept that I'm depressed because I'll be overwhelmed and unable to deal with my feelings.
4. I can't let the people around me know that I'm down.
5. If I were a stronger person I wouldn't get down or depressed.
6. If I say that I'm depressed, it means that I'm not a happy person or that I'm not happy with my life.
7. If I say I'm depressed it might mean that I'll have to change things about myself and my life.
8. I have to keep myself from feeling down in order to be a good mother/wife/professional/employee.
9. Getting depressed means that there is something wrong with me psychologically.
10. I should never get depressed.

11. Accepting depression means giving in to it and *being* depressed.
12. If I let myself get depressed it means that I'm choosing to feel that way or that I must really like it.

These beliefs are indicative of a resistance approach to your mood problem. Prior to reading this book, you may have felt that this kind of "tough" or "strong" thinking would protect you from getting down. But your experience probably has shown you that, despite your resistance beliefs, you have had depressed moods and bouts of the blues anyway. Furthermore, your resistance has only served to strengthen the negative feelings while weakening you through depletion of energy and self-blame.

Fear of Depression

The most insidious form of resistance is fear of depression. This fear response is most common among women who have had prior experience with serious Depressive illness. Given the severe emotional pain that clinical Depression can entail, it is hardly surprising that even prodromal feelings of a down mood would evoke strong anxiety and resistance reactions in someone who had endured the illness previously.

But the fear of getting depressed is not limited to women with histories of clinical Depression. Even if your bouts of the blues last for only a few intense days, and you have no other clinical symptoms, you may dread the prospect of another bout or the possibility that one of these times, your blues may escalate into a far more severe condition.

Anxiety is born of uncertainty. Naturally, if you have not learned effective techniques for mood management in the past, you may well feel quite uncertain about your ability to control depression in the future. But with the mood-management program and sustained effort, your moods will improve and your self-confidence and sense of control will increase.

Uncertainty can be triggered by depression. When you feel yourself sliding down a dark tunnel, you don't know how deep the bottom will be. And that uncertainty causes anxiety. Depressive thoughts often focus on the future and on the question of when and how the bad feelings will ever stop. Since the future is inherently uncertain for everyone, thoughts and predictions about it create anxiety.

The case of Marjorie shows how troublesome anxiety and fear of Depression can be and how they operate to block acceptance. When Marjorie first came to see me in therapy she was 37 and had been off antidepressant medication for two years. Prior to stopping medication, she had been free of Depressive illness for four years. While in her early 30's, though, several extremely stressful life events precipitated her first attack of major Depression. Only six months after a miscarriage with her first and only pregnancy, Marjorie's husband of 10 years confessed that he had been having an affair with one of her closest (or so she thought) friends and that he was leaving the marriage for his lover. Shortly thereafter, the company that Marjorie had worked for as an executive secretary went bankrupt and she was suddenly unemployed.

"I really became incredibly depressed. I crawled into my shell and withdrew from everyone. My trust in men, women, employers, in just about everyone was shot. I wasn't sure if I could go on living."

Marjorie was treated with antidepressants and psychotherapy and was able to pull herself back together and start to rebuild her life. At the age of 35 she left Chicago and came out to Los Angeles, where she could be closer to her mother and three sisters, all of whom lived in California.

"I've been doing really well and I am honestly in love again," she told me. "Mark and I met about eight months ago, and he wants to get married. It took me a long time to acknowledge that I loved him too, and especially to trust a man again, but I think he's a wonderful guy. I'm working as a computer programmer with a rock-solid company here, so my career is in good shape. And we're even talking about the possibility of having children together."

Marjorie went on to describe that her only problem now was that she lived in "dire fear" of getting Depressed again.

"It scares me so much that I panic even when I just feel normal 'blues.' My doctor in Chicago told me that I would have down times, and I don't really have any of the serious symptoms that I had five years ago. But when I start to feel down, I get incredibly nervous. I don't want to go back on the medication because I want to get pregnant. Actually, I don't even think I need the medication, but when I get down for a day or two, I feel like the Depression is starting again, and I start seeing disaster movies in my head."

Marjorie had excellent insight into her dilemma. She was educated enough about the illness of Depression to differentiate her experiences of low moods from the full-blown clinical syndrome. She realized that her problem wasn't the illness of Depression, but rather her *fear* of becoming Depressed again.

"Mark doesn't understand why I get so nervous and upset with myself for being in a bad mood. He always reminds me that I'm just human, and that he loves me if I'm up or down. But my anxiety makes me irritable, and I start picking on him. Then I start worrying about ruining this relationship, or driving him to another woman and I really get on my own case."

Marjorie was having trouble dealing with her normal depressions because her anxiety and fear of what they might be signaling were keeping her from accepting them. Working through the mood-management program helped Marjorie to reduce her anxiety dramatically, since she felt more in control and able to reverse the downward swings. By learning to monitor her moods, she reassured herself that she would be the first to know if she was indeed sinking into another more serious episode and that she would know how to respond if she found that she needed psychiatric consultation and medication.

Marjorie's case is illustrative of fear of Depression and the resistance problems that anxiety creates. It is also interesting as an example of another kind of acceptance issue—the problem many women have accepting good times, positive moods, and being happy. This latter acceptance problem appears to be the flip side of not being able to accept Depression, although the motivation is actually much the same. The discomfort with happiness stems from a fear that the inevitable "crash" will occur and depression will follow. We'll talk about this more in a later chapter.

Overcoming Resistance and Accepting Your Depressed Moods

Understanding and accepting the ups and downs of your mood and your life is a little like accepting changes in the weather. You undoubtedly prefer clear, sunny days, but you know that the weather must inevitably change. It will rain, or snow, or cloud over, and all the resistance and protest that you mount will do nothing to alter the fact that the weather has changed; resistance will only tire you out, make you feel inadequate, or create disappointment.

The comparison stops, though, with the issue of control. Whereas you cannot deny *or* change the weather, you can respond to a cloudy mood in ways that serve to drive the clouds away and restore sunshine. But to exercise your control, you must start by accepting the current reality. Then and only then can you respond appropriately to the problem. Misplacing your energy in futile efforts to deny that you feel down or that your mood is becoming depressed will only result in an intensification of the negative feelings. Moreover, by getting stuck in resistance, you will only procrastinate on initiating the behaviors that really will alleviate your emotional discomfort.

Accepting your depression does *not* mean giving in to your low mood. Nor does it mean that you must assume the identity of a depressed person. Acceptance means that you are ready to respond to the reality of feeling depressed with the trust and self-confidence that you can control the course your mood will take.

9

◆

Accepting What You Can't Change, Changing What You Can

◆

Two things a man should never be angry at: What he can help, and what he cannot help.

—THOMAS FULLER

As you work through the step of accepting your depressed mood, you are likely to confront some broader psychological issues that also involve the process of acceptance.

You will, for example, face circumstances that upset you, anger you, cause you emotional pain, or just drag you down—circumstances over which, in the end, you have very little or no control. If you rail against the universe, protesting such realities, your depressed mood will deepen. If you lack the knowledge, insight, or perspective to understand that your control is limited or negligible, you will be prone to mistakenly blame yourself and your inadequacies for your failure to make things different. Self-flagellation and punitive self-reproach will only intensify and amplify your low mood but will not serve to change unchangeable events.

101

Conversely, there will be times when your depressed mood develops because you feel helpless to change something over which you truly do have a degree of control but fail to recognize your options or deny your responsibility to behave differently. Under these circumstances, your depression is perpetuated not only because the negative situation persists, but also because you do not exercise your control to make things better.

In Alcoholics Anonymous, there is a serenity prayer that asks for divine guidance to sort out these complex dilemmas: "Lord," it begins, "grant me the peace to accept the things I cannot change, the courage to change the things I can, and the wisdom to know the difference."

Trying to Rewrite Personal History

I know that you know that the past cannot be changed. But I also know that some of your depressed moods are due, in part, to your lack of acceptance of this truism.

Keep in mind that acceptance, as a psychological process, is different from mere acknowledgment. While you probably can readily acknowledge the futility of trying to rewrite your personal history, the fact that you occasionally dwell on prior mistakes, or experience remorse and regrets over missed opportunities or errors in judgment, or hear yourself saying, "I just wish I had done [fill in the blank] instead," is evidence that you haven't accepted that the past is unchangeable. You are still putting effort and psychological energy into trying somehow to undo things that you can see, in retrospect, would have been better left undone, and into faulting yourself for things you omitted but now know should have been accomplished or said.

How can I be so sure that you waste time making yourself feel down over things past? Because everybody does. We are all both blessed and cursed with a lifetime of memories— good and bad—and the uniquely human ability to analyze, review, and critique our actions and deeds.

Of course, some introspection and life review is healthy and necessary, especially if the outcome is learning from your mistakes. But what I want you to become more sensitive to is the obsessive tendency to go over and over the same mental territory, continually scratching and poking at the psychological scabs that will inevitably leave scars, but never seem to heal because you won't allow them to do so.

Susan had her life on hold for 10 months. She was paralyzed by her bouts of depression, while she ruminated over the past.

For seven years Susan and Mike had been lovers. At 33, Susan was anxious to end the "on again, off again" pattern of their relationship and get married. She was ready to have a family and reminded Mike that her biological clock was ticking away. But Mike, a 45-year-old divorced man, was a study in ambivalence. He told Susan that he loved her, but he vacillated constantly on whether or not to remarry, and remained dubious about the wisdom of starting another family "so late" in their lives.

Mike had been married once, in his 20's, for seven years and he had two sons from his first marriage. But his ex-wife had left him abruptly for a wealthy older man and had moved out of state with his boys. He saw his sons irregularly and felt both saddened and guilty over withdrawing from their lives because of the wounded pride and anger he felt toward their mother. As a result of his marital trauma, Mike had big problems trusting women.

But Susan thought she could change him. During the first five years of their relationship, she was faithful to Mike, "waiting for him to change and come around to the idea of getting married." During the last few years, though, their relationship had reached more than one crisis point. In particular, Susan and Mike had broken up for a period during which she started dating. Peter came into Susan's life about this time and fell very much in love with her, offering marriage, family, and anything else he could to make her happy.

But Susan still loved Mike. And when Mike learned about Peter, he asked Susan for one more chance, promising to get married within a year. Susan chose Mike, broke off her relationship with Peter and convinced herself that "this time, he would really change."

But at the end of the year Mike reneged on the marriage proposal. He told Susan that he just couldn't get married to her or anyone else, and in order to resolve the children issue, he had had a vasectomy. Susan was crushed.

When Susan came to see me, she was riddled with indecision and feelings of failure and loss.

"I don't know what to do now," she began. "Maybe I should just stay with Mike and give up on ever having a family or even getting married. It's all my fault anyway. I'm so depressed. I can't believe I've wasted all these years with him. I feel like I should stay in the relationship just to avoid facing the fact that it was all such a waste. I wish I had married Peter when I had the chance, but he's married to someone else. By now, I could have had a family. He won't even talk to me or be my friend because I hurt him so much. What a horrible mistake! I just wish I could turn back the clock and do things differently."

Susan repeated the same monologue each time I saw her for the first few weeks. And she assured me that these thoughts filled her consciousness to the point that she could think of nothing else. When she spent time with her friends, she cried to them over her mistakes and misjudgments. When she talked to Mike, she blamed herself over and over again for staying with him and trusting him, and tried to convince him that he could still have the vasectomy surgically reversed. Mike, of course, only became more angry, guilty, and rejecting while Susan's alternative of staying involved with him became less and less of a possibility.

For a total of 10 months (the last three in therapy), Susan dwelled on her past mistakes and indulged in self-punitive blame and remorse. Eventually, I was able to reach her and help her to see that she was only perpetuating her mistakes by staying so depressed. During the 10 months since breaking up with Mike, Susan had avoided all social contacts, refused to date anyone, and dropped out of a night school program in which she was pursuing an MBA that would have been rewarded with an immediate and automatic 20 percent salary increase and promotion in her job.

Susan and I discussed the fact that by ruminating about the past, she was not succeeding in changing anything. She agreed, although somewhat reluctantly, that punishing herself would not make her any younger, or alter the events of her personal history. By staying so depressed and low, she was expending energy on things she could not control—including the past, Peter's feelings, and Mike's ambivalence and choices about children—while failing to recognize and choose to take responsibility for changing her current life circumstances. Focusing on the past was only obscuring her opportunities to make her future better and different by meeting new men, going back to night school, and immediately acting to restore a more positive mood and state of mind, even if nothing she did involved or affected Mike in any way.

Susan did, eventually, let go of her ruminations and accept the realities of her own past. "It wasn't really all bad," she was able to say. "Mike and I did have a lot of love and good times but he just wasn't the right guy to marry." The postscript to the story is that Susan is now finishing her MBA and is dating one of her professors who, she says, "is very single, and very ready to get married. This time I won't make the same mistakes."

Trying to Change Others

Learning to accept that you really can't do much about changing other people is an even harder lesson than letting go of past mistakes and unhappy memories.

As Susan's story illustrates, the most addictive and destructive love relationships feed off of the mistaken belief that you can change the other person. This is not to say that you have no control or influence over men with whom you are involved in love relationships or over other people in your life as well. But the control that you can properly exercise involves changing *your* actions and responses. The other person may elect to change or not in response to your behavior; but you *cannot* directly change him or her.

With the exception of your own children, what other people say, feel, and do is their responsibility, not yours. Accepting that you cannot change other people as a general principle will release you from much of the frustration and negative energy expenditure that contributes to your low moods.

What you *can* change is the way you choose to respond to what other people in your life do and say. You are certainly free to communicate how you feel and even that you would be happier in certain respects if the other person did, in fact, choose to change himself or herself. Ultimately, you can choose to terminate a relationship or withdraw your love, attention, participation, or time if the other person does not elect to change in ways that you believe are essential. That, of course, is your prerogative. Or you may choose to stay in the relationship and decide to accept the other person as he or she is.

But getting obsessively hooked on changing another person's feelings or behaviors is a formula for frustration, resentment, and depression.

Women like Susan who stay in relationships trying to change ambivalent men suffer enormously from a debilitating erosion of their self-esteem. Whenever you are the object of another person's ambivalence, it is inevitable that you will wind up feeling that there is something flawed or undesirable in you. Otherwise, you erroneously reason, the other person's feelings would be unequivocally positive. And if your efforts at changing the other person are unsuccessful—as they almost always are—your mood is clouded by the inadequacy you feel.

Laura and her mother, for example, have been entangled in a psychological web of ambivalence for as long as Laura, now 27, can remember.

"I guess I love my mother because she's my mother. But we've never gotten along well. She was always resentful of the attention and praise my dad gave me and felt jealous that I received the education and career training she never had. She has always been critical of me. I just wish I could change her."

Whenever Laura started dating a new man, or received

praise from her supervisor at work, she would call her mother to share the news. And each time Laura's mother would find something to criticize and some way to inject negativity into the conversation.

After a typical conversation with her mother the night before our therapy session, Laura came to see me feeling very low and defeated.

"I just can't change her. I try to make her proud of me and make her feel a part of my life. But I never do it right, I guess. She just won't allow me to feel good about myself no matter what positive things are going on in my life."

Laura's mistaken approach of trying to change her mother was behind her low moods. In therapy, Laura learned to accept that her 60-year-old mother was not likely to change very much, and if she was going to change, the responsibility to do so was her mother's, not Laura's. Laura needed to learn that she was keeping herself from feeling good in part by repeating the same ritual of seeking approval from her chronically ambivalent and withholding mother.

By focusing her energy on trying to change her mother, Laura was merely deflecting her responsibility to change herself and her own reactions and behaviors. If you think some of your unhappiness or down moods are due to your inability to change someone else, then you, like Laura, need to work on changing yourself. *Accept the fact that you cannot change others.* To try to do so is misplaced and misdirected energy.

Accept that *you can only directly change your own actions and responses*. Think about the alternatives you have rather than about what the other person *should* do. This shift in focus will enhance rather than diminish your sense of control and result in actions that are far more likely to meet your objectives.

Bitter Pills to Swallow

There are, of course, many other aspects and circumstances in life over which you have little or no direct control. Coming to terms with where your control begins and ends will be enormously helpful to you in achieving mastery over your low moods. Over and over again, I hear my patients deplete their energies and talk themselves into negative mood states by uselessly protesting realities of life they do not like but, alas, cannot alter directly. By misdirecting their efforts onto changing what cannot be altered, they deflect attention from their responsibility to choose to react, respond, or cope with those realities in ways that will make them feel better.

For example, one of my patients became quite depressed when she turned 50. During the month following her birthday, she stayed home, wandering around the house bemoaning the fact that she "hated getting old," and staring at herself in the mirror to detect wrinkles, sagging body parts, and other dreaded signs of age. After a few weeks of this behavior, she pronounced, "I hate getting older. I want to stop the process. There's nothing for me to look forward to, and nothing I can do to have fun. I'm really old now. I can't stop thinking about how much I wish I were younger."

This woman was protesting one of life's inescapable realities. Obviously, nothing can be done to halt the march of time. But by draining off her vital energies in a futile protest of the fact of aging, she failed to embrace her opportunities to respond in ways that would maintain or enhance the quality of her life. The reason she didn't have anything to look forward to or any way to have fun was not because she was now 50; in the month preceding her birthday, she had been very active socially and had made lots of fun plans. Now, simply because the calendar had turned past her birthday, she suddenly opted to act like a house-bound geriatric case. This woman felt older because she elected to act differently—in ways that made her feel old and believe that life had lost its luster.

Growing older is only one example of a host of issues that, collectively, represent difficult and bitter pills for many women to swallow. Some other examples are: Life is inherently uncertain and risky; you make mistakes; you do not do things perfectly; there are limitations to your physical and psychological energy; and almost everything and everybody change with time.

While these statements may be truisms, they nevertheless are often quite problematic to accept psychologically. But acceptance will release you from the pain and frustration you may now feel if you are engaged in resistance struggles against some of life's basic realities.

Acceptance and Choice

Accepting the hard realities in your own life that you cannot change will free you to examine and embrace the choices that you do have to respond differently.

No one's life, however protected and privileged, is immune from stress. People who cope relatively better in life are not necessarily exposed to less difficult situations. Instead, they are able to cut rapidly through their resistances to accepting the things that they cannot change, and to channel their energies toward finding ways to act, think, or feel that will improve their mood and make them more resilient to the stressful events of their lives.

As you learn to manage your moods more effectively, you also will be learning the difference between responding to a situation in a *futile* change mode and a more productive and appropriate *acceptance* mode; between a passive *helpless* mode and an *active* choice and constructive change mode. Let me explain.

When Susan was mired in her passive depression, her mode of thinking and acting was geared toward *futilely* trying to change Mike as well as her own past actions and decisions. The woman who turned 50 and hit a crisis was also operating in a *futile* change mode. By protesting, she was ineffectually trying to change the immutable process of aging. Laura continued to suffer from bouts of low self-esteem and depression as long as she stayed in the *futile* change mode, trying to alter her mother's ambivalent response and gain her unequivocal approval.

When you approach the life issues that underlie your depressed moods by futilely trying to change what is not within your control to alter, your depression will only become more intense. Inevitably, you will feel frustrated, inadequate, and defeated.

If, however, you accept the reality of what is happening and focus on the choices you can make to respond behaviorally, emotionally, or cognitively (in your thoughts), your mood will improve as a direct result of your enhanced sense of control.

You can retrain your thinking in this regard with the use of a simple paper-and-pencil exercise called the Acceptance and Choice worksheet. Take a sheet of paper and divide it vertically into two columns. Label the column on the left, "I accept that I can't change the fact that . . ."; label the right column, "But I can choose to . . ."

Think about a problem or situation in your current life circumstances about which you sometimes get down or depressed. Is this a problem that you really can't control or change? Is there another person involved in your problem who must be responsible for deciding what and how he or she will change? With these thoughts in mind, complete the sentence in the left-hand column.

Then, give some careful thought to that portion of your problem over which you do have control: Your own actions, thoughts, and feelings. You might choose, for example, to change your reactions to the problem described in Column One so that you don't become as bothered, upset, or unhappy as you have in the past. Or you might choose to disassociate yourself from the situation that is causing you to be unhappy, thereby removing yourself from exposure to the thing or person that seems to be causing you discomfort.

You should experiment with various alternative responses in Column Two. Write out as many completions to the sentences in the right-hand column as you possibly can. Don't worry about whether they are logical, plausible, or even desirable. Just brainstorm about all the choices you have—actions, feelings, and thoughts—in response to the statement of the unchangeable fact in Column One.

The process of brainstorming and focusing on all of your alternatives is itself corrective toward producing a more positive emotional outlook. The reason for this has to do with the effects of stress on thought processes. Remember, depression and low moods are psychologically uncomfortable or painful, and this discomfort is inherently stressful.

When you feel stressed—by depression or any other circumstance or emotion—your tendency will be to think that you have no choices or very few "ways out" of your problem. In other words, your mental search for alternatives will be superficial at best, stopping short of a full identification and delineation of possible solutions. This systematic error in thinking that stress produces is called "premature closure."

Premature closure explains why you often feel "trapped" and therefore hopeless and helpless in response to stressful and depressing problems and situations. You feel trapped because your mind fails to explore all alternative ways of responding due to the stress you are feeling. Using the sentence heading in Column Two as a prompter, force yourself to keep seeking alternative answers until you have satisfied yourself that all possibilities are truly exhausted. Don't reject any alternative out of hand because it may appear ridiculous, or absurd, or simply out of the question at first. Remember, too, that choosing to do nothing or electing to keep on doing what you have been doing should be included in your list of responses. By generating as many alternatives as possible, you will correct for the tendency to prematurely close off your search for solutions as well as the perception that you are trapped in your unhappiness.

Let's take a look at how the Acceptance and Choice worksheet helped in the cases of the women we have been discussing. Here is what Susan wrote:

I accept that I can't change the fact that . . .	*But I can choose to . . .*
1. Mike doesn't want to get married to me or have children.	**1a.** Accept that fact and try to be happy with the relationship on his terms.
	1b. Not feel rejected because it is Mike's

I accept that I can't change the fact that . . .	*But I can choose to . . .*
	problem that he can't trust women.
	1c. Feel relieved, since the relationship has caused me a lot of pain for seven years.
	1d. Go out socially and try to do whatever I can to meet a man who does want marriage and a family.
	1e. Do things that will make me feel better about myself that don't have anything to do with men—like going back to school.
	1f. Keep on being depressed and moaning over the past.
2. I broke up with Peter and made some bad mistakes in my past.	**2a.** Put the past behind me and move forward, wiser for my mistakes.
	2b. Really appreciate another man—if I'm lucky enough to meet one— who is as crazy about me as Peter was.
	2c. Remember that I really wasn't in love with Peter at the time and congratulate myself for not marrying the wrong

I accept that I can't change the fact that . . .	But I can choose to . . .
	man for the wrong reasons.
	2d. Keep beating myself over the head with all my self-hate and make sure that nobody else will want me in the future.

When Susan wrote out her alternative responses, she could see how counterproductive her depressive behavior and thoughts were, especially in the context of other choices she could identify.

"Before this exercise," Susan admitted, "I couldn't see my way out of any of my bad feelings. I didn't think I had any choices because I couldn't get Mike to change and I couldn't get Peter back. Now I realize that by focusing on the two men, I wasn't looking at what I could do to improve my mood and situation."

Laura used the Acceptance and Choice exercise to analyze her difficult relationship with her mother. These were Laura's responses:

I accept that I can't change the fact that . . .	But I can choose to . . .
1. My mother is a negative, critical person who has a lot of trouble ever giving me approval or showing me her love.	**1a.** Tell my mother how much her behavior hurts me.
	1b. Forgive my mother and accept her as she is, knowing that she loves me in her own way.
	1c. Be totally different with my own children.

I accept that I can't change the fact that . . .	*But I can choose to . . .*
	1d. Share my success with good friends and/or people I admire whose honest feedback I trust more than my mother's.
	1e. Stop asking my mother for her opinion and just tell her that she has reason to feel happy and proud because I'm doing so well.
	1f. Keep on crying and getting down every time I talk to her.
	1g. Give my mother more support and approval for her efforts.
	1h. Rely more on my own approval and praise for building my self-esteem.
	1i. Cut my mother out of my life.

Laura's list is exemplary in representing all the alternatives that she could imagine, including ones that were unacceptable. With the exception of alternatives "1f" and "1i," Laura implemented all of her responses at various times, and kept a mood rating of how she felt after doing each. In this way, Laura discovered how much control she really did have over the problem which she had previously cast as chronic and hopeless. Her depressed moods diminished markedly and, since she felt far less vulnerable, she was able to deflect her mother's negativity by making it somewhat humorous.

"Leave it to my mom." Laura chuckled, "I told her that I came in second in my company for gross sales volume this year, and she wanted to know why I hadn't made it to first place! She's actually pretty funny when you think about it."

Finally, here is the Acceptance and Choice worksheet for the 50-year-old patient who was fighting a bout of birthday blues:

I accept that I can't change the fact that . . .	*But I can choose to . . .*
1. I'm getting older.	**1a.** Be damned glad about it since the alternative is dying!
	1b. Feel pretty good about how nice my life has been so far and do things to make my future more exciting—like plan trips, have parties, etc.
	1c. Forget the stupid number (50), and act the way I felt when I was 38—that was a great time in my life!
	1d. Have plastic surgery if I don't like how I look.
	1e. Exercise more to stay in shape and feel energetic.
	1f. Start feeling grateful that I'm 50 and still healthy.

I accept that I can't change the fact that . . .	But I can choose to . . .
	1g. Stop thinking about myself so much and get more involved with other people.
	1h. Stay in the house for the rest of my life and get so depressed that I don't care about getting older or anything else.

◆

This patient took her list of responses, circled the ones she liked best, and taped it to her bathroom mirror.

"Everytime I start looking for wrinkles and getting into the 'old and ugly' frame of mind, I read over my choices. Then I repeat this sentence like a form of meditation, 'I can't change the fact that I'm getting older in years, but I can choose to keep a young attitude and make every precious year that I have to live count.' "

Gaining the Courage to Change What You Can

Some of your moods may reflect discouragement and disappointment with yourself for not mustering the courage or the willpower to change something about yourself that is making you unhappy. In this case, the acceptance to strive for is not the same as when your power to change is minimal or indirect. This time, you must work toward accepting the responsibility to make yourself happier.

For example, you may have one or several habits that are damaging to your health and self-esteem and represent self-control deficiencies. If you smoke cigarettes, eat excessively, fail to exercise, drink too much, and so forth, your bad habits are themselves indicators that you are not controlling something that is within your power to regulate. The fact that you are not controlling yourself may be one source of depression for you; and the resultant overweight, low energy, poor appearance, and other consequences of your bad habits also may be making you unhappy.

Acknowledging that you have an addictive habit is insufficient to excuse yourself from committing to change. You may even be rationalizing that, whereas you want to stop smoking, or lose weight, you simply *can't* as proved by your repeated failures in the past.

In these cases, as well as with parallel issues like staying in an addictive love relationship because you are afraid to go through the withdrawal of breaking up, or pushing yourself too hard and becoming dangerously stressed because you are not recognizing your limitations, the real problem is that you have not fully accepted the *responsibility* to make necessary changes in your life.

Here again, it is useful to become very conscious of your choices. This time, you will need a triple-column Responsibility Acceptance worksheet. At the top of the left-hand column, write the heading, "I want to change . . .". On the heading of the second column write, "Currently, I am choosing to . . .". On the third column write, "When I accept the responsibility to make myself happier I will . . .".

Using these sentence leads, select something about yourself that you want to change, but that you are currently unable or seemingly unable to control. Your responses to Columns One and Two should be straightforward descriptions of your thoughts, feelings, and behavior vis-à-vis the problem over which you have become depressed. By being candid with yourself about the choices that your current behavior reflects, you will take the necessary first step toward mustering the courage and commitment to change: being honest about your own contribution to your problem and unhappiness.

After examining your responses in Column Two, make a decision to stop giving yourself reasons to feel down and depressed. If you feel low because you are overweight, or are in a bad, addictive relationship, or you are a compulsive, addicted smoker, then you owe it to yourself to change the behaviors about which you feel disappointed and negative.

Focus on your responsibility to feel better about yourself, to be happier, to feel prouder, and to maintain a more positive mood. Replace thoughts about dieting, or quitting smoking, or whatever your particular problem is, with a focus on the negative mood consequences of your bad habit.

Diane was a heavy smoker and an overeater with 30 extra pounds to prove it. She was willing to acknowledge that her smoking and overeating were responses to anxiety but was steadfast in her belief that she was "out of control" and an "addictive personality."

I told Diane in therapy that, while I agreed that her smoking and overeating were bad for her health and negative for her appearance, the main issue was that she had not accepted the responsibility to do what was necessary to improve her mood and make herself happier.

"I always think of a bowl of ice cream as a way of being nice to myself," Diane mused; "then thirty minutes after I'm done, I hate myself for being so indulgent. Then I start smoking as a way to keep myself from eating more. And that makes me even more upset with myself. But I never thought about any of these habits as connected to making myself depressed. I thought I ate and smoked in response to feeling depressed, not the other way around, although it's clear to me that my lack of control makes me unhappy with myself."

Diane's worksheet looked like this:

I want to change . . .	Currently, I am choosing to . . .	When I accept the responsibility to make myself happier, I will . . .
1. My overeating	1. Rationalize and excuse my bad habits.	1. Not want to give myself reasons to feel down.
2. My smoking.	2. Stay fat.	2. Make me proud of myself.

I want to change . . .	Currently, I am choosing to . . .	When I accept the responsibility to make myself happier, I will . . .
3. My anxiety.	3. Be a smoker and tempt the fates.	3. Understand that smoking and eating make me unhappy and depressed in addition to fat and unhealthy.
4. My low self-esteem and depression.	4. Give myself reasons to be disappointed with myself.	4. Not tolerate my own excuses.
	5. Use the depression and anxiety as reasons to continue smoking and eating.	5. Not give in to quick-fix impulses.
	6. Be weak.	6. Know what to do about smoking and eating.
	7. Be too easy on myself regarding my lack of control.	
	8. Be too hard on myself with self-criticism.	

◆

Two weeks after completing her triple-column worksheet, Diane told me that the decision "to accept responsibility for my own health and happiness clicked in." Consistent with her proclamation, she stopped smoking, boosted her exercise, went on a healthy eating plan and, with the assistance of a nutritional counselor, lost 35 pounds within three months.

"The key," said Diane, "was confronting myself with the fact that choosing not to change was the same as choosing to keep myself depressed. I hated feeling depressed more than I hated being fat. Once I thought about how it was my responsibility to get happier by knocking off my bad habits, my life started to fall into place."

The Wisdom to Know the Difference

The most difficult problems are those where the responsibility for change is ambiguous. There are situations, for example, where the control rests with two people who are linked by bonds of interdependence. In a marriage or relationship, for example, fights often develop from mutual provocation. The leverage to stop the destructive pattern rests with the self-control of both partners. Still, even where the control is shared, one partner can choose to change unilaterally, hoping that the other will follow suit.

There are other situations where you may decide that the cost or price of changing—financially, emotionally, physically, or otherwise—is simply too high relative to the benefits that might be realized. Laura's alternative to stop all contact with her mother would remove her from exposure to her mother's negativity, but the emotional price in terms of guilt, loneliness, and loss of family contact was too high in Laura's psychological calculus and the choice was therefore rejected.

The wisdom to know the difference between situations where you have no control and must accept the fact and those where you do have control and need the courage to exercise it judiciously is acquired through trial-and-error learning and careful observation. Wisdom develops gradually over time.

When you feel down over a situation that you would like to see changed, focus on *your control*. Even in those situations where your direct control is negligible, you can still choose to respond in ways that lessen your frustration, upset, and depressed feelings. Where you have a substantial degree of control in changing the circumstances that are contributing to your negative feelings, focus on your responsibility to yourself to do what you can to be happier. Where the control issues are unclear, remember that developing your alternatives and choosing to take some action has a value independent of whether or not the actions you take completely remedy the problematic situation. That value is to lessen your sense of helplessness.

Accepting your depressed mood, then, means also that you take a hard honest look at the situations from which your low moods arise and decide where you can productively exercise choice and control. Accepting what you can't change may sometimes imply that you must accept and experience sad feelings. But, as you will see in the next chapter, you can still choose to appreciate the upside of your down moods.

10

◆

The Upside of Down Moods

◆

What soap is for the body, tears are for the soul.

—ANCIENT PROVERB

There I was, by myself in a strange hotel room, watching this romantic movie on the cable channel," Joanne described, "and I was suddenly overcome by a tremendous sense of sadness and an overwhelming desire to cry. Normally, you see, I just don't let myself give in to those kinds of feelings. When I'm at work, it simply wouldn't be appropriate, and when I'm at home, I feel obligated to be up all the time so that my husband feels reassured that I am happy with our life together.

"But, all alone, away from home on this business trip, I could let myself feel depressed. I honestly can't remember the last time I cried, though I feel low and sad more than I'm willing to admit. And, you know, it felt great. Not only did I get a major sense of release from crying, but I was able to get in touch with something that has been making me feel sad for a long time.

"Away from my husband, probably because of the romantic scenes in the movie, I was able to acknowledge that our relationship really isn't as good or close as it was when we

122

first got married. I know my career takes a huge amount of time and I try to compensate by putting on a cheerful act all the time when I am home. But I think he feels that I'm faking it, though neither one of us has been willing to let on to any negative feelings.

"After my cry, I picked up the phone and called my husband. I told him what I had been thinking, and he was very receptive to discussing our relationship. I think one of the reasons we haven't been as close recently is that I try so hard to avoid and deny any depressed feelings because I know how sensitive he is and that he'll blame himself totally for my unhappiness, which is something he needs to work on changing. But I haven't been *real* or completely honest with him, or with myself, either, for that matter.

"I have this idea that being depressed is a very bad thing. My husband's mother was depressed a lot when he was growing up and I know he hated it. So I always feel like I should cover up my low moods. The problem is that I was covering up so much, I didn't even know what was bothering me anymore. I can really see the value of letting myself feel sad and down once in awhile, even to the point of having a good cry. I just want to be sure I can control my feelings once they begin. I sure can't afford to stay depressed."

Joanne's experience taught her to become more accepting of her depressed moods because she discovered that her sadness carried a significant message about a problem that needed addressing. While I have said repeatedly that acceptance of your depressions doesn't necessarily mean giving in to them or giving up control over your negative feelings, you may discover, like Joanne, that letting yourself experience sadness sometimes can have a corrective value.

"I used to be so afraid of getting depressed," another of my patients said, "that when I started to feel weepy I immediately panicked. The panic made me cry. But instead of trying to understand or deal with what was making me feel sad, I only criticized myself for being out of control. Now that I know I can control my moods better, I'm not afraid to cry once in a while. In fact, I must admit that I actually look forward to it."

What Joanne and my other patient did, in effect, was to give themselves permission to feel sad and depressed. On occasion, as part of your first step of acceptance, you may decide also to let yourself feel the sadness associated with your depressed mood. While feeling and acting depressed are emphatically not a necessary part of accepting your depressed mood, there are times when doing so may be desirable.

The operative word here is *choice*. You have the choice as to whether or not you want to indulge yourself in a good cry, in a bout of nostalgic memories, or in a few hours of solitude and social withdrawal. You may also choose to bypass experiencing your moodiness and sadness altogether, and move quickly through the steps of acceptance and attribution on to the action program designed to restore a more positive mood state.

Why do I suggest that you may actually want to feel and act depressed once in a while? Because, as you may have suspected from your own experience, there sometimes is an upside to a down mood.

But completely abdicating control and letting the depressed feelings take over and take hold is a dangerous practice. If you are going to indulge in some sadness and tears, therefore, it is wise and prudent to have a plan for how long you will allow yourself to do so and for what steps you will take to move off the sadness and on to the behaviors that are incompatible with staying down. Left uncontrolled, crying and other expressions of sadness too easily can trigger rumination and inactivity which, as we have already seen, deepen and amplify depression.

Crying as an Anxiety and Stress Release

"Sometimes I wish that I could just let myself go and have a good cry. A hard sob, like when I was a kid, would help me feel better. But I can't find the release valve," a male patient complained.

His wife responded, "That should be my problem. I cry too easily. And then I get so upset with myself for crying that I feel even more anxious and uptight. So I don't really get any release from the experience at all."

These two contrasting sentiments, quite stereotypical for men and women, respectively, reveal both the difficulties and potential value of gaining voluntary control over the crying response and of using tears as a vehicle for lowering stress and anxiety. Like most men, this husband was sorry that through the years he had learned to overcontrol his crying response, so much so that now, even when he yearned to turn on the tears, he was unable to weep. In contrast, his wife, like many women, had never learned to control crying adequately. As a consequence, her inability to stop the flow of tears in situations where crying was deemed wholly inappropriate—such as at her office—was a tremendous source of emotional distress for her. Because of the self-criticism that crying elicited in this woman, it had lost its value to her as a useful form of anxiety and stress release.

In a later chapter, you will learn some effective behavioral techniques for bringing your own crying response under better voluntary control. For now, however, let's look at the stress reduction and anxiety release value of having what is colloquially referred to as a "good cry."

In the first place, crying is simply a wonderfully cathartic experience. By cathartic I mean a releasing, unloading, outpouring of emotional tension. After you have really cried or sobbed, your body is loose and relaxed. The tightness that you typically retain in your muscles is drained away in the flood of tears.

But the relaxation and cartharsis will be positive only if you want to cry or give yourself permission to weep. If you are fighting the response, and mentally criticizing yourself for the tears, you are merely producing new tensions to replace whatever is released by the crying.

Crying as Emotional Punctuation

When you cry, you also are providing emotional punctuation to the content of what you are saying. Obviously, you may shed tears silently in an emphatic response to a sad movie or story on television. But when the tears come in conjunction with something you are saying or expressing, they serve to underline the depth of your feeling and/or the sadness, emotionality, frustration, or even anger that is behind or contained in your words.

In my office, I always keep a box of tissues on the small table that stands between the two comfortable armchairs on which my patient and I sit. But, when a patient—particularly a new patient—starts crying, she (or he) almost always apologizes for the tears as though crying were somehow unexpected, unacceptable, improper, embarrassing, or unnatural. Obviously, crying to a psychotherapist is expected, natural, and fully acceptable—hence the available tissue.

"Don't even think about it," I generally respond. "If you want or need to cry, just go ahead. I'll consider it a punctuation to what you are saying." This reassurance generally elicits a smile amidst the tears, and the embarrassment rapidly diminishes.

One of my patients talked to me about the concept of crying as emotional punctuation and how it helped her to better understand her feelings. "When I was telling you about what my boss did," she said, "I felt the tears rolling down my cheek. And I thought about the idea that the crying was really emphasizing my hurt and humiliation. In retelling the story, the tears also underlined how enraged and simultaneously passive and helpless I felt to do anything to stop his obnoxious behavior."

You can use your tears as an aid to reading your own emotional message more clearly. At what point in the telling of an upsetting story, for example, do the tears start? What kinds of emotional expressions turn off your tears? Looking at how your crying punctuates your communication may help you to realize more precisely what it is in the content of your message that is most upsetting or painful to you.

The Aesthetics of Moodiness

The upside of down moods extends beyond the notion of having a good, releasing cry. There is a way in which moodiness—especially as associated with depression, sadness, or gloominess—can actually induce sensations of aesthetic pleasure.

Consider, for example, the pleasure you experience when you listen to a particularly moody, emotional piece of music. The music may be from the classical genre or from jazz, popular songs, or even country-western lyrics. Something inside of all of us resonates to the experience of sadness and loss, or just to the induction of moody, introspective, quiet feelings. It is difficult to put words around this experience since it is inherently nonverbal.

The aesthetics of moodiness is expressed frequently in photography, painting, and drawing. Poetry and works of literature have traditionally been vehicles for expressing strong passions—both positive and negative.

What these artistic and musical expressions suggest is that sad or moody feelings can be aesthetically pleasing. While nobody leaves a concert of expressive, moody music laughing and telling jokes, you can feel uplifted by "down" pieces of music, or moved in a gratifying way by emotionally "heavy" plays, movies, or sad, evocative works of art.

This emotional tug that most of us feel in response to various representations of moodiness may help explain why some people report actually feeling better after they have allowed themselves to be depressed or sad for a limited period of time.

"I just needed to be quiet, pensive, and down for a few hours," a patient said. "It felt good to me in some strange way. It's like I sometimes need to exercise that part of me— the part that can be moody and sad. Letting myself feel that way opens me up to feelings and thoughts that I keep buried most of the time."

This woman invites an experience of depression into her life once in a while. She trusts that she can control the experience and knows when the value of being down for her begins to diminish and the need to restore a more positive emotional state arises. Of critical importance, she knows what actions to take to terminate the sad feelings and to make herself feel happier again.

Paradoxical Intentions

Many years ago, Viennese psychoanalyst Victor Frankel introduced an intriguing and successful psychotherapeutic technique for patients who suffered from persistent insomnia. He instructed the insomniacs, paradoxically, to try to stay awake. Essentially, Frankel told his patients to stop trying to go to sleep and to put all their efforts into making sure that they did *not* sleep. The insomniacs put their best efforts into trying to stay awake and, as a result, they slept.

This technique, called Paradoxical Intention, has been used more recently for the treatment of a host of other psychological conditions. The method is closely allied to the concept of acceptance. Recall that Step One of the program involves a paradox: You have to accept your depressed mood before you can successfully let go of it.

In some circumstances, the upside of a bout of depression can be, paradoxically, to cure the blues.

Lisa came to see me after she broke up with Bobby, her boyfriend of two years. "It was my idea to end the relationship," she explained, "because I knew that I didn't love Bobby enough to marry him, and at twenty-five I figured I shouldn't be wasting time. But what really kills me is that I'm so down. I know I did the right thing and I think I should just be able to go out and have a good time, but I feel this sense of sadness. It's so stupid."

Lisa told me that she hadn't spent any time at all letting herself experience the sadness and loss associated with the end of her relationship because the breakup was her choice. "I think it would be ridiculous to feel sad or cry. I'm actually relieved that we're moving on to other people and I think Bobby is, too. It's just that I feel this sadness that keeps creeping into every situation when I'm with a new man. I don't get it, but I sure wish it would go away. I'm trying like crazy to fight it, or ignore it, but it's there like a black cloud. I don't know what to do."

Because Lisa was essentially well balanced emotionally and had an excellent support system of friends and family as well as a stable job, she seemed like a good candidate for a trial of Paradoxical Intention. I told Lisa to set aside the next weekend and instructed her to act very sad over breaking up with Bobby. After her initial surprise and resistance, Lisa was willing to go along with my suggestion. "Nothing else seems to work so I might as well give it a try," she agreed.

At my encouragement, Lisa assembled music and memorabilia that she associated with her relationship with Bobby. At my recommendation, she even bought an album of Billie Holiday's blues music. And she recovered some love letters from Bobby that she had "stashed at the bottom of a stack of old papers and junk so that I wouldn't see them for a long time."

Then, from Friday night through Sunday morning, Lisa tried as hard as she could to feel sad over the end of her relationship. "I never thought about wanting to get back together," she recalled later, "I just did what you said and got into being nostalgic—hauling up old memories, reading those corny letters, crying to some of the music. By Sunday morning, I was sick of the whole thing. But I felt that I had dealt with letting the sadness come out. Before then, I was trying so hard to prevent myself from feeling anything that I think I was just making the sadness a lot worse. I haven't cried once since that weekend. I've even talked to Bobby and we both feel fine about being good friends. Now I'm ready to start going out with someone else."

Paradoxical Intention with depression and sadness should be used selectively and judiciously. Obviously, if the result is to reinforce rumination and obsessive depressed thinking, the technique will backfire. But on occasion you may find, as Lisa did, that instead of resisting your sad feelings and attempting to fight off a depressed mood, you may actually overcome the feelings by accepting and indulging yourself in the blues for a predetermined period of time. At the end of the period, however, it is vitally important that you distract yourself with other thoughts and activities: Go out and be among friends, take in a funny movie, and engage in other depression-incompatible behaviors (D.I.B.'s).

Ups and Downs:
Experiencing the Contrast

One clear upside of getting in down moods is the appreciation they can give you of the times when you do feel happy and up. After enduring several months of Depressive illness, one of my patients remarked when she began to feel better, "I never have felt so grateful. I'm sure that I always liked feeling happy or good in the past, but I just took it for granted like a lot of people do. Now that I've felt what it's like to really be Depressed, the up mood and good feelings I have are so much sweeter. When you've been down for a long time, you really appreciate what it feels like to be happy—or just not to be Depressed."

The sentiment expressed by my patient is similar to that felt by people who have undergone a serious illness and recovered their good health. To such people, the trauma of illness heightens their awareness of the precariousness of life and the precious gift that is good health.

Fortunately, you don't have to experience either serious illness or an episode of clinical Depression to raise your own awareness and appreciation of physical and emotional health. But if you do struggle with Depression or confront bouts of the blues and depressed moods, you can take heart in the promise that when your emotional cycle turns upward again—as up-and-down mood cycles always do—you'll have a renewed and awakened sense of how good your good moods really feel.

Moods and Creativity

There has always been a mystique surrounding the emotional upheavals and moodiness of great artists, writers, and musicians. Recently, Dr. Kay Jamison, a psychologist who specializes in the study and treatment of major mood disorders such as manic-depressive illness and clinical Depression, has turned her attention to uncovering the relationship between creativity and moods.

Dr. Jamison's work includes interviews with living artists and writers as well as historical-biographical analyses, and her studies have revealed that compared to the general population, a highly disproportionate number of creative people indeed do suffer from mood disorders. In many instances such individuals credit their forays into the dark side of life—into Depression—with adding a meaningful and poignant dimension to their creative process. But in a large number of cases they also have endured such enormous pain from their Depressions that they have taken or attempted to take their own lives. So if their Depression contributed to their creativity, the price has been very high indeed.

Of greatest interest for our purposes is Dr. Jamison's finding that these highly gifted people report that the quality of their work is higher after they have found successful methods (including treatment) for controlling their illness and harnessing their moods so that their creativity is channeled effectively. It appears that extreme mood swings left uncontrolled become so disruptive as to seriously impair creative discipline and productivity.

To put these findings in a context relevant to your own mood problems, emotional downswings and bouts with depressed moods and the blues may, in fact, have a positive value in fueling your creative talents. If you have a creative vocation or creative avocations, you might try using your down moods as a source of inspiration for your work. Encourage your creative juices to flow when you feel moody. Remember, though, that by exercising the control methods you will learn in the mood-management program, you will be putting necessary reins on your depression so as to establish the structure, discipline, and concentration required to turn creative ideas into completed products.

A Note on the
Down Side of Up Moods

Curiously, some women have difficulty accepting and fully enjoying their good moods and times of relative happiness. Notwithstanding the fact that the contrast between the lowness of depressed moods and the highness of good moods makes many women all the more grateful for the latter, some still insist that they have uneasy feelings when their moods are up.

"I'm afraid to really let myself go and feel good," one such patient said. "It's a superstitious notion, I suppose, that if I acknowledge I'm in a terrific mood, somehow I'll spoil it and my spirits will crash." This woman, it seemed, was so familiar with the up-and-down nature of her mood cycles that she became unable to enjoy the upswings because of her strong anticipation and dread of what she felt was inexorably going to follow. "As soon as I start to feel happy," she explained, "I immediately expect the depression that I know will come next. And in anticipation of the awful down mood that's coming, I start acting and feeling like I'm already depressed. I can really see how I bring this whole thing on myself."

I worked intensively with this patient over a period of time to teach her the concept of *mood protection*. Instead of letting her good mood trigger anticipation and fear of an inevitable depression, she retrained herself so that her good mood instead triggered behaviors and thoughts that were designed to keep her positive feelings in place and protect herself against input that would disrupt her positivity and lower her spirits.

"Now when I feel happy," she commented, "I know I can do things to keep myself in a good mood for a longer period of time. I don't allow myself to focus any attention at all on thoughts of getting depressed. I concentrate on positive images and memories that make me feel good. I do things like sing, or exercise, or bake some goodies—the kinds of things I love to do when I feel happy. I've learned that it's okay to minimize conversation and activities that can get me into a funk. I know that it's my responsibility to protect my good

132

feelings and to avoid getting into the kind of superstitious thinking that just makes the depressed mood come on faster and stronger. By protecting my mood, I've even learned that the inevitable downturn doesn't feel quite so inevitable. I know I'll always be prone to moodiness and depressed times, but I don't feel so afraid because I can control how low and bad they get."

If your fear of depressed moods has compromised your ability to freely and fully enjoy happy moods when you have them, then you are, in effect, doubling your trouble. Accepting all of your moods, in their various shades and colors, will increase your acceptance and understanding of yourself and the unique experience that is your own life.

The opportunities you have to feel happy, just like the joys of good health, should be embraced and enlarged. When you are feeling good, select activities and focus on thoughts that will protect your happy state, prolong it, and contribute to even better feelings. Don't allow your thoughts to wander off to anxieties and fears about losing your good feelings. If you start to worry about what you will do or how you will feel when the good mood ceases, you will merely bring on the low feelings that much sooner. You have the right and ability to feel high on life and up on yourself as much of the time as you possibly can arrange or achieve. Don't waste it.

Setting the Limits on Acting Depressed

Depressed moods, as you can now see, are not a wholly useless or even entirely negative experience. Without some of life's pain, you might not be able to value its pleasures quite as dearly. A good cry or an intentionally chosen date with the blues might be just what you need to discharge some tension, understand yourself better, or cure yourself of the need to be down any longer.

Since there is an upside to a down mood, you may accomplish the step of acceptance more easily if, on occasion, you give yourself permission to be and act depressed, looking all the while for the value and meaning you seek in the experience.

But since mood control and management are your ultimate goals in this program, you must predetermine some limits on the amount of time and the level of intensity of the depression you elect to let yourself feel. You probably have already had the experience of indulging in a crying bout, and then forcing yourself to stop crying so that you could go to work, or make an appointment, or just answer the telephone and have a conversation. While you may have had to wear dark glasses to hide swollen, reddened eyes or apologize for "sounding bad," you have demonstrated to yourself—albeit inadvertently or unwittingly—that you can make your tears stop if necessary and proceed to other activities.

When you choose to feel and act depressed for a while either because you simply want to or because you suspect that you might uncover a meaning or message in the experience, you should plan to set a limit on the time you'll indulge your negative mood. Have an action plan for counteracting rumination and inactivity at the end of the allowed period.

It is understandable if this all seems to require a degree of control over your emotions and behavior that you have lacked in the past and doubt being able to muster in the future. You should be aiming for increased control. You want to be in control of your depressed moods, not allow them to take control of you. Deciding to impose time limits on how long you will let yourself cry, for example, is a way to exercise control. Engaging in behaviors that are incompatible with depression (D.I.B.'s), after your predetermined depression time has elapsed, is a method for using active means to combat low feelings. Waiting for the depressed feelings to go away before you behave differently merely puts your low mood in charge, and this is what you must strive to avoid.

One of my patients described how she practiced the time-limit method after a stressful, upsetting week: "I had gone through a terrible time with about six crises happening all at once. Standing over the kitchen sink on Friday morning, I decided that I had a darn good reason to cry. But I knew that I had to set some limits or I'd get washed away in a flood of tears and that was the last thing I needed. So I set a schedule for myself. I decided that starting at ten A.M., I would do several pleasurable activities such as going shopping, getting a haircut, and stopping in to see some friends. I decided to dress nicely and put on my makeup carefully so that I'd look as good as possible. I even planned this down to the point of getting some cold compresses ready in case my eyes swelled from crying.

"Ten minutes before my pleasurable activities were set to begin, at exactly nine-fifty, I just let myself start to cry and feel sorry for myself and furious about the unfairness of all the bad things that had happened to me during the week. I closed the door to my bedroom, took the phone off the hook, and grabbed the Kleenex. But at ten o'clock—ten minutes later—I determined that I had to stop crying and start getting dressed. It even astonished me that I had such good control. I felt much better and more relaxed from the cry, got dressed, and by noon I was actually in a much improved state of mind."

Another patient handled a socially barren period between relationships in a similar way. "I hate getting down in the dumps on the weekends. Then I really have trouble getting myself up out of the pits. So I try to set aside Thursday nights as my time to lick my wounds, feel sad about being alone, and even cry if I need to. I've learned that if I give in to feeling down when I choose to on Thursday night, and get rid of the need to cry for myself, I'll be fine for the weekend. I always make sure that I have plans for Saturday night with friends, and if I do start to feel at all low on Friday or Sunday, I turn on some good rock music and dance around, or go to the gym, or write some funny letters to friends."

These examples demonstrate that you *can* choose to feel and act sad, not merely lose control and give in to overwhelming feelings. By setting predetermined limits on the amount of time you allow for the depressed behavior and planning to do activities subsequently that are not compatible with staying depressed, you will lessen the sense of helplessness and the uncertainty associated with bouts of the blues over which you fail to exercise any intentional control.

Not everyone recognizes or needs to find the upside of down moods. You certainly may opt not to indulge in depressed behavior even though your mood is down. The Triple A Program simply allows you to give yourself permission to be and act depressed for a limited period if you so desire. Whatever you decide to do for a particular bout of the blues, your depressed mood will be easier to accept when you assure yourself that, with the mood-management program, you will be able to maintain control.

PART THREE

Attribution

11

◆

Searching for Agent Blue

◆

Blue is not merely a color; it is a mystery.

—ISRALL BEN MOSES NAJARA

When depression strikes, most of us feel a natural impulse to search for the causes behind our emotional slump. If we can discover what is causing our depression, we reason, we will know what to do to solve our problems and, thus, how to restore a more positive state of mind.

In theory, the search for "agent blue"—the causal factor in your depressed mood—should fruitfully lead to effective action plans and solutions. Unfortunately, the mental search in fact often leads you down the wrong paths into a darker and darker mood and around in unproductive, confusing circles. In short, you worry instead of reason.

As a consequence, the search for a cause can become so frustrating, depleting, and demoralizing that you either give up trying to do anything to reverse your depression or reactively and prematurely grasp at radical or ill-conceived solutions that emanate from negative thinking and promise immediate relief but don't, in fact, work. All too often, the attribution process becomes an end rather than a means to the proper end of acting to restore a more positive mood. In other words, you stop short of action and stay stuck in a state of analysis paralysis.

The search for agent blue is basically a natural impulse in psychologically minded people. But you need to learn a productive way to engage your analytical powers so that you avoid getting bogged down by becoming overly introspective, obsessively worried, paralyzed by analysis, or discouraged by the negatively biased thinking that depression typically produces.

The main objective of Step Two, then, is to learn *how* to find the causes of your depressed mood without becoming more depressed or confused by the process.

The Attributional Triad: Events, Thoughts, and Feelings

Before embarking on the search for agent blue, it is necessary that you be fully prepared with a roadmap and guidelines for your analysis. You will need to know how to direct yourself to the right answers and where, precisely, the causes for your depressed moods can be found.

There are three basic sources from which feelings of depression arise. First, the cause of your low mood may be your interpretation, perception, or reaction to an *event* that has occurred in your life. Note that I have not said that the event itself is the causal factor. Whereas some life events directly elicit or evoke depression—like the death of a loved one, a serious financial setback, or a life-threatening illness—most of the events in life do not, in and of themselves, cause depression.

If a telephone fails to ring, or another person scowls at you, or a particular number registers on a bathroom scale, you do not necessarily have reason or cause to be depressed. But if you are awaiting a phone call from a man to whom you are very attracted, or from a prospective employer with whom you desire an interview, or from your husband with whom you have had an argument and from whom you hope for an apology, your interpretation of the quiet telephone may indeed produce feelings of depression.

Your unsupported interpretation may be that the man you like is rejecting you, or that the employer is not interested in interviewing you, or that your husband is contemplating a divorce. Not surprisingly, such interpretations would weigh down your mood. Similarly, your interpretation of the scowling expression, if it was on your boss's face, could be that he or she hates you and plans to fire you. Or the number on the scale could signify confirming evidence that you are fat and that your eating is hopelessly out of control. In all these examples, your *interpretations* determine your low mood.

Remember, then, it is not merely the events in life that cause you to be unhappy but your interpretations, perceptions, and reactions to those events. Nevertheless, when you seek to determine the reason for your depressed mood, your attribution will be to the events themselves as the initial cause of your low mood.

Therefore, when your answer to the question "Why do I feel depressed?" elicits an attribution to an external event— that is, something that happened outside or external to your emotional, cognitive, or physiological functioning—we will call that attribution an *Event-Centered* cause.

The second factor in the attributional triad is a *Thought-Centered* cause. In this case, the cause of your down mood seems to arise out of the particular content or pattern of your *thoughts*.

For example, if you are away from your family during the Thanksgiving and Christmas holidays, you may feel quite down. Your thoughts would likely center on your loneliness, or nostalgic memories of times past when the family was all together. Or a particular date on the calendar, like a wedding anniversary or a birthday, might trigger unhappy thoughts if the marriage in question has ended in divorce, or if the date is the birthday of someone you loved who has passed away. In these instances, the event would not be the main reason for your low mood; your thoughts would be more salient as the cause of why you are feeling down. You would not be likely to say, for example, that you feel down "because it is Christmas or Thanksgiving" but rather "because I am thinking about my family and miss them during the holidays" or "because the date of my anniversary makes me think about my ex-husband."

You probably have had the experience of watching your

mood take a dive after what you know and believe to be a truly insignificant event or comment by another person sets off a barrage of negative thinking and self-criticism. "I asked my husband if he liked the dress I bought," a patient explained, "and I honestly wasn't sure myself whether I looked good in it or even whether I liked it. But when he said that I should exchange it for something else, I immediately got down in the dumps. I started thinking about how other husbands probably always like how their wives look, or how I used to look so much better when I was thinner. And then I even started imagining that my husband might be looking at other women. I know it wasn't the fact that he didn't like the dress that got me so down. It was the negative way that I started thinking. I do that a lot." This patient, then, attributed her mood to a Thought-Centered cause.

Third, your mood may be primarily *Feeling-Centered*. This means the source of your depression is in the *feelings* themselves, as opposed to your thoughts or to a particular external event that elicited a depressed reaction. Like Thought-Centered causes, Feeling-Centered causes pertain to factors internal to you rather than to external events. Down moods that seem to arise for no apparent or obvious reason are generally Feeling-Centered.

A prime example of a Feeling-Centered depression is Premenstrual Syndrome. During the premenstrual time of your cycle, you may sometimes—though not always or necessarily ever—find that your mood is just down, irritable, or particularly sensitive. The reason for your depressed state is primarily attributable to a biochemical impact on your feelings. The specific cause is hormonal; but the impression you have is that the source of your low mood just comes from within—that the attribution for why you are down is simply that you *feel* depressed.

There are, of course, other occasions that are not related to systematic variations in your hormones or times of the month. You may be overly fatigued, stressed, or under the weather physically—having the flu or a cold, or enduring significant levels of pain. In these cases, while the attributions can be made to more specific causes, the essential experience you have is that your mood is centered at the pure feeling level. In a sense, this attribution is often made by exclusion of the other two sources in the attributional triad. You feel down, but you can't pinpoint any particular external event or identify a pattern of negative thinking. By exclusion, then, you can say that the cause of your blue mood seems to reside primarily with the feelings themselves.

Causal Chain Reactions

Categorizing your depressed mood as arising primarily out of Event-Centered, Thought-Centered, or Feeling-Centered causes provides a useful model for organizing your attributions. In reality, though, no one source exists without affecting or pulling in parts of the other two. This is because your psychological wiring consists of intricate interconnections among your emotions or feelings, your thoughts, and your interpretations of events in your life.

Consider the example of a woman anxiously awaiting a telephone call from a prospective employer. The phone call eventually comes, but the personnel manager tells her that there will be no interview, since the position has already been filled. She finds herself feeling down even before hanging up the phone. The conversation and news from the caller presumably are the reasons for her depressed mood. In our model, her mood is primarily Event-Centered in origin. Had the call been more encouraging, her mood probably wouldn't have plummeted.

Almost at the same time she hangs up the telephone, however, the woman's thoughts immediately begin focusing on what this event means about her desirability as an employment candidate, her prospect for other jobs, or about mistakes she made in her résumé.

Because her thoughts are negatively tilted as a result of her sinking mood, the attributions now also extend to Thought-Centered causes. That is, the woman's negative thoughts are now contributing to and perpetuating her low mood and disappointment in response to the event.

The combined impact of the disappointing telephone call and her negative thoughts will deepen her mood. Within a relatively short time, she will be caught in a downward mood spiral. Perhaps she calls a friend for moral support. Her first response to the friend's voice might be, "I feel so demoralized and down, I just need to talk to you." Now, her feelings are most salient. She is not saying that her thinking is distorted and negative, nor that a disappointing event has transpired. The source of her problem as she relates it to her friend is now centered in the depressed feelings themselves.

The interconnections among events, thoughts, and feelings operate to produce a rapid chain reaction in all directions. Your depressed mood might be primarily Thought-Centered, but the thoughts, naturally, will produce negative feelings. Your negative thoughts and feelings might, in turn, precipitate a negative interpersonal event. For example, another woman might be thinking critical thoughts about the way she performed at a recent meeting at work. These thoughts make her feel low and irritable. When her husband comes home that evening, he makes an offhand, insignificant remark about the fact that the light was left on in the garage. Because of the woman's lousy mood and short fuse, she reacts strongly, accusing him of always criticizing her or of picking on her for stupid things that he could take care of himself without bothering her. The result might then be that she and her husband have a fight, thereby producing an event over which she is likely to become even more upset and down.

These scenarios may or may not fit your experience directly, but they serve to make the point. The diagram below shows schematically how Event-Centered, Thought-Centered, and Feeling-Centered causes for depressed moods overlap. In almost every instance, all three sources of low moods will become involved in your causal analysis because they all get stimulated whenever one of them is primarily activated. As the diagram shows, wherever your depressed mood is centered primarily in terms of its originating cause—events, thoughts, or feelings—portions of two or all three intersecting circles are affected as indicated by the shaded areas. Depending on the particular circumstances, the degree

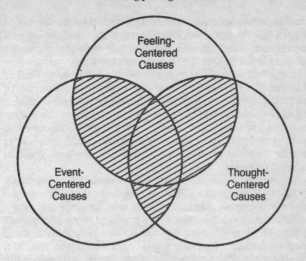

of overlap among the three circles may be relatively greater or smaller than in the diagram.

Understanding the nature of the relationship between the attributional sources of your low moods will suggest ways to break the chain reaction and counteract feelings of helplessness.

As an example, assume that you have a depressed mood that seems to be Event-Centered. Further, assume that you determine you have no control over the event in question, so there is nothing you can do directly to alter the circumstances that are causing you to feel depressed. But since your thoughts and feelings also play a role in your blue mood, you do have some leverage in reducing your discomfort by changing the way you think and emotionally react to the event.

Assume, for example, that a woman's depressed mood arises out of feelings of guilt. Her mood, by her analysis, is primarily Feeling-Centered. When she thinks about why she feels guilty, her thoughts turn to the fact that recently her job has required that she travel and consequently has kept her from spending as much time with her family as she would like. In her thoughts she labels herself an "inadequate wife and mother," and wonders whether her ambition is causing her to lose the people that matter most to her.

In this instance she may not be able to alter her feelings of guilt directly. But she might be able to improve the quality of the time that she does spend at home, or arrange to take a few days' vacation just to go away and be together as a family. Or she might work on stopping her self-punitive labeling and become aware of the erroneous negative predictions she is making that are causing her to feel anxious and upset in addition to guilty.

As another example, suppose a woman has a primarily Thought-Centered low mood. She is depressed because she has been filling her waking thoughts with longings and desire for an intimate relationship with a man and reminding herself of how alone and empty her life is. The thoughts, in turn, bring on feelings of unworthiness, rejection, loneliness, and abandonment. The background event, in this instance, is the fact that currently she is not dating anyone special.

To break the chain reaction, she may elect to intervene by directly working on lifting her spirits. To do so, she might decide to call a friend and go out to a movie. Or she might rent a video of a comedian in concert just so that she can have a few laughs. She might go for a brisk walk and try to get her mind off her loneliness and onto more positive thoughts about her life. In any event, while the results won't change her love life immediately, her overall mood is likely to improve.

Apply the Attributional Model

In order to halt or slow down the negative chain reaction among events, thoughts, and feelings, try doing an attributional analysis of your depressed mood. Consider the first and primary reason for your low feelings. Generally, Event-Centered and Thought-Centered causes will be more apparent to you than Feeling-Centered Causes, since, as I have said, you may deduce the latter by exclusion of the other two.

Then, starting with your attributed primary source, see if you can identify how the other two attributional centers have been activated. If, for example, your mood is primarily Event-Centered, what thoughts about the event or about yourself have also been triggered? What is the effect on your feelings?

Just becoming aware of how your thoughts and feelings and events play off each other to amplify depression will help you to gain control because you will better understand what is happening both externally and internally to make you feel as you do. Remember, the main purpose of the attribution step in the mood-management program is for you to develop a sense that you understand the causes of your depression sufficiently well to move on to action.

As you dissect your blue mood, try to imagine how you would react if you were able to think about what was going on in a less negative or more positive way. For example, the woman who did not get an interview with a prospective employer might entertain alternative ideas that perhaps the job wasn't right for her in the first place, or that a company that didn't recognize her value from her experience on the résumé might not appreciate her enough if she did go to work for them. While these alternative explanations may, in part, be rationalizations, they nevertheless will help her to feel better and cope better with the disappointment.

Give consideration to how you might choose to respond with alternative feelings and how your entire mood, therefore, would be positively affected. For example, if you can find the humor in an undesirable situation and laugh at your dilemma, your overall mood will improve.

Finally, ask yourself if your interpretation or perception of the event you believe is upsetting you can be altered. For example, in the case where the woman started a fight with her husband because she was in a lousy, irritable mood, might it be possible that he really isn't as upset with her as she imagines? Perhaps, if she simply explained to him what happened during her day and how her thoughts were making her feel depressed and oversensitive, he might be willing to forget the fight altogether.

Also, if the cause of your blue mood is Event-Centered, ask yourself what, if anything, you can do to change the event. If, for example, you feel down because a friend misinterpreted something you said and is angry with you, you might decide to call her and discuss what went wrong with your communication. In this instance, your depressed feelings might dissipate when you act to change the event that is making you unhappy.

As you apply the basic attributional framework in your search for agent blue, keep in mind that you are trying intentionally to engage your mind in a linear, analytic process in order to break it out of repetitive thinking and perpetual chain reactions among the triad of causes. When you examine your depression from this vantage point, you probably will arrive at attributional answers relatively quickly and with reasonable facility, as most of my patients do. And you will be one step closer to action.

12

◆

Helplessness and Low Self-esteem

◆

> *Despair exaggerates not only our misery but also our weakness.*
> —LUC DE VAUVENARGUES

There are two toxic emotions that lie at the core of depression: helplessness and low self-esteem.

It should come as an immediate relief to you to learn that these feelings, which may have seemed like your own private shame, are shared by everyone who goes through bouts of down moods and the blues. Even more reassuring is the knowledge that these intensely uncomfortable and totally dysfunctional feelings are more a reflection of erroneous—*and correctable*—ways of thinking than of the reality of your particular personality or life circumstances.

Understanding the thought patterns that produce helplessness and low self-esteem will diffuse their intensity and weaken their debilitating grip on your mood. With your increased awareness of the link among thought patterns, helplessness, and low self-esteem will come the opportunity to increase your sense of control and enhance your self-esteem by modifying and correcting your thoughts and behavior.

149

Expectations of No Control
and Unattainable Goals

Diane, 32, came to consult me about her career goals and objectives. After spending eight years as a midlevel manager in the data-processing division of a large heavy equipment–manufacturing company, Diane believed that she had "topped out" in her professional field and was confronting a career crisis.

"I've gone as far as I can go in my career," she explained. "I'm feeling very unhappy, frustrated, and like I need a change. But there's really nothing I can do to get a better job. I would love to be a senior manager, but I know I don't have the kind of personality or abilities to reach that goal. If I did, I'm sure I would have been promoted by now in my company.

"The worst part is that I can never really be happy or successful unless I have the respect and approval of all the people I work with *and* earn a huge salary. I know that my career goals are just not going to come true, but I'm having a lot of trouble accepting my failure. I'm depressed about the way I've handled my whole life."

As Diane and I came to know one another, it became apparent to me that she was exceedingly intelligent, articulate, analytical, amiable, assertive, and well educated. Clearly, I had difficulty understanding what it was about her personality and abilities that was lacking with respect to qualifying her for a senior-level position. Moreover, I learned from Diane as well as from independent research that the company she worked for had absolutely no women in senior-management positions, and only two others besides Diane among a middle-management staff of 75.

Since Diane believed that she was deficient in "personality and abilities," she had not contacted any executive search firms, nor had she sent her résumé out to any other companies. She interpreted the fact that she had not been promoted within her own company as evidence of her "failure" to meet senior-management requirements generally and therefore erroneously reasoned that she would have no better chance of moving into upper-management ranks at any other company or in another environment.

Diane's attributions for her depressed feelings were that she was helpless to improve her career situation ("There's really nothing I can do to get a better job") and that she really didn't have what it takes to achieve a senior-management position (low self-esteem). Because she made these attributions, Diane failed to initiate a job search outside her company or to make her aspirations for a senior-level position known to the appropriate people within her own firm. In fact, she had no information to either confirm or contradict her negative beliefs and predictions.

Diane's attributions were characteristically depressed. In the first place, she misperceived that she had no control over an important career goal in her life. Moreover, she was convinced that her desired goal would therefore be unattainable to her. This attributional combination—the misperception of having no control over important outcomes or goals and the expectation that the desired important goals will not be attained—produces the sense of helplessness and the syndrome of passivity, negative thinking, low mood, and deflated self-esteem that is the essence of depression.

In addition to judging an important goal as unattainable, Diane also demonstrated other thought patterns that actually caused her to feel depressed. Apart from her desire to be a top manager—a goal that in fact may have been attainable—Diane also expressed criteria for happiness and success that were inherently extreme and largely unrealistic: "I can never really be happy or successful unless I have the respect and approval of all the people I work with *and* earn a huge salary."

Stating the criteria for the attainment of happiness or success in life in such inflated terms is a prescription for failure and a passport to depression. Desiring *universal* respect, admiration, or approval—especially if you are an ambitious woman—is simply unrealistic; aspiring to earn the respect of *most* of your colleagues, or of those people for whom you have respect, is a far more reasonable, realistic, and attainable goal. Similarly, linking the ability to be happy or to feel successful at what you do to a dollar figure—especially one that is defined as nebulously and probably unrealistically as "huge"—is equally self-defeating for attaining happiness and success. In short, Diane's goal setting was flawed and unrealistic. At the same time, since she never attempted to test the job market elsewhere, her perception that her goal of landing a senior-management position anywhere was unattainable probably was distorted in a negative direction.

Debilitating Attributions

Diane's formulation of her career crisis and depression demonstrates how profoundly certain types of attributions can damage self-esteem and produce a sense of helplessness and hopelessness.[1] Obviously, there are many different ways to explain the reasons for events that occur in your life—especially why undesirable or negative things happen to you. In particular, self-esteem is most affected by whether you see the cause or reason for a negative event as something *internal* or within you as opposed to something outside of you.

When you *blame yourself* for something bad that happens, you are making an *internal attribution*. When you *blame someone else,* or account for the event as being due to other outside factors such as the weather, the economy, bad fortune, and so forth, you are making an *external attribution*.

In general, whenever you make an internal attribution for a negative event or outcome in life, your self-esteem will be injured. And, in creating a vicious cycle, low self-esteem increases the likelihood that you will blame yourself for undesirable occurrences. The force of the blow to your self-esteem that comes from internal attributions for negative events will be greater when you make invidious comparisons between yourself and others. In other words, if you blame yourself for an undesirable outcome while also believing that

---

1. S. R. H. Beach, L. Y. Abramson, and F. M. Levine, "Attributional Reformulation of Learned Helplessness and Depression." In J. F. Clarkin and H. I. Glazer, eds. *Depression: Behavioral and Directive Intervention Strategies* (New York: Garland, 1981).

most other people are able to attain desirable outcomes, your self-esteem will be especially deflated.[2]

A common example will serve to illustrate how internal attributions for undesirable events damage self-esteem. Assume, as a case in point, that an intelligent, attractive woman has been jilted by the man she has been dating. This undesirable event makes her feel depressed and ultimately she asks herself why he left her. Now, if the woman attributes her being jilted to something within her such as "I'm too old for him" or "I'm ten pounds overweight" or "I'm not sexy enough," her self-esteem is likely to be impaired and her depressed mood will stubbornly persist.

On the other hand, if she says, "He's intimidated by smart women," or "He has trouble staying committed to any woman for very long," she is far less likely to let the event bruise her sense of self-worth. On the contrary, by attributing the negative event to things largely *outside* herself, she can maintain her self-esteem and recover more quickly from her depressive reaction.

Similarly, certain types of attributions are more likely than others to produce feelings of helplessness and hopelessness. This time the relevant comparison concerns whether you see the reason for a negative event as something that is basically stable and not subject to change or whether you see the reason as something that can be changed—by either you or someone else.

If the cause for a negative event is, in your view, not changeable, there will be little that you or anyone else can do to alter things now or in the future. Hence, you will feel helpless and without much hope. If, on the other hand, you explain a negative event as being due to something that might change, you will feel less helpless and more hopeful, since conditions can be made better.

If the woman who was jilted by her boyfriend believes he left her because she is somewhat overweight, her attribution is to a changeable cause. Clearly, if 10 excess pounds is the reason that her relationship ended, she has no basis to feel

---

2. Ibid.

helpless, even though her self-esteem might be wounded. On the contrary, she can easily help herself by simply losing the weight, thereby standing a chance of getting back her man. But if she makes the attribution that she is too intelligent for this man, her sense of helplessness is bound to increase. Intelligence is a fixed trait. The woman cannot become less intelligent, nor would she presumably want to, so her chances of winning back the man in question would be slim. Hope would come from seeking another kind of man, who prefers smart women.

The most debilitating combination, then, is when you attribute the cause of an undesirable event in your life to a reason that is both internal to you and unchangeable in nature. In this case, your attribution says, in effect, "It's my fault and there's nothing that I or anybody else can do to change things." On the other hand, if the attributional mix is to something or somebody outside of you and is changeable, your mood should be less depressed, since you are unlikely to experience either low self-esteem or the crippling sense of helplessness. In the latter case, while the event would be no less undesirable, the attribution would say, in effect, "I'm not to blame for this, and things will be different in the future."

Let's examine Diane's depressed feelings in the context of her attributions. Diane's low mood now becomes eminently understandable and even predictable, since her attributions reflect the most debilitating combination: She blamed herself (internal attribution) for her lack of promotion to senior management and believed that her personality (internal and unchangeable) and lack of ability (internal and largely unchangeable) accounted for her company's decision.

In therapy, Diane learned—as you are learning now—about the importance of attributions in influencing how she felt about herself, her future, and life in general. Together, Diane and I developed some alternative formulations that would make her less vulnerable to depression and that she subsequently could test for accuracy herself. Specifically, Diane reattributed her career crisis this way:

"Okay, maybe it's not me," she tentatively began. "I certainly used to think that I had the ability and personality that it takes to make it to the top of any corporate ladder—

provided that there are women there, or that they at least are allowed to get there. I guess I just wanted to think better of my company, or that I could get them to change. But maybe the more correct attribution is that I haven't been promoted to senior management because there is really a 'glass ceiling' in my company that prevents women from going any farther than I have gone already."

Once Diane stopped blaming herself and began to see the company's policies as discriminatory toward women, her self-esteem was on the mend and her motivation gained momentum.

"You know, there might be hope after all. If it's the company's problem, another, more enlightened, firm might really appreciate someone with my skills and ambition. I should do some research and check into which companies have women that have crossed over into senior management."

To test her new analysis, Diane registered with three national executive search firms and decided to actively pursue a position with another company. After a few interviews, she determined that some additional training and an MBA (she already had a Master's degree in mathematics and computer science) would boost her desirability. When last I spoke with her, Diane had started negotiations with a fashion firm owned and managed by women that was offering to underwrite the cost of her education if she immediately accepted the position, with a guaranteed promotion to vice-president upon completion of her degree.

In addition to changing her attributional style, Diane also modified her unrealistic goals and the importance she placed on attaining what was, essentially, unattainable.

"I understand now how undermining my inflated goals were. I thought it was typically 'yuppie' and motivating to go after a huge salary. And I think my self-esteem problem had something to do with needing approval from *everyone*. I laugh at myself now. I don't approve of everyone else, so why should they all like me? I'll probably always aim for a big salary, but I know I can be happy if I'm doing well, making good money, and feeling productive and appreciated. I feel successful just being offered such a great opportunity with the fashion firm."

Diane's case had a very positive outcome. The way you explain the causes of good, positive outcomes in your life also has important implications for mood, self-esteem, and expectations for the future. If you don't take adequate credit for positive outcomes, neither your self-esteem nor confidence will be bolstered. When you explain away your success as being due to good luck or a break someone gave you, you don't take the credit you deserve for your performance. And your confidence in the likelihood that you will succeed in the future is not enhanced by your attribution, since luck is inherently unpredictable. Conversely, if you attribute your success to your ability, your self-esteem will be appropriately nourished and you will gain added confidence in approaching similar tasks in the future.

Research on the attributional styles of women versus men, and of depressed individuals versus nondepressed people, has revealed some fascinating, though disconcerting, parallels. Women, as a group, tend to explain their successes as being due to good luck, whereas they attribute their failure to their lack of ability. Men, in contrast, attribute their successes to ability while they explain their failures as being due to bad luck or other external causes.

Attributions that depressed individuals make closely parallel those made by women, but in an even broader, more far-reaching way. Among depressed individuals, all negative events, including failure, are attributed to internal causes like lack of ability, unworthiness, and so forth. Positive outcomes, including success, are attributed to outside factors; since no credit is taken, no enhancement to their self-esteem results.

This means that if you are a woman who experiences bouts of low moods and depressions, you have a particular vulnerability to ways of attributing and thinking that (a) cause you to feel helpless and out of control, (b) produce low self-esteem, and (c) lead you to believe that highly important outcomes and goals are unattainable to you.

Changing Your
Attributional Style

You can and should directly target the goal of changing the tendency to blame yourself for negative outcomes and events, especially when they are particularly important or significant. This does not mean that you should dodge responsibility or blame for the things that you indeed have caused. In reality, though, you are not likely to be solely responsible for causing all or even the majority of the bad things that happen to you. The self-blame you assume for negative events is more likely to be a reflection of your negative mood than an accurate mirror of reality.

An Exercise in Reattribution:
Developing Alternative Explanations

Think about two significant negative events that happened to you during the past few months and made you feel really depressed or down. Try to recall how you accounted for what happened at the time, or reconstruct now what you think were the causal explanations. Review your attributions and look for examples of self-blame.

Now try to come up with at least two alternative explanations for each event, preferably more weighted to factors outside of yourself *and* to things that can be changed. This process—called *reattribution*—is very effective in reducing depressed feelings and thinking.

Modifying Unrealistic
Expectations and Goals

Depression often results from comparing your current status in life with expectations and goals that are unrealistic, unattainable, and self-defeating. This is not to say that you should lower your ambition, your achievement drive, or your hopes and dreams for a fulfilling, successful life. But like

Diane's, your assumptions about what is necessary in order for you to be happy or to feel successful may be unrealistically inflated. Your goals, like those of many women, may be defined in terms that are overly long-term (e.g., be happy with a man some day), or so abstract (be more successful; do better at work) as to provide inadequate direction and thereby undermine your motivation.

Two exercises are effective in modifying unrealistic or seemingly unattainable goals. Both are designed to help you to redefine your expectations and goals in terms that are more easily attainable so that your efforts are rewarded, your motivation is stimulated and reinforced, and your depressed mood is alleviated.

EVALUATING CURRENT GOALS

Write down your expectations of yourself and/or your goals in each of the following five areas:

1. Personal appearance
2. Career success
3. Success and happiness in a personal relationship
4. Attitudes of other people toward you
5. Daily accomplishments and quality of the things you do

These five areas generally tap the unrealistic expectations and goals of most of the women whom I have treated or known. As you write down your personal answers, try to be completely candid. This exercise is for your eyes only, so editing or censoring your answers will serve nobody's interest—least of all your own. Write down your automatic thoughts about the goals or expectations you have of yourself in each area.

Now, take a closer look at each of your current expectations. Whenever you can identify unrealistically high or too-distant goals, rewrite your expectations in terms that are still motivating while being more realistic and attainable.

158

SETTING ATTAINABLE SUBGOALS

When you feel down, you tend to focus on long-range goals that may seem so far off that they appear unattainable. Or the abstract nature of your defined goal (e.g., "be happier," "have a good life," "be a good mother," "get thin," and so on) can feel overwhelming and unattainable because the behavioral steps that lead to success are not spelled out. While the goals are fine, their abstract, general terms don't tell you how to go about achieving them—such as exactly *how* to become a good mother, or what to do or feel that would mean that you were happier, and so on—which then makes them seem out of reach.

In order to bring distant, long-range, or abstract goals into an attainable range, redefine your goals into smaller *subgoals*—concrete, attainable behaviors that you can watch yourself accomplishing on your way to reaching longer-term objectives.

For example, if your goal is to "have a better marriage," three attainable subgoals might be (1) spend three evenings per week doing a relaxing, pleasurable activity together with your husband; (2) set aside at least 30 minutes every evening to spend alone together, without children, television, telephone, or other interruptions, to talk about the events of the day; (3) give each other three statements of appreciation each week to reward the efforts both of you have made toward improving the quality of your relationship.

If your goal is to take better care of yourself, your subgoals might be (1) have a complete physical; (2) follow a nutritionally sound diet plan every day; (3) give yourself a special treat like a massage, facial, or new hairstyle.

By defining subgoals, out-of-range aspirations are broken down into manageable steps. Remember to reward yourself with self-praise or other reinforcements in order to strengthen your motivation and induce feelings of success and accomplishment along the way.

Depression as
Its Own Attribution

You will recall from Chapter 6, "Blue Alert," that depression produces a bias toward pessimism and negativity, as well as a host of systematic cognitive errors and distortions, which will be discussed further in the next chapter. Of central importance in your attributional efforts is the recognition that your depressed mood is the product of depressed thinking and misinterpretation of information. In short, the attribution of why you so often feel helpless and down on yourself is that feelings of helplessness and low self-esteem are symptoms of depression.

Sometimes it comes as a big relief just to know that the uncomfortable symptoms you feel when you are depressed, such as tearfulness, inability to concentrate, low energy, or pessimism, are precisely that, *symptoms,* as opposed to evidence of some permanent physiological deficiency, malfunction, or character failing. When you hear yourself expressing derogatory comments about yourself, or stating that you are helpless in the face of what seem to be overwhelming problems, *that is your depression talking.* Knowing what you now do about attributional thinking that counteracts helplessness and low self-esteem, you can talk back to your depression and reverse its disquieting effects.

In addition to the attributions that lead to helplessness and low self-esteem, there are other systematic and predictable distortions that affect your thought processes when you get depressed, which you also can reverse once you gain an awareness of how such distortions operate. Repairing your mood by "debugging" and correcting your internal mental computer is the subject of the next chapter and your next phase in working through the attributional step of the mood-management program.

13

♦

Bugs in Your Mental Computer

♦

Get your facts first, then you can distort them as you please.

—MARK TWAIN

When you try to answer the question "Why do I feel so depressed?" you engage your mental or cognitive equipment searching for the right answer. But because of your depressed mood, the equipment you are using—your own thoughts—is already malfunctioning. Based as it is on negatively biased and distorted thinking, the logic of your answers is necessarily suspect. This is why, if undertaken without guidance, the attributional step in mood management can be a treacherous one.

The fact that depression distorts your thought processes has important behavioral consequences. If you think that you have no alternatives or ways out of a problematic situation, for example, you are likely to become passive; if your thinking becomes self-flagellating, you are likely to engage in self-punitive actions; and if you think you are doing everything wrong or inadequately, your motivation will flag and your achievement drive and efforts will plummet.

The Repair Manual:
The Ten Most Common
Cognitive Errors

The simplest and most accurate attribution you can make about why you feel depressed is that you are perceiving, evaluating, and interpreting your experience in a distorted way. I can say this with confidence because a great deal of research and clinical observation over the past decade in a field known as cognitive therapy has produced unequivocal and compelling evidence to support the relationship between depression and cognitive, or thinking, errors.

In brief, this work, spearheaded by psychiatrist Aaron Beck and his colleagues at the University of Pennsylvania, indicates that (1) depressed moods result from distorted, negative ways of thinking about the self, other people, and the future; (2) the mood of depression, in turn, creates a tendency to think in systematically distorted ways that operate to confirm, amplify, and prolong the depression; and (3) by identifying and correcting what have become automatic or second-nature thought patterns, a depressed mood can be improved rapidly and dramatically.

Fortunately, the kinds of cognitive errors that depression produces are identifiable, recognizable, and fairly consistent among individuals. What this means is that you will not only be relieved to recognize your own ways of thinking in these common errors, thereby reducing your concern that you are alone in experiencing depressing thoughts, but also will be able to correct the errors by using the techniques that have been successfully developed for the treatment of depressed patients through cognitive therapy.

There are 10 basic errors in thinking produced by depression. To analogize your cognitive apparatus to a computer, these errors constitute the "bugs" or flaws in your mental program. The bugs cause the phenomenon known in computer jargon as "garbage in, garbage out," or, perhaps more accurately, "data in, bugs in the processing, garbage out." The "garbage" that is generated by cognitive errors are conclusions or attributions that you make about yourself, other people, and your future that lead you to feel defeated and depressed.

But with the benefit and guidance of a debugging manual, your mood can be repaired by correcting the cognitive errors. Following is a list, with definitions, of the 10 most common cognitive distortions that depression produces.[1]

◆

Definitions of Cognitive Distortions

1. **All-or-nothing thinking:** You see things in black and white categories. If your performance falls short of perfect, you see yourself as a total failure.
2. **Overgeneralization:** You see a single negative event as a never-ending pattern of defeat.
3. **Mental Filter:** You pick out a single negative detail and dwell on it exclusively so that your vision of all reality becomes darkened, like the drop of ink that discolors the entire beaker of water.
4. **Disqualifying the positive:** You reject positive experiences by insisting they "don't count" for some reason or other. In this way you can maintain a negative belief that is contradicted by your everyday experiences.
5. **Jumping to conclusions:** You make a negative interpretation, even though there are no definite facts that convincingly support your conclusion.
   a. *Mind reading.* You arbitrarily conclude that someone is reacting negatively to you, and you don't bother to check this out.
   b. *The fortune-teller error.* You anticipate that things will turn out badly, and you feel convinced that your prediction is an already established fact.

---

1. David D. Burns, "Definitions of Cognitive Distortions," *Feeling Good: The New Mood Therapy* (New York: William Morrow, 1980). Copyright © 1980 by David D. Burns, M.D. Reprinted with permission of William Morrow & Co., Inc.

6. **Magnification (catastrophizing) or minimization:** You exaggerate the importance of things (such as your goof-up or someone else's achievement), or you inappropriately shrink things until they appear tiny (your own desirable qualities or the other fellow's imperfections). This also is called the "binocular trick."

7. **Emotional reasoning:** You assume that your negative emotions necessarily reflect the way things really are: "I feel it, therefore it must be true."

8. **"Should" statements:** You try to motivate yourself with "shoulds" and "shouldn'ts," as if you had to be whipped and punished before you could be expected to do anything. "Musts" and "oughts" are also offenders. The emotional consequence is guilt. When you direct "should" statements toward others, you feel anger, frustration, and resentment.

9. **Labeling and mislabeling:** This is an extreme form of overgeneralization. Instead of describing your error, you attach a negative label to yourself: "I'm a loser." When someone else's behavior rubs you the wrong way, you attach a negative label to him or her: "He's a goddamn louse." Mislabeling involves describing an event with language that is highly colored and emotionally loaded.

10. **Personalization:** You see yourself as the cause of some negative external event that you were not in fact primarily responsible for.

❖

Read over the list and definitions carefully and try in each instance to think of ways that your thinking tends in the direction of the cognitive distortion. Your purpose should be to understand these cognitive errors sufficiently well that you are able to spot them in a sample of your own thought processes when you feel blue or depressed.

Recording and
Correcting Thinking Errors

In Chapter 11, as you began your search for agent blue, you learned that your attributions will center around three areas: events or situations, thoughts, and feelings or emotions. In the cognitive-therapy approach to depression, the focus is on thoughts—specifically on erroneous thoughts—as reactions to events that in turn cause feelings and uncomfortable emotions—principally, depression and anxiety.

The central concept is that if you can tap into the automatic train of your thoughts, triggered by a situation or event that upsets you, (e.g., makes you feel angry, unhappy, guilty, and so on), you will be able to identify where the "bugs" in the programming exist by referring to the repair manual of cognitive distortions. Your repair work entails correcting the errors, specifically by replacing the flawed and distorted thinking with more rational, logical, and functional responses.

In cognitive therapy the therapist must assume a collaborative relationship with the patient. The patient plays a major, active role in reporting her or his automatic thinking without censoring, and by working together with the therapist to uncover and challenge what is flawed and illogical about her reasoning. With practice, the patient becomes adept at identifying and correcting irrational, distorted thinking on her own and thus becomes an effective manager of her periodic low moods and depression.

You and I are going to collaborate in "busting" the self-defeating ways of thinking that are making you feel depressed and in developing more appropriate, rational thoughts that will make you feel better. Let's begin by having you think about a situation, event, or a recollection of an event that you associate with depressed or negative feelings. Write down a brief description of the event, sticking as closely as you can to the *facts*.

Now, identify as precisely as possible how the event made you feel, or seemed to make you feel. For example, did you feel rejected? Victimized? Stupid? Or just plain down in the dumps? Write down your feelings.

The next question is, how intense were those feelings? Rate the intensity on a 10-point scale where 1 equals just a trace of emotion or extremely low intensity and 10 equals the most intense feelings or emotions you can imagine.

Now I want you to close your eyes and visualize the situation you have described. Try to feel now just as intensely as the situation made you feel; let yourself experience the negative emotions associated with the depressing event you are recalling to mind.

Okay. What are you thinking? Why do you feel depressed? What is your interpretation of the event? Write down the immediate, automatic thoughts that come to your mind. Don't hesitate or edit your writing. Let the thoughts simply transfer from your mind onto paper in as direct a way as you can. After your thoughts are recorded, read them back to yourself. Still visualizing and recreating how you feel or felt in the upsetting situation, decide the extent to which you have confidence that your thoughts are accurate. In other words, rate the extent to which you believe in your own automatic thoughts on a scale of 0 to 100 percent.

The next step is to reread your thoughts. This time, using a colored pen or highlighter, indicate those portions of your automatic thinking that look as though they are logically flawed. Refer back to your repair manual. Search for evidence in your thinking of any or all of the common cognitive distortions.

For each portion of your thinking that you suspect as being flawed or erroneous, assign one of the 10 cognitive distortion labels. For example, does your thinking contain admonishments that you "should" or "shouldn't" do something? If so, assign the label "Should Statement" (Number Eight). Are you having thoughts that the situation means something terrible because your emotional reaction involves a lot of anxiety or fear? In this case, your cognitive error would be Number Seven, "Emotional Reasoning": Because you feel anxious, you assume that the situation is dangerous or bad, when in fact your reasoning is based on your feelings rather than on what is factually true.

Your thinking probably contains at least three elements that are cognitively distorted, and very likely many more. If you find only one error, review the list of distortions and search again for evidence of flaws in your thinking. Don't be at all discouraged if this exercise is difficult at first. The idea that your thinking is irrational has probably not occurred to you before. Since you feel depressed, you are looking at events through gray-colored lenses, in the fog of depression. You probably believe that your thinking is unbiased and accurately reflects the depressing nature of your life circumstances. Depression makes you believe in your own negative thinking, and your negative thinking makes you hold on to your depression. This is the vicious cycle you must break.

The ability to recognize and identify cognitive errors will become quite easy for you with time and diligent practice. My patients become proficient at identifying distortions in their thinking within a few weeks of learning the technique. Interestingly, they become acutely sensitive and adept at picking up on the distortions in the communications of other people, often under circumstances in which helpful feedback can be offered. When you can teach those with whom you live or work about cognitive distortions, you will establish an effective, supportive atmosphere for helping yourselves to manage your respective moods.

The next step in the process requires reinterpreting and reattributing the situation that produced the depressed, upsetting feelings. By uncovering what is flawed or wrong with your thinking, you are now in a position to develop more rational, logical responses. If, for example, you found evidence of All-or-Nothing Thinking (Number One) in your record, write a more rational response based on the fact that reality exists in many shades of gray rather than in the extremes of black and white. Instead of thinking about an experience as a "total failure," you might develop a response such as "I didn't do as well at this as I would have liked but there were some things that I did do right. I certainly can't expect myself to be perfect. And, by learning from whatever mistakes I made, I can try to be more successful in the future."

Write a more rational response to correct each of the cognitive errors you identified. A useful mindset to adopt for this part of the exercise is to talk to yourself as you would to your best friend or to someone else whom you love. Rarely, and especially when you are down, will you treat yourself as kindly, supportively, and helpfully as you do other people. This is merely another example of your proneness to be hard on yourself when you are depressed. Therefore, program your mindset so that you say to yourself the supportive, rational, and accurate kinds of things you would say to your best friend if she felt depressed because of engaging in erroneous thinking.

But just as you wouldn't deceive a friend, don't assume that undoing your erroneous, critical thinking means that you should fool yourself into feeling better by making up responses that are not truthful. Be accurate and honest in your rational responses. You don't have to be a Pollyanna to counter negative, distorted thinking. You do have to be temperate, well-reasoned, and convincing while maintaining a benevolent attitude toward yourself.

Read over your rational responses to the situation or event that initially upset you. Do you have confidence in these more logical thoughts? To what extent would you say you have convinced yourself that the rational responses are an accurate way of looking at the event? Rate the extent to which you believe in your rational responses on a percentage scale from 0 to 100 percent, where 100 percent means total belief and 1 percent means virtually no belief at all.

Finally, compare your original line of thought about the event with your reattributed responses. Now ask yourself to what extent you now believe in your initial automatic thoughts in light of your more rational responses. Your belief in the original interpretations, in all likelihood, will diminish markedly if not completely.

Review the emotional reaction you originally had to the event that was triggered by your now refuted automatic, distorted thinking. Ask yourself if you still feel the same way in light of your more rational responses. How do you feel about the situation when you react through the filter of your rational responses? Again, rate the intensity of your new feelings from 1 to 10.

I have just walked you through the mental debugging procedure. With some practice, you'll become a capable mood mechanic on your own, able to repair "broken" or flawed thought processes that disrupt smooth, positive, emotional functioning.

14

◆

Mismanaging Yourself

◆

Nobody can make you feel inferior without your consent.
—ELEANOR ROOSEVELT

Because of the erroneous ways in which you process information when you feel depressed, the quality of how you manage yourself can be severely compromised. You can develop a significant morale problem with respect to your attitudes, motivation, and performance in life because the person who is in charge of managing that performance has the deck stacked against you. And that unfair, biased manager is *you.*

When you are down, you are quite likely to behave toward yourself as an arbitrary, biased, hypercritical, and demotivating supervisor would toward his or her employees. This is because your capacity to monitor, evaluate, and reward your actions and performance is crippled by your depressed mood. In addition to the cognitive distortions discussed in the last chapter, when you feel down, you also are prone to make other systematic mistakes in the information and feedback operations that you use to regulate and control your behavior and emotions.

Nothing else drives home the point of self-mismanagement caused by the blues as well as depersonalizing the issues and

170

placing it instead in the context of organizational management. The organizational analogues to depressive symptoms include low productivity, poor employee morale, high absenteeism and attrition rates, and lack of initiative or creativity.

Women in business, especially if they are in management, know the value of constructive, balanced feedback, consistent positive reward and praise, and realistic, attainable and fair performance standards in bringing out the best in employees. Yet these are precisely what women in the throes of a down mood fail to do for themselves.

Martha is an attractive 33-year-old woman with about 15 to 20 extra pounds on her frame, gained during her pregnancy with her second child. As the director of human resources for a major corporation, she knows the principles of good management. She is highly regarded among both employees and senior management as someone whose excellent "people skills" motivate, encourage, and succeed in helping others to live up to their fullest potential.

But when Martha came to see me in therapy one afternoon, she spent the first 20 minutes of her session regaling me with details of how she had utterly failed in her attempt to lose weight during the past week. In the course of her monologue, she described herself as a "fat nobody who never does anything right," pointed out every time during the week when she had "cheated" on her diet or sloughed off on her exercise. She "hated" herself so much, she continued, that she had sworn that she wouldn't buy herself new clothes or do anything fun with her friends until she was "totally thin." She stated categorically that she was now "so ugly, disgusting, and creepy" that her husband probably was just going through the motions of making love to her and is secretly "completely turned off."

When Martha exhausted her tirade of self-deprecation, I asked her to sit back for a few minutes and ponder a management problem. I told her that I had been called in as a management consultant by a company that was having serious problems with one of its divisions.

Over the past six months, since the time that a new division manager was installed, the employees had been evidencing a major morale slump. The division as a whole was well off its normal productivity standard, and quality problems such as errors and shoddy workmanship had been reported frequently. The absenteeism rate was twice as high as in other company divisions, and several key employees had quit. In psychological and production terms, the division was depressed.

The new division manager, I continued to tell Martha, had a practice of calling in each employee once a week and telling her or him everything that she or he had done wrong. Only shortcomings and errors were noticed; positive work and high-quality output (though clearly present in some instances) were ignored. The manager told employees that he ran "a tight ship," that he would settle for nothing less than total perfection, and that he had no tolerance whatsoever for anyone learning on the job. Furthermore, he said he was already convinced that nobody in the division could possibly live up to his standards and regularly called employees names like "loser," "disaster," "doo-fus," and "dumbo."

"So, what do you think I should recommend?" I asked Martha with a straight face.

"Obviously this manager either has to go or his entire management style needs revamping. What a jerk!" Martha responded. "How can he possibly expect anybody to do well under those kinds of psychological conditions? He sounds like Captain Bligh in *Mutiny on the Bounty*."

"I thought you might see it that way," I smiled. "But what you don't seem to realize is that you manage yourself as harshly as the division manager. You focus on your failures exclusively, call yourself names, make all sorts of negative predictions and demand nothing short of perfection from yourself. It's no wonder you feel demoralized."

Clearly, in the context of organizational management Martha could readily see what she could not see about her own self-management style. Had Martha been a full-time mother or a schoolteacher I would have made the same point with an analogy to a critical and arbitrary teacher or coach who runs his kids' performance into the ground by name-calling, selective attention to mistakes, and withholding encouragement, support, and reinforcement.

Martha's poor self-management style reflects the typical thinking and regulatory errors that depression causes. Specifically, there are *three areas* of deficits in self-control processes that creep insidiously into the way you monitor, evaluate, and reinforce your behavior when you feel down.[1]

The monitoring errors include giving selective attention to negative events while discounting positive experiences or feedback on the grounds that somehow the latter doesn't count as much as the things that have gone wrong. Further, when you are feeling the pain of depression, you will be inclined to attend to the immediate as opposed to delayed consequences of your behavior.

This means that when you are down, you observe or monitor your behavior in a distorted and unfair way. You will pay attention to and remember those things that happen in the course of a day that represent criticism, failure, your own shortcomings, or anything else that you encode as a negative experience, while discounting, ignoring, or selectively forgetting positive things that people may have said to give you compliments, evidence of your competence and successful performance at home or work, and other feedback that would balance or offset the weight of the bad things that occurred.

In a similar monitoring distortion, you will tend to examine or think about only the immediate or short-term value of your actions when you are depressed and to ignore or overlook their longer-term effects. It is this error that accounted for Martha's tendency to binge on chocolate as a short-term relief to her frustration at work, for example, while failing to anticipate how aggravated she would be two days later when her favorite skirt would not zip. Staying in bed and pulling the covers over your head as a way to avoid facing the world and its pressures when you are depressed is another common example of grasping at short-term relief while overlooking the cost in terms of a longer-term backlog of work, festering of unsolved problems, absenteeism, and so forth.

---

1. L. P. Rehm, A self-control model of depression, *Behavior Therapy 8*, 1977, 787–804.

The evaluation errors you will tend to make when you are feeling down include setting perfectionistic, unrealistic standards for judging your performance, engaging in all-or-nothing thinking (e.g., total success versus complete failure), and assuming total blame for negative events while refusing to accept full or even partial credit for the positive things that happen. These errors account for why it is so easy to become discouraged and to want to just give up, even when you think you are trying to do something to make yourself feel better. Martha, for example, had actually lost one pound during the week that preceded her self-flagellation tirade in my office. But her evaluation errors led her to encode that one pound loss as a *total* failure.

"Can you believe I only lost one pound in a whole week?" Martha wailed. "I should have lost at least five pounds if I'd been perfect at my diet! There's no point to any of this. I might as well just throw in the towel and stay fat . . . or get even fatter. It's my fault that I didn't find some indoor exercise to do during that rainstorm we had last week."

The third set of self-control deficits caused by depression concerns the way you reinforce or fail to reward yourself for your actions. Consistent with the negativity bias that depressed moods produce, you will tend to influence your behavior in a negative direction—albeit unconsciously or unwittingly—when you feel down. So when you do something "wrong" (a judgment which is already distorted by evaluation errors), you are likely to punish yourself in an excessive way by indulging in punitive name-calling and self-reproach, and even by engaging in self-destructive behaviors and habits such as binge eating or excessive drinking.

In addition, you also will tend to be very miserly with yourself when it comes to giving yourself rewards, while at the same time overadministering punishments. Would you treat a child or your best friend or a valued employee in this way? Of course not. But you do it to yourself when you feel depressed. And you wonder why you feel so down?

174

Strategies for
Improving Self-Management

After Martha and I discussed how her depressed mood was distorting her ability to control her thoughts and behavior, which in turn perpetuated her blues, we turned to strategies for reversing her errors and improving her self-management style. That week, Martha's homework was to keep a record of all the things that she did right or correctly on her diet and exercise program. She was also instructed to write out three positive statements of praise for complying with her weight-loss program and to read them after each meal or exercise period when she had eaten or exercised pretty well (*not* perfectly). Finally, she was assigned the task of coming up with a list of rewards—such as enjoyable activities, new clothes, or gifts for herself—to use as positive reinforcers for every three pounds she lost.

The final exercise in Chapter 12, in which you broke down long-term or seemingly unattainable goals into attainable, measurable subgoals, also is applicable to correcting evaluation and reward self-control errors. In addition to the subgoal exercise, here are two other strategies that will help to counteract the tendency to demoralize yourself by monitoring, evaluating, and rewarding yourself unfairly:

1. POSITIVE FEEDBACK LOG

This exercise is designed to counteract the tendency to selectively notice negative feedback and events. Keep a daily journal of all the positive things that people have said to you during the day. Record all the things that you did properly, well, or correctly. Be sure to include all the things that you probably do well every day but disregard because they are merely part of your routine or because you expect yourself to do them well. When a low mood hits and you begin to obsess over negative events or details, read over your positive feedback log for the past week.

2. REWARDS REPERTOIRE

Compose a list of easily accomplished positive activities that can be used as rewards when you accomplish more difficult activities or goals. For example, your list might include going to a movie, indulging yourself by buying yourself a gift, getting a new hairstyle, and so forth. Select an activity or item from your rewards repertoire whenever you do something difficult or something you didn't feel like doing because you felt down. Remember to keep the rate of positive reinforcement much higher than is your natural tendency when you have the blues.

Confusing a Data Point With a Downward Trend

One final cognitive error deserves special mention, since it is so common and is endemic to the experience of up-and-down mood cycles. This mistake occurs when you forecast that your current feelings of discouragement, pessimism, and depression are valid predictors of a continued downward trend in the course of your life circumstances and emotions.

This confusion between a specific data point on a cycle—how you feel at a given time—and an overall downward trend is a central cause of the hopelessness so common and pervasive in depression. If you believe that your current blue feelings are predictive of a crash in the future, there indeed would be little reason for hope. On the other hand, if you believe either that your current feelings simply have no predictive value—that they tell you nothing about how things are likely to be in the future—or that your low feelings mean that things have only one way to go and that is up, then you are likely to feel far more hopeful and less pessimistic.

There are two relatively simple and effective corrections for the confusion of a data point with a continued downward trend. The first is to draw a mood cycle on a piece of paper. Your drawing will look something like the one below, since this is the inherent form of an up-and-down cycle.

When you feel depressed, indicate the point on the cycle that represents your current feelings. The point might be at A as indicated in the second drawing. Your sense of hopelessness and depression comes from believing (mistakenly) that the fact of being at point A is predictive that the future trend will follow the broken arrow in a downward direction.

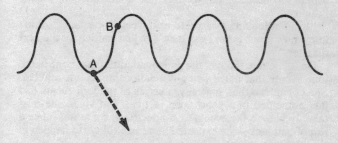

However, you have already drawn the mood cycle that indicates that the most likely prediction of your mood in the future is that it will turn upward, to point B, for example. Thus, as you can demonstrate to yourself, believing that a temporary downward swing in your mood or life circumstances necessarily means that everything henceforward is doomed is clearly a reflection of a cognitive distortion rather than a more accurate prediction based on prior experience with life and emotional swings.

Correcting
the Gambler's Fallacy

The second correction lies in exposing what statisticians call the Gambler's Fallacy. This corrective point of logic is useful when you are making the negative and erroneous prediction that you are having a "run of bad luck." In other words, if a few or several irritating, stressful, or even damaging events have occurred within a short period of time, you may feel that you have a black cloud hanging over your head and begin to wait for the "other shoe to drop" or for the next bad thing to happen.

For example, in the course of one week, the car of one of my patients had required major, costly repairs, her house roof sprung a serious leak during a heavy rainstorm, her daughter fell and broke her arm, and her computer went down at the office four hours before a pressing deadline. When she saw me for therapy she complained of feeling "doomed."

"I'm not looking forward to next week," she said. "I don't know how much more I can take. I'm just waiting for the next disaster."

On reflection, though, the patient admitted that none of the four events that befell had any relationship to one another. She concurred that, logically, a series of random events had just coincided in a short span of time. But since she mistakenly viewed the events as connected in some way—like a run of bad luck—she expected more bad things to happen in the coming week.

The Gambler's Fallacy is that an event or outcome that is statistically random has some predictive relationship to the likelihood of another random event occurring next. For example, if the number 22-black comes up on a given spin of a roulette wheel, the chances might seem slim that the number 22 will come up again on the next spin. In fact, on an honest wheel, the chance that any of the 39 numbers will come up on any given spin is exactly the same: one in 39. Logically, therefore, the chance that 22-black will come up again after it has just paid off is exactly equal to the chance that any other number will win.

Similarly, if a coin toss produces five "heads" in five tosses, the gambler believes that the chances that "tails" will come up in the sixth toss must be pretty good. But, logically and in fact, the odds on the sixth toss of heads or tails are exactly the same: fifty-fifty.

I explained the Gambler's Fallacy to my patient in the context of her recent apparent string of bad luck. The chance that something bad will happen to you next week, I said, is the same as it was last week or the week before, if the bad event is really something random like an accident or other unfortunate experience. When she could see that her reasoning was superstitious and logically flawed, she reported feeling much better and more confident about facing the week ahead. Moreover, in therapy I worked with her on refocusing her attention away from the events themselves and onto the good job she did, in each case, of coping calmly and capably with the problem. Since her coping abilities were not random but rather intentional and predictable, my patient also could see that even if some further misfortune did occur, she could forecast that she would be able to handle it.

Through the application of logic and mental discipline, you have learned throughout the last few chapters how much of your depressed mood is truly "in your head" and how effective your guided and corrective thinking can be in reversing low moods and the blues.

Sometimes, however, even with dedicated mental effort your mood can seem intractable. Or the depression lifts only to be replaced by one or another difficult, unpleasant feeling. Understanding how depression gets embedded in nasty vicious cycles is the subject of our next chapter.

15

♦

Hard Feelings and Vicious Cycles

♦

When one link snaps, the whole chain collapses.

—ANCIENT PROVERB

I'm utterly confused and depressed at this point," Michelle confessed. "I'm an intelligent woman, but I can't seem to think my way out of the mess I've created with my marriage. My efficiency at work is getting worse and worse. I'm really down about everything."

Michelle explained to me that her sex life with her husband had "dwindled down to just about zilch." And the frequency of fighting in what previously had been a mellow, sexually gratifying, and basically happy relationship was on a meteoric rise.

"I wish I could get a handle on this thing. I have all kinds of different feelings and one seems to trigger the other—I can't sort it out. In the first piace, I can't deal with the guilt I feel over not wanting to make love often enough to my husband. I love him, but I must be getting turned off or something. I feel unattractive because I'm not in good physical shape so I don't really like the thought of him touching my body. I feel so guilty and I just don't handle guilt well at all—I wish it weren't such a problem for me."

Michelle described a typical problematic episode this way: "I get home at about five-thirty from what is almost always a frustrating, aggravating day at the office. My boss infuriates me, and of course I don't dare say anything to him. So I'm already fuming before I even get in the house. Then Don comes home, and invariably he says something that just sets me off. In fairness, he's probably no different than the way he was before I took this miserable job, but now I have no fuse for his sarcasm and teasing. I really get mad. But because I already feel so guilty about my nasty mood lately and the fact that I don't feel like I'm being a good enough wife, it seems like I don't have a right to yell at him. So I keep my mouth shut and my anger stuffed down.

"Then I start having thoughts like our marriage is over or something, and that gets me more depressed. I usually start to cry, which then makes Don feel guilty that he hurt my feelings. So to try to salvage the evening, I decide to cook something terrific, which is totally fattening.

"We both love good food, so dinner goes along fine. But after dinner, I feel bloated and even guiltier that I blew my good intentions to stick with a diet of some kind. Naturally, I'm too tired and full to even think about working off the calories with exercise, let alone of having sex. So I turn into a couch potato, watch television, and fall asleep by ten in the den.

"If Don tries to wake me up to make love I get furious. I tell him that he doesn't appreciate how hard I work, how tired I am from cooking the big dinner and so forth. The worst part is that I know I'm being unfair—he has a right to have sex with his wife!

"The next morning he'll say something to tease me about falling asleep and rejecting him again. But I'm so overly sensitive that I start a fight, or I just start to cry because I feel so guilty. By the time I hit the office, I'm down in the dumps, which just sets my boss off on another round of criticism."

Michelle concluded, "You see, it's hopeless. It's all a big vicious cycle and there's no way out. Even if we go away on a romantic vacation it won't do any good, because I'll have to face the same mess again as soon as we get back home. Now do you see why I'm so depressed?"

Michelle's dilemma and sense of helplessness illustrate a central fact about low moods: Depression rarely exists in isolation from other uncomfortable, often painful, emotions and behaviors. Together, these "hard" feelings and ways of behaving comprise a tangled, interconnected web—in which depression is invariably embedded and enmeshed—that revolves in vicious, self-perpetuating circles. Because of the complex mechanism in which emotional reactions trigger depression, which in turn triggers actions that then produce more emotions, the already highly uncomfortable state of affairs is severely compounded by the added stress of feeling confused, out of control, helpless, chaotic and overwhelmed.

As you proceed through the attributional analysis of your low moods and the situations from which they arise, you too will likely be pulled into the vortex of hard feelings and vicious cycles. As Michelle learned in therapy, you will discover that becoming aware of the triggering mechanisms and becoming conscious of your *choices* to respond in ways that will halt the cycle are key to gaining control over depressed moods.

Hard Feelings

Just about every woman (and man, for that matter) has a hard time with guilt, anger, powerlessness, failure, grief, low self-esteem, insecurity, frustration, conflict (both interpersonal and internal), anxiety, and rejection.

Virtually by definition, these emotions create discomfort, pain, fear, and a general debilitation or compromising of all levels of psychological functioning. I would venture to say that to one degree or another every patient who has ever come to see me for psychotherapy has done so because of being troubled by one or more of these intensely difficult but very human emotions.

For purposes of correcting attributional errors, it is worth emphasizing that (a) such feelings are inherently difficult and uncomfortable, (b) they frequently accompany or produce depression, and therefore (c) expecting yourself to handle any one of these hard feelings with ease and facility is precisely the kind of unrealistic and unattainable expectation that amplifies and prolongs your low moods.

While these points may appear obvious and logical, I assure you that, psychologically, people operate otherwise. Repeatedly, I hear patients, friends, and even colleagues say things like "I just can't handle the guilt I feel" or "Being rejected is really hard for me" or "I hate feeling angry. I don't deal with it well."

Time and again, the fundamental attributional error is made that the feeling in question is difficult or problematic for the person speaking but not, by implication, difficult for others. Furthermore, since an internal attribution is made, along with an invidious comparison to presumably more psychologically capable "others," self-esteem is attacked. As a result, the problem escalates from the initial experience of the hard feeling to the inference that inadequacy or poor coping skills must account for the difficulty and discomfort associated with an emotion that, as I have noted, is inherently and universally difficult and painful.

Let's examine how this insidious feedback loop operates. Assume that a woman gets into a terrible argument with her mother. Assume further that the woman feels guilty and remorseful because of the things she said to her mother in anger. She criticizes herself for losing her temper, for having hot reactions, and for not dealing better with her mother. Although she is remorseful about her anger, she is disgusted with herself for feeling guilty and, like Michelle, for not dealing at all well with that emotion, either.

Soon the woman begins to feel inadequate and her self-esteem plummets. She berates herself for not "growing up" and defines maturity as being "above anger" and "beyond guilt." Since, by her criteria, she has failed to sufficiently grow up, she flagellates herself with name-calling ("baby," "infantile outbursts," "childish," etc.). She is overwhelmed by feelings of depression, and the ire toward her mother is dwarfed by the intensity of her inner-directed anger.

Anger and guilt—especially when directed toward a parent—are difficult emotions. Had our hypothetical woman been able to acknowledge and accept that fact, she might not also have suffered the compounding punitive effects of depression. Instead, she fell into the attributional trap of harshly blaming herself for finding the angry situation uncomfortable and for having a quite normal—though, to our woman thoroughly unacceptable—guilt reaction. Hence, her depression.

In my work with Michelle, a major focus of her early therapy was to stop blaming herself for having trouble with hard feelings. Her self-criticism for not easily handling complex and painful emotions was entirely misplaced and overstated.

In your own case, you may have an accurate basis for identifying anger or low self-esteem or certain behavioral responses as targets for self-improvement and change. That is fine and undoubtedly to your benefit. However, take a look as well at whether or not you fault yourself for finding any or all of the hard feelings difficult. If you do, then be aware that your critical self-judgments are fueling a vicious cycle of depression.

Anger, guilt, rejection, and the other hard feelings are difficult for you because they are difficult for human beings generally, not because you are inadequate, immature, or emotionally underdeveloped. The ways in which you may respond to the hard feelings behaviorally, however, may indeed need alteration, especially if you hope to break out of the vicious cycle of depression and self-perpetuating actions that merely fuel and reinforce harmful emotional patterns.

The Dynamics of Hard Feelings

Since, as I have said, hard feelings account for or play a part in virtually every case I have ever treated in psychotherapy, a book could be written on each one of them alone. But I want to encourage you to begin untangling your own complex knot of hard feelings and blue moods. My purpose here is to simplify and focus that ray of insight about these hard feelings and their relationship to depression, which I have seen turn on a mental lightbulb in the eyes of my patients.

184

GUILT

You feel guilty when you (a) accept full or major responsibility for a negative event or outcome in your own life or someone else's, and (b) you invoke the reprimand that you "should" or "shouldn't" have done or said something. In some cases, specifically where issues of morality apply, guilt may be appropriate. In other words, if you indeed have violated a moral dictate or legal statute and as a direct consequence caused harm to yourself or another person, it is appropriate to suffer pangs of conscience and remorse, especially if their effect is to deter you from repeating the violations in the future.

But more often than not, your guilt probably is inappropriate and essentially useless. In particular, your guilt is inappropriate when it is based on your assumption of responsibility for people or things for which you are not, in fact, responsible. In this sense, guilt springs from an excessive and misplaced sense of responsibility. Or guilt can develop from the "should" admonition that is directed toward unrealistic, perfectionistic, and unattainable standards for judging your performance and behavior. Generally, guilt serves little purpose other than self-punishment. But this purpose it serves as well as any self-inflicted mental torment. Guilt feels awful and almost invariably brings on feelings of depression.

The dynamics of guilt are complex. Essentially, guilt is the internalized parental instruction that as adults we label conscience. Guilt occurs when your internal, parental voice scolds you for doing something wrong or failing to do something right, and it is a voice that will cut you no slack.

When you use guilt as a form of interpersonal manipulation, you are very likely to arouse anger in another person. While you may get the compliance you seek, the person being manipulated by your guilt induction won't like you very much for your methods. In a similar vein, you will respond angrily to the guilt that you induce in yourself. *It is your own angry response to the guilt that is the trigger for depression.*

The dynamic, then, is that you feel guilty when an excessive sense of responsibility and/or unrealistic expectation leads you to punish yourself for a negative event or outcome that has occurred (or for the absence of a positive outcome). The guilt you induce in yourself creates angry feelings, which are directed back at yourself, since you are the person making yourself feel guilty. The internalized anger is felt as depression.

ANGER

There are basically three things you can do with your anger: (1) direct it toward the person (or object) whom you perceive to be its cause, (2) direct it back on yourself, or (3) direct it on another person or object not directly related to its cause—a process known as displacement.

Anger is a frightening emotion for many women, especially if they are accustomed to suppressing its expression. Because the anger builds up internally—like a pressure cooker—when it begins to bubble to the surface it can feel explosive. In fact, anger whose expression is overly suppressed or denied can erupt as dangerous, explosive, and inappropriate rage. For this reason it is important to learn how to identify your anger when it is stimulated, and to learn methods for communicating your anger without an excessive display of emotion so that the pressure is immediately released and a dangerous buildup avoided or prevented.

Anger is problematic for women in another way as well. For many, conversation that is fueled by anger is the stimulus for tears. As a consequence, women who cry when they feel angry—especially in business settings—know that the strength of their message is diluted. Further, they become angry with themselves for crying, which compounds their frustration and negative feelings and produces depression.

But if you have reasonably good communication skills and a grasp of the mechanisms that trigger your anger, directing the anger, provided it is appropriately controlled, toward its correct object is preferable to suppressing it. So if your husband, boyfriend, child, work associate, or someone else with whom you interact regularly and with whom you have a fundamentally solid relationship steps on your emotional toes and elicits an angry response in you, you are best advised to discuss your reactions and be open to a constructive dialogue aimed at problem resolution.

If, however, you are afraid to confront the object of your anger (for valid or invalid reasons), or if you avoid dealing directly with your anger for other reasons, you will be left only with the other two options. Displacement works most effectively and safely when the anger is directed toward an inanimate object, such as a tennis ball that you smash around, a pillow that you punch, or a piece of furniture that you select as an audience for your yelling. These are time-tested methods for "blowing off steam." In general, physical exercise also is useful for lowering adrenaline levels that are stimulated by anger.

More dangerous is the widely practiced and ill-advised method of displacing anger and hostility on another person who is not directly, or often even indirectly, involved in the arousal of your anger in the first place. Displaced hostility, such as Michelle's anger toward her husband, which was displaced from the real target—her boss—can get you into a lot of hot water. To begin with, the person on whom your anger is being unjustly displaced is bound to feel righteously angry in return. After all, you're getting angry and hostile when he or she has done either nothing or nothing sufficiently provocative to warrant your attack. The displacement, then, becomes the source of another interpersonal problem, which generally either heightens tension and anger or elicits guilt.

If you are like most women, internalizing the anger is likely to be your preferred mode of dealing with hostile feelings. This choice is most closely connected to feelings of depression. (In fact, depression has been defined in the psychological literature as anger directed toward the self.)

Often, then, depression is really disguised or masquerading anger. Consciously or unconsciously, the blues you experience may be angry reactions toward other people, the expression of which you block or suppress. In particular, when you feel angry with another person but act passively because you are either afraid to express your emotions or prohibited from doing so for one reason or another, the consequences are feelings of helplessness and internalized anger—the combined effects of which you will recognize and experience as depression.

Some of your anger toward others may arise from "shoulds" and "shouldn'ts" that reflect unrealistic, misplaced, or unfulfillable expectations of them. You will be effective in reducing your anger if you can logically examine those expectations and adjust them down or away altogether. In other words, other people won't be likely to make you as angry if you remove as a source of irritation the fact that they have violated some excessive or inappropriate expectation that you hold for their behavior.

On the other hand, some angry reactions are natural, appropriate, and inevitable. However you choose to deal with or respond to your anger, it probably will continue to seem like a "hot potato" to you. Remember, anger is a difficult feeling for everyone. Even for people who seem to be readily able to express it or are naturally hostile, anger exacts a continual toll on them and those around them in both emotional and physical terms.

Anger, then, is best handled when it is still small enough to be manageable. Angry feelings that are denied and suppressed over time manifest themselves as a weighty and oppressive depression or as eruptive, volcanic, and destructive rage. Anger displaced on others is often the occasion for further anger and/or guilt and perpetuated negative feelings. Anger turned against yourself is an immediate trigger for depression.

POWERLESSNESS

Nobody likes to feel that they are out of control of the things that happen to them, particularly if the events or outcomes are negative. In fact, according to some, powerlessness equals depression.

To cope, we block from our conscious awareness a great number of potentially catastrophic events over which we genuinely have little or no control. For example, we intentionally try to think about the possibility of imminent nuclear war, or major natural disasters, or of our own eventual mortality. We board airplanes or get behind the wheel of a car trying to keep the fear of calamity at bay by pushing the uncomfortable thoughts to the back of our minds or out of them entirely.

Nevertheless, there are many times when the recognition of your powerlessness or lack of control over negative events or outcomes is unavoidable or simply too immediate to deny. Sometimes, though, the feeling of powerlessness results not from an accurate analysis but rather from misattributions that lead you to conclude you are helpless when there may in fact be measures of control that you can exert.

Powerlessness is a hard feeling for at least two reasons. In the first place, if you believe you cannot control bad things from happening, you have less ability to predict when, where, and what could happen than if you are in control. Psychologically, the uncertainty that results produces feelings of anxiety. Second, the lack of control makes you feel frustrated, since you would like to be able to do something to avoid the negativity and cannot. In this case frustration breeds aggression and hostility.

With powerlessness come two other equally compelling and highly distressing emotions: anxiety and aggression. When those forces are directed inward, you will experience a sense of agitated or nervous depression.

The worst combination is when your perception of powerlessness triggers depression and makes you believe that you are also powerless to do anything to control or reverse your low mood. The passive behavior that results only serves to perpetuate and amplify the depression. Therefore, taking an active stance toward your mood will help to dispel overwhelming feelings of powerlessness and depression. Working on correcting misattributions and on identifying areas in your life in which you can exercise control and act in ways that enhance your overall sense of being in charge also will help to offset the negative effects of powerlessness.

FAILURE

It is a bad sign if you become too comfortable with failure. When you get used to failing, you will create self-fulfilling prophecies in which your prediction of failure will lower your motivation, lessen your initiative, cripple your self-esteem, and induce self-sabotaging behaviors. Failure, then, is best when it remains a hard and foreign feeling.

Ultimately, the hardest failures to accept are not those where you have extended your best effort and fallen short of success but rather where you have avoided the risk of failing by not even trying at all. With a resilient spirit, failure need not be a trigger for depression. Many, and in my view, the most, admirable people commit to trying again after they have failed or not succeeded. They view failure—which we *all* experience from time to time—as merely a temporary setback on the road to ultimate success. So should you.

Failure is also, of course, a relative term, subject to cognitive misinterpretations and redefinition. As you have learned in a previous chapter, when you are feeling down, you tend to view things in all-or-nothing terms so that partial successes are mistakenly encoded as total failures. Your depressive reaction to failure can be greatly mitigated if you learn to look for the partial successes (sort of a subgoal) inside of your efforts that have not been met with total success. The most important partial success to note within a failure experience is the fact that you have made an effort in the first place.

The sense of failure, particularly as it relates to depression, can occur as a result of excessively high, unrealistic expectations. The most dangerous expectation, in this regard is that you expect yourself *never* to fail. You may approach situations or challenges confidently with a generalized expectation of doing well or your best. That is healthy and productive. But to hold as a personal standard that you will never fail at anything is to set yourself up for a crashing depression when the inevitable occurs. For the same reasons that perfectionism is unrealistic, expecting never to fail at anything, anytime is a standard that ought not to apply to plain mortals, however able, talented, determined, or successful they may be.

Fear of failure is a trigger for depression in yet another way. If the fear of failure is strong, the result is that you will be passive and avoid taking any initiative that might yield negative results but that might also produce positive outcomes. To avoid failing, then, you avoid trying, doing, or risking. Without effort or initiative on your part, the feedback you receive will be devoid of successes. In other words, the passive behavior that fear of failure produces becomes the cause for the very thing it is designed to avoid.

GRIEF

The pain of loss that occurs through death or the termination of a relationship is the hard feeling of grief. But grief is unique among the hard feelings in that, appropriately handled and expressed, it is self-limiting and eventually healing. The most important thing to say about grief is that you must let yourself experience the sadness, pain, and even helplessness associated with the loss of a loved one when it occurs in order to avoid a later depression.

People who try to deny their grief or who push it aside in order to be stoic and go forward without tears or without a backward glance are quite vulnerable to the debilitating effects of a delayed grief reaction which often manifests itself as a *severe* Depression. Sometimes the delayed depression appears such a long time after the death or separation event that the two may seem unrelated. In fact, though, the depression is very likely to be directly caused by the grief that was suppressed at the time.

A number of cultural and religious practices related to death have survived over millennia precisely because they assist people to grieve appropriately. Holding and attending a funeral service, being among friends and family members who talk with nostalgic fondness about the person who has passed away, and putting ritualized time frames around the active grieving period are psychologically helpful in working through grief and loss.

Unfortunately, there are precious few rituals or practices that help or instruct people in grieving over the loss of a relationship. In fact, well-intended suggestions from friends or family members can be counterproductive in this regard. "Try to just put the jerk behind you," or "Cheer up, you're better off out of the relationship" typically serve only to block the necessary grief process and, further, to induce feelings of guilt and greater depression over not being able to let go as easily as others would prefer.

Grief is a natural form of depression. Denied grief or overextended grief, however, can trigger or transform itself into unnatural or dysfunctional forms of depression. A good rule of thumb is that the acute stage of a psychological crisis—including grief—generally lasts for about six weeks. While this is certainly not to say that the loss or the sadness should completely disappear after six weeks, it does provide some time frame for when it is healthy and appropriate to refocus on life and the living, on the future and on the determination that you have suffered acute grief for long enough.

LOW SELF-ESTEEM AND INSECURITY

Low self-esteem and low self-confidence (insecurity) are symptoms of depression that also make all of the other hard feelings even more difficult to handle. One of the most insidious effects of low self-esteem is that you can come to feel that depression and other negative feelings are what you "deserve" to feel. In other words, if you don't like yourself much, you are unlikely to believe that you deserve to have good things happen in your life or to be happy. Moreover, if your low self-esteem is accompanied—as it usually is—with low self-confidence and insecurity, your expectations that you will be able to do anything to produce positive outcomes (even if you don't deserve them) will be low.

Together, low self-esteem and insecurity become fertile psychological soil in which depressed feelings breed prolifically.

While it is possible in theory to have low self-esteem and

not be depressed, or to be down without experiencing low self-esteem, the two generally go hand in hand. To overcome low self-esteem and insecurity, you have to be willing to engage in proactive behaviors that will reverse the negative feedback cycle. What this means is that despite your lack of confidence and your sense of unworthiness, you must extend yourself toward actions and people that hold the promise of providing positive feedback and success experiences.

FRUSTRATION

The route from frustration to depression goes via the arousal of hostility, anger, and aggression. Psychologically, the relationship between frustration and anger is exceedingly strong. Even an infant will evince rageful tears when a bottle is taken from its mouth before hunger has been sated. An otherwise sweet-tempered animal will begin to snarl and bite if it is teased and tormented by having food held in front of its face and then pulled away when the animal reaches for it.

Circumstances that cause frustration in adult life, though generally more subtle, also produce hostile reactions. The stress response—physiologically a fight-or-flight reaction—can result in feelings of anger because the desire to fight back or to flee the scene are frustrated. For example, being stuck in a gridlock traffic jam when you are trying to make an appointment produces enormous stress with the accompanying frustration that you can neither attack the other cars, nor remove yourself from the situation. The frustration of having your impulses blocked produces hostility and anger.

If the hostility that the frustration engenders is directed inward, depression results. Depression, especially if strong feelings of helplessness are involved, can itself produce frustration. And so the negative feedback cycle is again established.

Frustration can trigger depression via other routes than hostility. Or the hostility may be unconsciously experienced. In sexual frustration, for example, sad, unhappy feelings or a profoundly felt inadequacy may swamp any recognizable anger.

You might respond to sexual frustration as well as a host of other frustrating situations by choosing a behavior, such as eating or going on a shopping spree, that is designed to deliver short-term relief. While short-term relief may occur, the longer-term consequences of gaining weight or of spending too much money are likely to heighten your sense of frustration and lead to self-disparaging attacks that lower self-esteem and produce further depression.

Frustration is another hard feeling, like anger, that can be somewhat dissipated by a good workout and offset by refocusing your energy on tasks or relationships where your efforts are likely to be rewarded. Constant exposure to frustration over the long term is not only difficult but damaging to both emotional and physical health. Therefore, situations or relationships that you experience as consistently frustrating should be analyzed carefully so you can determine whether some alternatives exist that could reduce the frustration. Keep in mind that the perception of limited alternatives—feeling trapped or that there is no way out—not only is the essence of frustration but also reflects the stress that frustration produces.

Stress, as you will recall, causes a narrowing of perceived alternatives because of a process called premature closure. When you are in a frustrating situation, it is important to search for alternative ways of responding to reduce the discomfort. Force yourself to brainstorm all possible alternatives so that you don't prematurely close off the search and create the sensation of entrapment.

While nobody likes to feel frustrated, there are individual differences in tolerance for frustration. Such differences are related to another important psychological concept known as tolerance for ambiguity. For some people, situations, relationships, or circumstances whose meaning remains unclearly defined are intensely frustrating; for others, ambiguous events are more easily tolerated and are not as painfully frustrating.

Your tendency to get depressed may be partially related to a low tolerance for ambiguity. Impatience and intolerance for ambiguity is a frequent problem in male-female relationships, where one party has a need to know how things are going to turn out—such as whether a commitment is forthcoming—before the other is ready to decide or even before the other person even knows how he or she feels.

By working on becoming more tolerant of ambiguity, more patient, and therefore less frustrated, you can reduce the tendency to trigger a depressed reaction.

CONFLICT

Interpersonal conflict is often a trigger for depression because it involves so many of the other hard feelings, including guilt, anger, and frustration. Conflict in a relationship that arises from the partners' having widely divergent expectations is particularly difficult. I have often had the experience of realizing that a couple in therapy, married for 10 or 20 years, is functioning or seeing things as if the individuals were in two entirely different relationships.

The expectations you have of your relationship and/or of your partner will not serve you well unless you share them through open and clear communication. Otherwise, your disappointment or anger when expectations are violated will remain a private problem for you and will lead to depression. When expectations are not shared and mutual understandings do not productively evolve, an impasse is often reached. Such an impasse can involve mutual or one-sided withdrawal, a shutting down of communication, distrust, and a weakening of the relationship's bond.

But conflict is not necessarily bad or damaging to a relationship. The issue is whether the conflict is handled in a way that is constructive rather than destructive. Happy and unhappy couples do not necessarily differ in the degree to which they have conflicts or disagreements. Where they do differ is that happy couples resolve conflicts constructively and the same issues usually do not reappear as an occasion for renewed conflict in the future.

In unhappy couples, however, conflict is destructive. Communication is lessened, strategies of coercion, manipulation, and threat are used, and an impasse or a superficial resolution is reached that fails to address the real issues. Consequently, the same problems rear their ugly heads again and again and the relationhip deteriorates under the strain of destructive fights.

When you are in a relationship that is stuck in a cycle of destructive conflict, it is predictable that you will alternate between feelings of anger, frustration, and depression. Your depression can further aggravate the situation because of the tendency to withdraw emotionally, cry, or irritably provoke new arguments. Moreover, a love relationship that is going sour casts a gloomy shadow over the self-esteem of both partners.

The pain of unresolved, destructive interpersonal conflict can be exacerbated by the internal conflict that the state of hostilities can engender within each partner. When you feel internally conflicted, you engage in argumentative dialogues with yourself about the relationship, how you feel, and about the course of your life in general.

Inner conflict that remains unresolved causes stress and anxiety. Moreover, when the conflict is intense and the forces pulling you one way seem to be equal to those pulling you in the other direction, the result can be mental paralysis and behavioral passivity. In turn, these feelings rapidly deteriorate into helplessness and its companion, depression.

ANXIETY

In strictly psychological terms, anxiety is defined as fear without an object. In other words, anxiety is a kind of free-floating fear that isn't attached to any particular person or thing, but which, nevertheless, feels quite real and is generally highly disruptive.

Anxiety and depression frequently bounce off one another. Sometimes low moods are accompanied by high levels of agitation and the experience is felt as very unpleasant.

When anxiety is very high, concentration can become fragmented, and thoughts—which, when you are depressed, are often negative, worried, or morbid—can race. This kind of anxiety leads to the sensation expressed when a person says, "I can't think straight. My mind is wandering all over the place."

An agitated depression can be aggravated because confusion abounds and helplessness increases. An anxious depression can also feel extremely intense, since anxiety has the effect of amplifying your experience, turning up the volume of your emotional pain.

REJECTION

Rejection, like failure, is largely a matter of definition. If you interpret another person's decision not to hire you, or date you, or marry you, or be your friend as a rejection, you are likely to trigger depression, especially if the other person is someone whom you value highly.

If, on the other hand, you have a solid sense of your own self-worth and self-esteem, another person's decision to exclude you may be viewed as his or her choice; while it may disappoint, it does not detract from or negate what you know to be your essential value.

When a female patient of mine is struggling over feeling rejected by a man, I suggest that she might feel differently if she were to see the man's decision as a test of him, rather than a test of her. Rejection feels painful to her, I explain, because she makes the psychological interpretation that the man's choice represents a denouncement of her value. If he had said "yes," her value would have been confirmed; but because he said "no," her value was diminished in her own mind.

The test could be constructed the other way. The woman's value, in this alternative version, is a given. The man's choice would reveal whether or not he sees, appreciates, or adequately recognizes her value. If he chooses "yes," in this scenario, *his* value is confirmed—that is, he passes the test. If he chooses "no," he fails the test. Her value as a person (or as an employee, a lover, a potential wife, and so on) is not affected.

This distinction is far more than a semantic exercise. Your ability to venture forth into the world and seek experiences—be they in the career realm, in the romantic arena, or in other domains—without periodically capitulating to the devastating effects of rejection depends on being able to keep the attribution clear. I have treated many actors, actresses, performers, and writers whose self-esteem and mood have been severely injured by the chronic exposure to rejection or criticism which their chosen professions necessarily involve. Changing their way of viewing the meaning of rejection—by protecting their sense of self-worth while enduring a negative outcome of an audition, a manuscript or screenplay submission, or performance—was the correction that made it possible for them to proceed steadfastly with their careers.

You won't ever come to like rejection or to live easily with it. That is why I have included it in the list of hard feelings. But the trigger between rejection and depression depends on whether or not you allow another person's choice (which could possibly reflect poor judgment on their part, bad taste, or something utterly idiosyncratic that has nothing to do with you) to threaten the underpinnings of your self-esteem.

Vicious Cycles

The interrelationships among these hard feelings, depression, and behaviors are often complex and convoluted. For this reason, the experience of depression can seem like a vicious cycle of actions and reactions from which there is no apparent escape.

Michelle's story at the beginning of this chapter is a case in point. The cycle Michelle found herself caught up in is characteristically complex, and there are segments of it that you probably will recognize or find reminiscent of a repetitive pattern in your own history.

I see repeatedly at least four vicious cycles of hard feelings, depression, and dysfunctional behavior among my patients:

CYCLE ONE:
OVEREATING/DEPRESSION/LOW SELF-ESTEEM

The first cycle is a classic among women, including Michelle, especially those with chronic weight problems. Since the nature of a cycle is a closed circle, the beginning can be defined as anywhere in the pattern. Let's assume this cycle starts with feeling down.

In response to the blues, the woman becomes inactive and ruminates. Her depressed feelings intensify as she dwells on negative memories and inventories her faults. As her self-esteem falls and her discomfort increases, she seeks immediate gratification: food. But after she has eaten too much, her short-term relief is immediately replaced by guilt and further self-deprecation, which then feeds her depression so that she returns to the beginning of the cycle.

CYCLE TWO:
STRESS/OVERWORK/DEPRESSION

This cycle particularly affects women who are overburdened by the demands of a busy personal life and a busy career or job, along with involvement in other activities as well. The stress is caused by excessive demands on limited resources, and the woman's own reluctance or inability to say no to people, to delegate, to cut back on her activities, and her compulsion to be "everything to everybody"—the Type E stress pattern.

The Type E stress syndrome involves behavior in which the woman pushes herself beyond reasonable or healthy limits so that she becomes exhausted and even physically ill. But instead of resting or cutting back in response to the fatigue, the woman senses that she might be inadequate to meet her own expectations. The inadequacy creates depressed feelings, which are intensified by her exhaustion. But she uses the sense of inadequacy and the fear that she can't do it all as a goad to push herself even harder and to try to do even more. The inevitable result, of course, is that she is even more exhausted, and the vicious cycle continues.

CYCLE THREE:
FEAR OF REJECTION/
DEPRESSION/PREEMPTORY BREAKUP

Generally, this pattern begins after a woman has had at least a few unhappy relationships with men that have ended in what she perceives as rejection. She develops a fear of rejection, which creates anxiety and deep insecurity whenever she begins a relationship with a new man. As the relationship progresses, the woman's anxiety mounts and she begins to anticipate what feels to her to be inevitable: rejection and abandonment.

In response to her negative prediction and fears, the woman becomes depressed. The depressed feelings are manifested in the relationship with the man, who seeks either to understand or is provoked into an argument. In either event, the woman's behavior becomes a form of self-sabotage and she either breaks up with the man so as to preclude him from rejecting her (the preemptory breakup) or she pushes him into a position which forces him to end the relationship. The loss of the relationship then leads her into further depression and even greater fear of rejection in the future. The vicious cycle continues.

CYCLE FOUR: DEPRESSION
AND THE DEAD-END RELATIONSHIP OR JOB

This cycle begins with a situation in which a woman has a job or is involved in a relationship (or both) which is unsatisfactory to her. Because of the frustration she feels, she gets depressed and then down on herself (low self-esteem). Her depressed thinking distorts her logic into this flawed formulation: People get what they deserve; I am getting treated poorly by this man/employer/job; therefore, I must deserve this situation and nothing better.

Since her self-esteem is only further suppressed by this fallacious reasoning, she remains passive, settling for a relationship or job that fails to make her happy or fulfilled. Her lack of initiative keeps her alternatives narrow or absent and the self-perpetuating vicious cycle continues.

You may recognize your own feelings, thoughts, and behaviors in one or more of these patterns, or in some part of Michelle's story. Obviously, there are many, many more such cycles, their number limited only by the number of combinations and permutations of the hard feelings and depression.

To gain mastery over negative moods, you must become acutely aware of your particular pattern of hard feelings and vicious cycles. When you notice your mood turning downward, take note of how your emotional "buttons" may have been pushed and of how you have responded.

Breaking the cycle of depression and hard feelings requires that you focus on the *choices* you have at any point in the process to behave and/or feel differently. Have the courage to try out different ways of responding when your emotional buttons get pushed, and notice the effect on your mood.

As you become more aware of how your habitual reactions trigger depressed moods, and as you become conscious of your freedom to choose to behave and feel differently, the vicious cycles will loosen their grip while the frequency and intensity of your blue moods will diminish.

16

◆

Distression

◆

Durum est omnibus placere. (*It is hard to please everyone.*)

—LATIN PROVERB

Here's a thought: Maybe you're not really so much depressed as you are simply stressed out. Think about it.

Growing numbers of women today are working at full or part-time jobs, increasingly in the ranks of management and the professions, while they continue to pursue full, meaningful, and demanding personal lives in their more traditional roles as wives and/or mothers. The sum effect of women's blossoming achievements combined with the sheer weight of the economic imperative that commands dual sources of family income has become an avalanche of stress for women.

The reasons for this epidemic of stress among women are several. In the first place, success for contemporary women seems to imply a literal double standard: achievement in their personal lives *and* achievement in their work roles or careers. The dilemma, however, is that what most women perceive as the necessary behaviors and time commitments required to gain success in one arena are often in direct conflict with the requirements of the other.

If you work at a job, or as an active volunteer, even though you don't get paid, and you are trying to carve out a fulfilling personal life, you may feel stuck in a kind of no-win game. The distress associated with the rules of the game are no fun at all. Concentrating your energies on career priorities is likely to make you feel guilty or concerned that you are failing your family or husband, or missing out on a healthy and fulfilling personal life. On the other hand, focusing your energies primarily on the needs of your husband, boyfriend, or children might impede your chances for career advancement.

Of course, there are other strains as well out in the career world. Like it or not, the grim reality is that even today, when women display traits like assertiveness, leadership, competitiveness, or tenacity in an effort to succeed, they are often labeled pushy, aggressive, and just plain "bitchy." So the traits that are needed to get ahead in your work life clash with those that you—and most others—have been conditioned to associate with femininity.

Over the years in my work as a clinical psychologist with both men and women patients, it has often struck me that the concepts of success and achievement mean something different to the two groups. In general, men still confine their yardsticks for measuring success to the arenas of work, money, and professional or corporate status. Women, on the other hand, apply a dual standard. To feel "successful" as a contemporary woman means not only success in the workplace, but also achievement in the personal arena of life as well.

In conversations with my patients, for example, I have frequently noted that men will describe themselves as "successful" even though their personal lives, by their own ready admission, include a string of poor relationships with women and/or children. But while these men certainly are troubled and unhappy about their personal problems, they seem able to preserve their perceptions of themselves as successful people relatively uncontaminated by any personal failures.

In contrast, I have yet to hear a woman describe herself as "a success" if her personal life is, according to her own standards, unsuccessful. This is true even in cases where the woman's material or career success is equal to or greater than that of the man's. Women are far more likely than men to let shortcomings in their personal lives contaminate their entire perception of themselves as successful people.

For women who try to make it in both their career and personal lives, the success formula can be enormously frustrating and exhausting: be everything to everybody. In other words, you try to adapt to the pressure of "having it all" (whatever "all" means to you) by trying to *do* it all yourself. While you may believe that your solution is effective in the short term, I guarantee you that sooner or later, your physical and/or emotional health will suffer from the strain.

By trying to be everything to everybody, you are the proverbial candle burning at both ends. What's worse is that you are actually baiting a distress trap with your own competence. The more you demonstrate you can do, the more others demand of you. As you continue to prove compulsively that you can be everything to everybody, other people seem to expect it of you. In short, you become the victim of your own dazzling abilities, finding yourself caught in a damaging and self-perpetuating distress cycle.

You will recall from the last chapter that the Type E stress cycle is vicious indeed. As the distress begins to take its toll on your physical health, your moods, your personal and work relationships, and your career performance, you are likely to feel threatened and betrayed by your own limitations. Your self-esteem, precariously balanced on the delicate high wire of satisfying everyone's needs at work and at home, is likely to take a dangerous plunge; like other women caught in the same self-destructive Type E cycle, you may elect to fight back by pushing yourself even harder.

Inevitably though, the distress cycle will catch up with you. That's the bad news, but only if you don't get a handle on the core of the problem, which is trying to be everything to everybody. The good news is that you can maintain your desire to achieve in multiple areas of your life as long as you learn a few key skills that will permit you to prioritize and filter the onslaught of demands that threaten to overwhelm you every day.

Recall from the No Nonsense Women's Attitude survey,

discussed in Chapter 5, that 76 percent of respondents agreed that they personally suffer from the stress of trying to be everything to everybody. Type E stress results from two factors: (1) an overload of demands from multiple roles, many of which are in conflict with one another, and (2) an inability or unwillingness on the part of the Type E woman to take control of these demands by organizing them into manageable priorities and relinquishing the self-sabotaging and self-destructive compulsion to please everyone and to meet others' needs before she takes care of her own.

Research into working women's beliefs and behaviors has shown that endorsement of the following four statements put a woman at high risk for a host of stress-related physical and emotional symptoms.[1]

- "It's nearly impossible to have a family and a career and not be under constant pressure."
- "It seems like other people's approval and liking of me is dependent on the number of things I do for them."
- "It seems like I have to prove that I can be a good wife (or girlfriend or mother) in spite of the fact that I work."
- "My feelings about myself and my achievements seem to change and vacillate a lot."

The specific symptoms of distress that were found to be highly correlated with the Type E beliefs were "feelings of being emotionally unstable," "emotional ups and downs," and "talking faster than usual." While the latter symptom is indicative of agitation or anxiety, the other two are symptomatic of depression and low-mood problems.

Other data from the No Nonsense survey confirm the relationship between depression or the blues and Type E stress symptoms. In fact, as you will recall from Chapter 5,

---

1. G. Faulkner, "Type E Behavior and Distress Among Working Women," unpublished master's thesis, California State University, Chico, 1987.

the three most frequently cited reasons women gave for getting the blues were "having too many demands on my time," "feeling tired," and "feeling drained by the needs of others."

Taken together, these data suggest that if you regularly overextend yourself to the point of exhaustion in order to meet the needs and demands of others, Type E stress may be a major cause of your feelings of depression.

Depression or Distression?

The concept of stress, in my view, has an unfair reputation. Most of what you probably hear and read about stress and its management generally overlooks the fact that stress can play a positive role in your life. Actually, without stress you would be, in a word, dead.

The distinction to keep in mind is between *good* stress (technically called eustress—the prefix *eu* is Greek for "good") and *bad* stress or distress. Good stress is what we label excitement, motivation, purpose, enthusiasm, and so forth. It is bad stress—distress—that we experience as pressure, tension, frustration, or the sense that there is simply not enough of us to go around.

Distress, by the way, can result from overly high amounts of stress for too long a period, as well as from too little stress for a long time. Remember, a certain amount of challenge and change is necessary to keep you vital, healthy, and alive. Prolonged distress results in mental and physical exhaustion and is known to be associated with nervous and emotional disturbances, blood pressure problems, insomnia, heart palpitations, anxiety, anger, irritability, stomach pain, and feelings of depression.

It might be more appropriate for you to label the depression you are experiencing "distression."

The term "distression" is my invention and is intended to reflect a combination of depression and the condition of being distressed. The term distression, though, avoids the strong emotional connotation that is inherent in depression.

206

In other words, being in a state of distression can mean merely that you are depleted, exhausted, and overloaded but not that you are necessarily unhappy. Depression, on the other hand, almost always conveys sadness, unhappiness, and the inability to experience pleasure.

Labeling your temporarily depleted state as distression has an additional advantage. By focusing on the "stress" in distression—rather than on depression, *per se*—you should immediately aim your efforts at relaxing, taking time to do pleasurable activities, and renewing your overtaxed resources. Too often I see women who are strung out from distression but who label their state as depression, search for reasons to explain their unhappiness. As a result, they might grab prematurely and without adequate consideration at radical solutions to alleviate or alter what they mistakenly believe to be the causes of their depressed mood.

Nancy, a 43-year-old entrepreneur, and her new husband of six months decided to adopt an infant. Nancy was convinced that her characteristically high energy would make the early months of new motherhood "a breeze." Moreover, since she was the owner and manager of a popular clothing store, she expected to maintain a regular presence in the store by arranging for a half-day nurse to spell her times with the baby so that she could spend afternoons and evenings working.

Within six weeks of bringing the new baby home, Nancy started coming unraveled. Trying to function on two or three interrupted hours of sleep a night and still requiring herself to take full responsibility for merchandise buying and management of her business was simply not working. Her increasing irritability, moreover, was provoking arguments with her husband. Clearly, the honeymoon was over, and family life combined with a career was not the "breeze" she had predicted.

When Nancy came to see me she described herself as being "very depressed." She told me that she had always relied on herself to work out her own problems and she considered it a great weakness to have to consult a psychologist, an action to which she had only consented as a way to keep her husband off her back.

"I had a real soul-searching experience last night," Nancy

began. "I said to myself, 'Okay, so you're totally depressed. Why are you depressed?' I didn't like the answers that I came up with. But I'm not a kid and my success in life has been due to the fact that I have always faced reality—however painful—and have done what I needed to do to make things better.

"I realized that I must be so unhappy because, obviously, I've made some big mistakes. I'm just too old to raise a baby and I think marrying my husband was a huge error. The only thing that is still right for me is my store. At least there I'm succeeding. The solutions are pretty painful but I refuse to stay so depressed. The adoption isn't legal yet, so, as much as it hurts me, I think it's best to admit that I'm an unfit mother and give the baby to some younger woman who has the stamina to raise her. I also think I should ask Bill for a trial separation."

I explored with Nancy why she believed she was so unhappy with her life.

"I just look at how low I feel and the most apparent reasons are my family. I wasn't depressed before I got married and adopted the baby. Actually," Nancy began to cry, "I wish I were wrong. Maybe you can tell me that there's another way out of this crisis."

Following much more discussion, what I eventually told Nancy was that I thought she wasn't necessarily suffering from depression as much as from a whopping amount of stress. I suggested that she was injecting unhappiness into her experience by her choice of the label "depression," and that her radical solutions to alleviate the sources of her presumed unhappiness would look very different to her if she lowered her stress level and stopped trying to do so much.

"Basically," I said, "in my opinion, you're severely distressed more than you are depressed. You're so wiped out from trying to be everyplace and do everything on no sleep that you think you're unhappy, instead of recognizing that you have limitations and that nobody can adjust to a new baby without feeling a lot of stress."

Nancy and I agreed to focus on ways to alleviate the distress rather than the depression. Instead of looking for what she imagined must be making her unhappy, she examined the sources of her fatigue, depletion, and overload of responsibility. I convinced Nancy to put her radical solutions on hold for a month and to take another look at her life after she had made some adjustments that would dramatically lower her overall stress level.

Over the course of the next month, Nancy agreed to hire a manager and buyer for her store and limited her personal appearances to two a week, and then for only a few hours. Next, she hired a full-time, live-in nanny to help with the baby. And, since Nancy's financial position was very comfortable, she went to an elegant spa for five days to rest, pamper herself, and recharge her severely run-down batteries.

A month later, Nancy laughed at her earlier "solution." "I can't believe I was so strung out that I was ready to trade in the most important things in my life. I'm not at all unhappy. I was just so disappointed with myself for being tired. I was sure that dealing with a baby was something I could do without live-in help and without getting overly tired. Bill went through his own adjustments too. After all, to be a new father all over again at fifty wasn't easy for him. Now that I can see straight again, I know that agreeing to have a family is another measure of how much he loves me.

"I want you to know that I keep a card in my wallet that reads: *'Are you depressed or just distressed?'* I've taught the word *distression* to a lot of my friends. Taking the unhappiness out of the feelings by saying *distression* instead of *depression* makes all of us feel a lot better."

As Nancy and her friends learned, making the correct attribution that your down, depleted, and exhausted condition is due to being overly stressed rather than being unhappy about someone or something in your life can make a big difference. One cautionary note, however, is in order. Beware of the tendency to *get depressed* because you *are distressed*.

Part of Nancy's panicked reaction to her exhaustion and distression was the difference between what she had expected of herself and what she discovered was the reality.

Nancy felt inadequate in response to her fatigue, and her self-esteem took a dive, since her customary positive feelings about herself were founded on a belief that she had boundless energy and could take on any new challenge. Consequently, when she found herself in a state of distression, she criticized herself roundly and put herself down with such insults as "old lady," "lazy sloth," or "useless mother and wife." Naturally, Nancy developed depressed feelings on top of feeling distressed.

The same basic principles of acceptance that you learned in the first step of the Triple A Program apply here. When you feel yourself getting run-down and overloaded, accept your feelings—without unnecessary and damaging criticism—and turn immediately to the techniques at the end of this chapter that will help you to get a handle on Type E stress.

The New Woman and the New Depression

For a decade or more, the media have been filled with references to the "new woman." This phenomenon of the era after Women's Liberation is typically seen as an assertive, active, working woman whose life is often likened to an elaborate juggling feat.

Because women have indeed changed in many ways over recent years, the reasons for and even the nature of their depressive episodes have changed as well. Just as depressed feelings do not exist in isolation of other difficult emotions, the blues cannot be fully understood outside of the context of the blue woman's life.

Descriptions of depressed women from popular self-help books written in the 1950s, 1960s, and early 1970s typically feature subjects who are isolated, housebound, bored, and understimulated. But today's women suffer from depressed moods of a different kind. Their depressed moods are more closely related to the distression that arises from overstimulation, too much contact with and demands from too many people, and a frenzied, fragmented overstretching of their time, energy, and attention.

Distression describes the experience of many of my patients, as well as the thousands of Type E women I have met across the country as a public speaker and management consultant. If you recognize distression as a cause of your depressed moods, stress-management techniques should be an imperative part of your program for effective mood management.

The kinds of stress-management techniques that are most effective for Type E women extend beyond the traditional relaxation, deep-breathing approaches that were developed for the treatment of high-powered, overstressed men. While such relaxation skills are important and helpful for women to learn, the pressures on Type E women are far greater than what 10 minutes a day of deep breathing can adequately address.

Instead, the "new woman" needs new, proactive techniques for fighting back and regaining control of her own life and the demands that threaten to overwhelm her. A sampling follows of some of the most effective proactive techniques for combatting type E stress. Many more suggestions and methods can be found in my book, *The Type E Woman: How to Overcome the Stress of Being Everything to Everybody* (Dodd Mead and NAL/Signet Books).

Exercises to Combat
Type E Stress and Distression

RANK-ORDERING FOR
PRIORITIZING ACTIVITIES

This technique is effective as a general method for both time management and stress control. It is useful particularly for those days when your distression level and blues make you feel draggy and not up to meeting as many challenges of your typical day as usual.

Begin by making a list of everything that you have to do as well as anything else that you may want to do. Now put the entire list into rank order, starting with the item that will have the *worst* consequences if you don't actually accomplish it today. Assign Rank Two to the item that will have the next-worst consequences. Continue until you have a fully rank-ordered list. Every activity must have a number.

Now, beginning with Number One, tackle your list in rank order. Focus your concentration and energy on the first item until you have finished it, or gone as far as you can. Then turn your energy to the second-ranked item.

Recognize that, like other Type E women, you have probably set out a Herculean "to do" list for yourself. This merely reflects the excessive burdens you place on yourself, your demanding life, and the erroneous thinking that sets you up to feel as if you are not accomplishing enough. As a rule of thumb, if you can accomplish the three to five most pressing items on your list, you will have put a comfortable enough buffer between your list and tomorrow's stressors that you can sleep easily tonight.

Update your rank-ordered list, inserting new items every day.

LEARNING TO SAY NO

Every Type E woman I have ever met has trouble saying no. For this primary reason, she is distressed by an inordinate number of demands and needs from others and is deficient in time to spend taking care of herself.

This exercise requires, first, that you commit to decreasing the number of requests with which you will agree or comply, starting right now. This doesn't mean that you will turn into a selfish, hostile person. It merely means that you will start becoming realistic about your own limitations and remove one of the main reasons that you get distressed and depressed.

One of the greatest fears Type E women have about saying no is that they will be perceived as hostile. In fact, their fear is based on their own experience of saying yes to everybody for so long that when they finally do say no, the refusal comes out sounding angry. If you learn to say no comfortably, in a way that is assertive but not hostile, and if you prepare

212

yourself through anticipation and practice for the experience, you should have no reason to fear your own hostility or the negative reactions of others.

Write down three to five requests or sources of demand on you to which you would like to say no. Next, write out a way to deny each request that meets the criterion of being assertive but not apologetic, firm but not aggressive or angry.

When you have written out your scripts, practice saying no in the ways you have devised, either with the aid of a tape recorder or, preferably, with a friend who will role-play the other party. Ask for constructive feedback—or listen critically and carefully to your tape-recorded denials—to be sure that you sound neither weak nor angry, or as though you simply don't mean what you are saying.

Keep in mind that for Type E women, saying no is like speaking a foreign language. The way to get comfortable and proficient is to practice, practice, practice.

Also, remember that your purpose in saying no to some of the people some of the time, is to reduce the nature and amount of demands on your limited time and resources and to keep the requirements on your energies within attainable, accomplishable, and safe boundaries. Then, you will succeed in doing what you set out for yourself without excessive stress and without the inevitable sense of inadequacy and depression that unrealistic expectations create.

LEARNING TO DELEGATE

Type E women are notoriously poor delegators. Because they don't say no often enough and don't delegate to others, the sheer weight of their responsibilities drags down their moods.

Learning to delegate involves three steps. First, you must decide that you will delegate some tasks to others. Second, you must decide which of your several tasks and responsibilities you will delegate. This can be accomplished by itemizing each of your roles in terms of the particular jobs, chores, tasks and responsibilities that it comprises. Then, select at least one third of those tasks and target them for delegation. You may choose to supervise the delegation, but that means *supervise*—not do it yourself.

The third step in delegation is learning how to communicate your delegation request or instructions effectively. Time and again, I hear Type E women say something like this when they intend to delegate: "Gee, I *really* hate to ask you to do this. In fact, I feel awfully guilty. I know I should do it myself, but you know how disorganized I can be. If you'll do this for me, I'll be so grateful."

This may be a bit of a caricature, but not much of one. Most men, on the other hand, would make the same request by saying something like, "I'll need this by three o'clock. Thanks." P.S. Guess whose job gets done first?

Proceed to learn delegation in the same way that you practiced saying no. Identify the tasks you will need to delegate and select the people to whom you will give your delegation instructions. I recognize that the latter may not be an obvious or straightforward issue—you may feel that there aren't any options other than doing the job yourself. Look again. Perhaps you can hire someone; perhaps with improved communication and an explanation of how your distress is a factor in your blue moods, a member or members of your family might be recruited; or perhaps there is a way to pool the efforts of several women and institute a turn-taking or job-sharing system. *There are always solutions.* It is your high stress level that makes you believe that there are no alternatives. Then write out delegation scripts and practice until you are comfortable with nonapologetic, assertive, straightforward communication.

TAKING A MENTAL MINIVACATION

Because of your busy life and your important commitments, the very thing you probably need most is the thing you cannot afford to do. That, of course, is the luxury of a relaxing vacation to unwind, escape from it all, and fully recharge your batteries.

While it is imperative that you take time off and go away on a relaxing vacation at least once a year, I recognize that financial, family, job, and other constraints make frequent vacations relatively unrealistic. But your mind can go where your body cannot, and the stress-reduction effect can be substantial.

Using your powers of visual imagery, try to see in your mind's eye a scene that you associate with pure relaxation, beauty, serenity, or exhilaration. When you have captured the vision, talk into a tape recorder and let yourself free-associate, describing the scene and your positive feelings.

Begin with the lead "I am in [a locale] and I feel [a positive emotion]." Continue to monologue, letting your imagination wander, for as long as 10 minutes. You may invent a story, a conversation, or anything else as long as the imagery you use connotes a calm or relaxing mental picture for you.

After you have dictated your imagery, you will have in your possession your own tailor-made, personalized autohypnosis tape. To take a mental minivacation, lie down on a bed or sofa or lean back in a chair and close your eyes. Breathe in deeply through your nose and exhale through your mouth. Try to make your breathing slow and rhythmic. Many people find the image of waves rolling in to shore and back again to sea helpful in regulating their breathing.

After you have assumed rhythmic breathing and a relaxed position, turn on your tape. As the tape plays, let your voice transport you to the scene you are describing. Visualize what you hear; continue visualizing even after the tape has ended, all the while maintaining deep and rhythmic breathing.

This exercise is my patients' favorite stress reducer and one that you should come to rely on when you feel your emotional pressure cooker starting to erupt. After you tire of your imagery tape, simply invent a new one. You are limited only by your own creativity and imagination.

NEGOTIATING "HELP" CONTRACTS

The final exercise focuses on the need to ask for help and effectively to communicate what you need in the way of assistance so that your burdens are lessened. Most Type E women make the mistake of becoming overly self-reliant, expecting themselves to do everything and then resenting those they live and/or work with as a consequence.

One of the biggest objections women have to asking for help is the fear of nagging. Another is their anticipation that the attempt will be met with resistance; that possible disappointment is felt to be even more upsetting than just doing the task or work themselves. Both of these views are self-defeating.

Approach the job or task in question as you would a business negotiation. Obviously, you would like someone else to accept full responsibility and lighten your load; the other person may see his or her interest best served by continuing to have you do the work. What is needed, therefore, are acceptable compromises.

Begin by stating that you no longer are willing to do the chore, task or job unassisted all the time. This should be clearly labeled as a nonnegotiable position. The next step in the negotiation is to determine what, if anything, the other party might want in return for the assistance. (Perhaps, as is often the case, it is just for you to stop nagging.) Your goal is to strike a mutually acceptable deal in which you get more assistance than you are currently getting. You will find that your husband, children, work associates and others will be receptive to the idea of a negotiated contract far more than to a hostile confrontation or repetitive nagging. Honestly explain that your purposes are to reduce your stress level, with the intention of improving your overall productivity and, especially, your mood.

The important thing to keep in mind is that you *can* negotiate about things in your personal life just as you probably do in business. Too often, Type E women feel stressed because they respond to the needs or demands of others as if there simply is no room for negotiation, with the result that they feel either helpless, angry, or both. The net result is depression and increased stress.

Stress management is central to mood management if you count yourself among the ranks of "today's women" for whom distress is a major reason for depression and the blues. As you practice and incorporate stress management into your daily routine, your overall stress level will lower while your mood stabilizes and improves.

Just as a reminder, you might do what Nancy did: Put a sign somewhere in your home or office (or both) that asks the question: "Are you depressed, or are you distressed?"

17

◆

Holiday Blues and Other Calendar Slumps

◆

Hope ever tells us tomorrow will be better.

—TIBULLUS

Bah! Humbug!

—EBENEZER SCROOGE

Christmas: " 'Tis the season to be jolly." Right? Wrong.

According to every index of emotional distress and depression, the annual holiday season can be a very unjolly time indeed for a lot of people. In fact, so common is the experience of a mood slump around the traditionally festive season that the condition has been dubbed the "holiday blues" and should rank as a leading attributional suspect if you find yourself depressed anywhere from mid-November to the end of January.

But depressions linked to dates on the calendar are not limited only to the Christmas season. In every person's life, there are specific dates that evoke both happy and sad memories. And there are dates that used to be associated with celebrations but now may trigger feelings of loss or, perhaps, bitterness such as a wedding anniversary of a marriage that ended in divorce, or the birthday of a loved one who is now departed.

218

For many women, monthly calendar dates are predictive of the tension, irritability, depression, or hypersensitivity that accompanies the premenstrual phase of their cycle. Seasons of the year, especially in those parts of the world that are subject to severe winters, can be the calendar-linked triggers for otherwise unexplained feelings of depression. Even days of the week predictably affect mood.

The important recognition, from the standpoint of attributing your down mood to its proper cause, is that the explanation may be nothing more elaborate or complex than merely the date on the calendar. You may find, as many of my patients have, that attributing your low mood to a date or the time of week or year will come as a relief, especially if you have been troubled that something "more serious" might be wrong with you.

The Red and Green Blues

In the No Nonsense Women's Attitude Survey, several questions were asked about the major annual holidays—Thanksgiving, Christmas, and New Year's. In describing the holidays that the survey respondents typically celebrate with their immediate and/or extended families, 37 percent reported that the occasions produced stress for them, 15 percent acknowledged that the occasions caused them to feel sad, 30 percent acknowledged that the holidays involved conflict, 19 percent stated that the holidays were disappointing, and 23 percent admitted that the holidays were times that they anticipated with dread.

This suggests that a significant minority of the women surveyed experience less than idyllic holiday scenes and emotions. The women in the survey were all employed and their responses were specifically limited to holidays that were celebrated with their families. Women (and men) who are out of a job, without families altogether, or have families from whom they are alienated certainly would be expected to find the traditionally jolly holiday season even more stressful and sad than the survey sample.

There are several reasons why the holidays are associated

with feelings of stress and depression for many people. The most obvious sources of stress are the pressures of gift shopping, crowds, financial outlay, forthcoming bills, and the expenditure of time and effort in such activities as gift wrapping, addressing Christmas cards, cooking for company, and the social press of the party circuit. But these activities make up part of the positive stress or excitement of the season as well, and aside from those whose finances are too limited to permit the traditional purchasing frenzy, constitute much the same pressure for everyone. Why, then, are some people so prone to depression during the holidays while others revel in the joy of the season?

The answer, to a large extent, lies again with unrealistic expectations. I know many patients and other people who readily acknowledge marital or family disharmony throughout the year. But come Thanksgiving and Christmas, they hold the wholly unrealistic expectations that their families will suspend customary tensions and behave, instead, like live scenes from a Norman Rockwell painting.

The reality of their holiday experiences, not surprisingly, comes as a sharp and jolting contrast to the expectation that "everyone will get along because it's Christmas." Families or couples that don't get along well during any other time of the year cannot realistically be transformed suddenly by the date on the calendar and the exchange of some gifts. Nevertheless, the disappointment caused by the realization that the actuality of the holidays is a pale comparison to their idealized, unrealistic expectations can still trigger a significant sense of loss and depression.

Low moods can result from failure to live up to not only your own expectations, but to others' fantasies as well. Some women and men, for example, are faced with the anxiety that they will fail to live up to their parents' or other family members' expectations when they visit home for the holidays after an extended absence. In the survey, 26 percent of the respondents reported living more than 100 miles from their parents. For these women and others like them who live geographically separated from their parents and/or siblings, family reunions during the holidays can be occasions for tension and hurt, sometimes as much as or more than for joy and closeness.

Yvonne and her husband went home to visit her family in New Hampshire after being out in Los Angeles for seven years. Both Yvonne and her husband were anxious about the trip because they both had gained a lot of weight since leaving their hometown, and neither was doing very well in their careers. As they had feared, when they arrived home, the family teased them about their weight and repeatedly assaulted them with verbal barbs such as "The good life in California seems to be agreeing with you too much," and the like. The remarks about their appearance, as well as the incongruity between the reality of their financial struggles in Los Angeles and the family's assumption or implication that they were doing well enough to be living the "good life" led both of them to feel fraudulent, inadequate, and understandably depressed.

Another reason for the holiday blues is the almost unavoidable comparison that everyone makes between media and advertising images of the "holiday spirit" that are thrust upon them and the reality of their own lives. This is especially painful for people whose lives have recently been disrupted by divorce, separation, or termination of an important relationship. For single people who are without a meaningful intimate relationship altogether, the pervasive message of the season to be with the ones you love heightens painful feelings of loneliness.

The emphasis on families and friends during the holiday season means that the loss of a loved one through death or divorce can be a particularly difficult experience. All of the rituals and symbols that you associate with the holidays may serve to remind you that the person you have lost is no longer there to share the celebration with you. There is no easy remedy for this natural restimulation of grief and loss during special, nostalgic times of the year. The reappearance of grief and loss, or the pressure and trauma of trying to adjust to a Christmas with a separated or split family while trying to ensure a happy holiday for children, is sufficient to trigger a painful bout of the holiday blues.

Holiday depression is also caused by the collective sense that the end of the old year and the beginning of the new should signal resolutions for change and redirection. Inevitably, my appointment book begins to fill to capacity around the middle of January as patients who have postponed marital separation, job searches, or other significant stressful life changes until "after the holidays" must face their self-imposed deadlines.

The externally imposed pressure to be happy and cheerful is yet another source of mood strain for people who resent and resist "putting on an act." Going out to Christmas and New Year's parties as a "happy couple" when your relationship is in fact seriously on the skids can be stressful and upsetting.

Emotional trouble often results from the annual company Christmas parties in which alcohol and revelry combine to unleash inhibitions—sexual, verbal, and otherwise—that would better be kept in check. The proverbial "morning after" of such parties, when the realization that you have either humiliated yourself or let a potentially career-damaging secret out of the closet begins to sink in to your foggy and hung-over consciousness can be a gruesome emotional awakening. The inevitable remorse, guilt and anxiety of the holiday party gaffes and goofs can trigger a serious case of the blues.

Still another cause of the seasonal depression is the lengthy period of anticipation and buildup, followed by the rapid anticlimax and emptiness of the postholiday period. In most cities, Christmas music, ads, and displays go up well before the Thanksgiving turkey has been consumed. For more than a month, we are deluged with the anticipation of one 24-hour period on December 25.

Suddenly, after all the excitement and stress of shopping and preparing, the day is over and the reality of life, as usual, returns. Many people comment on the disquieting letdown of Christmas afternoon or the day after Christmas. Aside from the anticlimactic quiet, other realities can become salient. All that celebratory drinking and eating may now have turned into unwanted pounds gained or physical fitness gone to seed. Of course, none of this is permanent or necessarily reason for getting down, since a few disciplined weeks of January dieting and exercise will generally suffice to rectify the problem. But reason notwithstanding, many people suffer low moods because their holiday overindulgence has caught up with them.

What can be done to fight off the holiday blues? In the first place, simply giving yourself the permission to feel a realistic combination of both positive and negative feelings around the holidays will relieve some of the pressure you may feel to be constantly up and cheerful, against which your actual mood may seem depressingly negative or inadequate.

Guard against setting yourself up to be depressed by avoiding unrealistic expectations. Hopefully, your holidays will be a continuation of times in which close, happy relationships bring you the joys of love and sharing. But if your life is in a temporary downturn—and "temporary" is the key word to keep foremost in your mind—don't expect the holidays to magically suspend the conflict, loneliness, alienation, anger, tension, or whatever other hard feelings you may have been harboring or experiencing throughout the rest of the year.

If your customary or traditional ways of celebrating the holidays work well for you, then certainly continue in the same vein. But for many women I know and treat, the holidays are times in which they feel like square pegs trying to fit into round holes. Suzanne, for example, is a patient of mine, recently remarried to a man whose family rejects her for being a "divorcee" (his family are Italian, Old World Catholics). Nevertheless, despite the tension and rejection, Suzanne submits to spending Thanksgiving and Christmas Day with her husband's family. While Suzanne's motivations and intentions to try to please her husband are understandable and even admirable, the bottom line is that the holidays are a miserable, painful, insulting, and thoroughly depressing experience for her.

In a joint therapy session. Suzanne's husband, who is actually quite sympathetic to his wife and willing to do whatever will make her happy, agreed to a compromise whereby one of the two holidays each year would be spent away from his family. I emphasized to them the importance of developing their own traditions so that they did not feel empty or devoid of the rituals that make the season pleasurably nostalgic and memorable.

The holiday blues can be somewhat abated if you examine the possibility of alternative ways to celebrate that might involve developing some traditions of your own instead of following parental traditions that do not, in fact, produce happy feelings in you. Forcing yourself to do what others expect of you, in spite of the fact that to do so causes you discomfort or outright pain, is a major cause of holiday blues.

The most helpful things to remember about the holidays and the depression or blues that might accompany the season are these: (1) The "holiday blues" are, by definition, a temporary condition—reminding yourself of its temporary, transitory nature will help you endure it; (2) feeling stressed, ambivalent, or down around the holidays is quite normal and explainable for all the reasons discussed above and doesn't signal that there is something drastically wrong or abnormal about you and your reactions; and (3) stay tuned—next year (especially if you work at it) you will have another chance to spend the holidays in ways that make you a lot happier.

If the holidays are a happy and particularly joyful time of year for you, count yourself among the fortunate. The memory of your celebrations, especially if preserved in photographs, videos, letters, or journals, can be a source of pleasant restimulation of good feelings throughout the year. When you feel down and need a quick lift for your sagging spirits, think about the happy holidays you spent. Try to regain some of the good feelings that the period engendered and look forward to more cheer this coming season. If planning for Christmas is something you especially enjoy, feel free to start your anticipation as early as you like. You can extend the pleasure over the course of many months while eliminating the stress and pressure of last-minute hassles.

Other Calendar Slumps

While many people get the holiday blues simultaneously, other dates on the yearly calendar may be idiosyncratic triggers for depression. And there are other months or periods of the year that, while not necessarily holidays, evoke consistent reactions—including the blues—among many people.

Psychologists and psychiatrists call depressions that are triggered by the anniversary of significant painful memories "anniversary phenomena." The date of a loved one's death, the date that a marriage split up, the date that a job was terminated or that a large sum of money was lost are all examples of anniversary phenomena. The phenomenon, by the way, is not the inevitable recurrence of the date on the annual calendar cycle, but rather the sadness, irritability or general "out of sorts" feelings that occur during the week or two around the date. The person may or may not be consciously aware that these feelings are related to the anniversary event.

Mandy came to see me for her weekly therapy session reporting that she felt "really down," but that she had no idea what was bothering her.

"Sometimes I think I might be losing my grip," Mandy commented. "Everything is going fairly well in my life and I can't think of anything in particular that is troubling me. It's not time for my period and I feel okay physically. But for the last week I've started crying for no apparent reason when I've been with my boyfriend at a movie, or I feel this creepy sadness when I wake up in the morning. I have no idea why I'm so depressed."

The date of this session was June 10. I asked Mandy what memories she associated with late May to mid-June. Mandy thought for a minute or two, and then the light of insight appeared in her eyes.

"I can't believe I didn't realize this," she smiled in relief. Then, through tears, Mandy recounted a traumatic period of her childhood that occurred during early June. "I remember we were packing up the house to move to another part of town as soon as school ended and I was really sad about that. My parents and I had been fighting a lot because I was angry about being moved away from my friends and especially my first boyfriend. I was twelve at the time.

"Anyway, my older brother was very late getting home for dinner. About eight that evening, the police called to say that my brother had been killed in a car accident. I felt like the world was crumbling around me. On top of that—and this may seem minor to you but to me it was just huge—my dog died a week later and I felt like I was going to be without a friend in the world.

"I remember for years afterward just hating June because it reminded me of that terrible time. I guess I didn't realize how deep my memory of that period goes. I thought I had put all that behind me. But you know, I feel a lot better knowing I'm not depressed over anything in my life right now and I'm not going nuts. I just get weepy in June."

Many women find their own birthdays times of both celebration and intense discomfort—and often only the latter. The principle reason for this calendar-linked mood slump is that the passage of another birthday is a reminder of growing older. The reaction to birthdays, like other holidays, is affected by whether, in the overall context, your life is going well or whether you feel lonely or that you don't have a special person or relationship in your life that would make your birthday celebration more enjoyable.

Women who feel the press of the biological clock ticking away during their 30s while they remain childless despite their strong desire to have a baby often find that birthdays are particularly anxiety-ridden and depressing. The biological clock ticks away for everyone in the sense that life marches inexorably on to the inevitable end. Thoughts about growing older, about missing out on experiences you desire, or about not succeeding fully in areas that you would like, and ultimately about dying are the stuff of which depression is made. Needless to say, you can't stop the clock. But you can refocus on the life that you do have, rather than on what you morbidly anticipate losing.

The best way to counteract the depressing effects of your own birthday is to plan well in advance how and with whom you want to spend the day, and take special care to be good to yourself. If you depend on others to make your birthday happy, you may be let down; if you depend on yourself, you will have more control. You can't do a thing about growing older other than being the best you can be at every age of your life. Just consider the alternative.

There are a few other times of the year that seem to trigger collective depressions among many people. In parts of the country where the climate is harsh, for example, February is frequently felt as a depressing month. By February, the winter has lasted overly long, spring is still a few months away, the bills from holiday shopping are coming due, and spirits sag.

Over the years in my private practice, I have watched predictable seasonal cycles that affect the number of patients who book appointments each week. Like clockwork, my caseload drops each August, December, and April, reflecting the traditional summer vacation, the diversion of money and time into Christmas shopping, and income-tax season. Immediately after these lulls—in September, January, and May— my practice becomes much busier as people gear up for the fall, the New Year, and as they recover from the jolt of taxes. Generally, my patients report that August, December, and April are also times when they feel down or stressed again because the summer is ending and "vacation time" is over, income taxes must be paid, and the holiday blues cloud their moods.

Other seasonal variations affect business cycles and, consequently, have an effect on business people's moods. The early winter months, for example, are generally slow for business and can cause anxiety and mood slumps for entrepreneurs who rely on the ringing of the cash register for their financial welfare. Accountants are particularly stressed during the few months prior to April 15, when long working hours, grumbling clients, and other factors can strain otherwise even tempers and good natures.

Take a look at the calendar and reflect on the times of year when your mood generally takes a dive. Perhaps you are immune from seasonal slides, but most people are not. There is even a form of clinical Depression known by the acronym SAD, Seasonal Affective (mood) Disorder. This condition tends to affect people who live in climates where winters are long and their exposure to sunlight is consequently reduced. Such individuals show virtually all the symptoms of major Depression. The principle cause of their extremely low moods is thought to be the lack of light associated with winter. Not surprisingly, SAD is particularly prevalent in Alaska, where winter darkness and the shortness of days is most dramatic.

A treatment for SAD has been remarkably effective with an antidepressant therapy using exposure to infrared and ultraviolet rays of light. Within a matter of days, as soon as their bodies are essentially tricked into thinking that spring has arrived, SAD patients respond with a dramatic increase of energy and diminution of symptoms.

Other researchers who study major mood disorders such as manic-depressic illness and major Depression also report consistent patterns of mood swings occurring in the spring and fall of every year. This observation, like that of the existence of SAD, again confirms the importance of nature's calendar as an explanation for mood slumps.

PMS and Monthly Blues

Just a short decade ago, many people believed that the relationship between menstrual cycles, hormones, and moods was pure mythology. Today, there exists a mass of incontrovertible evidence that demonstrates the scientific validity of what has come to be known as PMS, or Premenstrual Syndrome, in a great number of women.

You may regularly suffer from symptoms of PMS such as water retention, irritability, nervous tension, weepiness, or depression. Or your PMS, like other women's, may be variable, troubling you greatly in some months but barely noticeable in others. Stress is thought to be the explanation for this variability. When you are under a lot of stress, you can expect your PMS symptoms to be more pronounced.

The fact that PMS is real, that it can suppress your mood, and that the origin of your low mood is biochemical (hormonal) should come as something of a relief to you if you have worried about your monthly depressions. But recognizing PMS and giving in to it or, worse, giving yourself either a reason or a suggestion to be depressed because of the time of the month are quite different.

Since the increase in amount of media attention and articles on PMS in women's magazines over recent years, I have noticed many of my patients making self-fulfilling predictions about their moods on the basis of their monthly cycles.

"I have a very important meeting next week and I just know I'm not going to do well because I'll be having PMS," one of my patients predicts. Another starts her therapy session by remarking, "Well, I guess I'm depressed because my period is due in a few days." This woman didn't even feel particularly troubed or blue. She was merely assuming and accepting depression as inevitable because of the time of the month.

These reactions to PMS are counterproductive to mood management. The observed variability in PMS symptoms means that you do not necessarily have to be affected at all, nor that you will be affected the same way each month. Most important, just because your hormones are operating to make you feel down doesn't mean that you can't do things that will counteract the negative PMS symptoms. All of the action techniques that you will learn in the next section can and should be applied to PMS-induced blues just as to any other kind of low mood that affects you. Once again, the key concept is *control*.

Just knowing that your down mood and dim outlook is a function of your menstrual cycle can be a significant attributional step toward feeling better. Whereas you may have lost track of the date, or have a somewhat erratic menstrual cycle, and may have started to believe that there must be some factors in your life situation that account for your low mood, recognizing and attributing your blues to "normal" PMS that is transitory and self-correcting by nature will lift your spirits.

Weekly Rhythms

One final calendar-linked mood slump is worth noting, and that is the way many people feel as a direct function of what day of the week it is. For example, almost everybody understands the concept of the Monday morning blues or blahs. When you have trouble getting motivated and energized at the top of the week, just saying "It's Monday" can be sufficient to end the attributional search for your listlessness and keep you from becoming overly critical of yourself. After all, lots of people have difficulty getting back into high gear on Monday mornings, and you simply may be no exception.

Other motivational and mood patterns are built into the weekly cycle. Just as most people have the blahs about starting the week on Monday, the anticipation of the coming weekend can start to raise spirits by Thursday evening. Fridays, then, are generally more "up" days in the workweek mood cycle; and Tuesdays, Wednesdays, and Thursdays often the most productive.

The way your mood is affected by the weekend has a great deal to do with the quality of your personal life and the extent to which you use your weekends to unwind, relax, and recharge your batteries as opposed to doing an endless stream of boring, tedious, unpleasant but seemingly unavoidable chores. If you store up all your chores for the weekend, you are probably not getting the lift in spirits that a less taxing few days could otherwise provide. You might consider adjusting your regimen so that you allocate every other weekend to getting caught up on chores and errands. That way, the alternate Saturdays and/or Sundays can be reserved for the important, restorative purpose of having a relaxing good time.

If your social or love life is currently at a low ebb, you may not experience the positive anticipation of Fridays and weekends that others around you do. Taking more control by planning and scheduling pleasurable activities with friends and/or family on weekends can offset at least some of the boredom or loneliness of an unplanned and empty few days.

Sundays—especially Sunday evenings—can trigger a mood slump because the weekend is coming to a close,

Monday morning is around the corner, and the week's stressors and pressures begin to intrude on your consciousness. In my family, we call the blues that hit right about the time that "Sixty Minutes" is over the "Sunday-nighters." Again, just having a name or label to which you can attribute the cause of the low mood that strikes because Sunday night is closing in may alleviate your concern about what your sudden drop in spirits means.

You may personally relate to the concept of mood cycles being linked to weekly cycles or know of others whose attitude and behavior parallel the calendar's repetitive progression. If you don't immediately recognize yourself in weekly patterns, try observing your mood fluctuations as a function of days of the week. Your Daily Mood Rating Form from Chapter 4 will be helpful for this purpose. When you know your own patterns and sensitivities, you will be in a better position to plan and implement mood-management strategies to counteract the demotivating or depressing effects of particular days.

When you understand how your mood and motivation operate as a function of time of the day, and day of the week (as well as other monthly cycles), you can capitalize on your most productive times by scheduling your work accordingly. The knowledge that your mood might take a predictable drop on Sunday evenings, for example, or any other day will allow you to plan either for pleasurable activities to protect your mood or for avoiding having to do unpleasant or overly demanding activities when your mood is already somewhat suppressed.

Know Your Own
Calendar Slumps

The march of time is beyond your control to influence. But knowing how your mood fluctuates according to seasons, dates, or days of the week or month will enhance your sense of control for a few reasons.

First, knowing your personal mood calendar patterns will

enable you to predict downward emotional slides and make preparations to do things that will buffer your discomfort and reverse your mood. Second, attributing the cause of your depressed mood to a widely shared phenomenon of the calendar will reduce your feelings of being alone with your blues. In fact, making a "quick" attribution of your mood slump to a date or time of the month may be all that is necessary to complete the second step of the mood-management program and move you forward to the critical action mode. Instead of starting to ruminate about why you feel down, you will know that your low mood is merely reflective of the calendar and that you are likely to feel better by distracting yourself with some pleasurable activity.

Finally, there is comfort in knowing that if your low mood is linked to time, then it, too, shall pass.

18

◆

Men and the Blues

◆

If they could put one man on the moon, why can't they put them all?

—ANONYMOUS ROMANTICALLY
DISILLUSIONED WOMAN

No discussion of why women get depressed would be complete without a chapter about men.

Let me hasten to add, however, that I do not want to join the legions of writers who have enjoyed wide readership of late through the explicit practice of "male bashing." I like men—a lot. And I still believe in love, romance, and the immense value of a healthy intimate relationship as the best haven against emotional distress and low moods.

But I wasn't born yesterday either, and I've known my share of unhealthy men—both personally and professionally—whose unresolved issues about intimacy, women, commitment, power, sexuality, and love make them downright dangerous partners in close relationships. Because of their mishandling of emotional issues and romantic malpractice, these men can be a primary cause of depression in their overcommitted partners.

The other side of the coin is that there are characteristic errors in the ways some women approach the meaning of their relationships with men, so that they set themselves up for recurrent bouts of the blues. This places at least a portion of the responsibility for the unhappiness in relationships in the laps of women. While doing so may not be as popular as male bashing, giving women the insight to recognize and change their ways of relating to men that ultimately cause both partners emotional pain is an essential component of effective mood management. Moreover, knowing what you are doing that is contributing to your mood problems and realizing that you can choose to behave and feel differently will immediately increase your real control over depression and the blues.

Dangerous Partners

My concern is with psychologically—as opposed to physically—dangerous men whose insidiously seductive but ultimately unhealthy patterns of relating to women in intimate relationships constitute identifiable forms of emotional abuse. While a solid argument can be made that women who stay involved with such men are colluding in their own mistreatment, the fact remains that the source of the behavior that gives rise to the women's depression is primarily the men.

I have repeatedly seen four basic types of men and patterns of relating that form the basis for depressed reactions in a great number of women I treat. Interestingly, I rarely actually see or meet the men; their clinical identification, however, is generally a rather easy matter, once I come to understand the effect that the relationships have had on the women's mood.

THE BIG FIX

This type of man relates to a woman in a way that causes her to become addicted to him and to the relationship. As a consequence of her addiction, she experiences a genuine loss of control over the status of her own mood and emotions. Ultimately, to save herself, the woman must endure the difficult and frequently depressing experience of withdrawal from the relationship.

Joan came to see me when her depression over the troubles in her relationship with her boyfriend of three years, Robert, was seriously interfering with her job performance as a loan officer for a major bank.

"I just can't continue to be as distracted and upset," Joan explained, "or I'll lose my job altogether. My boss actually insisted that I get help. She thinks I ought to get out of the relationship completely—and I think she might be right—but I'm afraid I can't do it. I've tried in the past to break up, but Robert needs me so much, he can't stay away. Somehow we always wind up getting back together.

"The thing that drives me crazy is that Robert is so inconsistent and unpredictable. There are times when he is the greatest man I could possibly hope for, but other times—probably, most of the time to be honest—he's a terrible jerk. There's no doubt in my mind that he loves me and needs me, but he also hurts me too much.

"It seems like it's always when our relationship is going well that he suddenly gets scared, backpedals, and distances himself from me. He'll say that he needs his 'space' and then he won't call me for several days. And I sit there, alone in my house, depressed, crying and staring at the phone, waiting for it to ring. As soon as it does, I'm so relieved and happy to hear from him. I keep hoping things will change, but they haven't in three years.

"Robert blames *me* for why he gets angry or withdraws. It's always something wrong that I did, but when I correct what I did wrong, the rules change and he blames me for something else. I can't ever make him happy on a consistent basis and I can't stand feeling so miserable and scared all the time that I'll lose him."

Joan is involved with the Big Fix. Robert's pattern of on-again, off-again behavior in which his occasionally very rewarding and giving behavior toward her alternates with apparently longer periods of capricious, random withholding behavior or anger creates what psychologists call an intermittent reinforcement schedule. This means that rewards in the relationship—such as affection, communication, lovemaking, intimacy, and so forth—are not given consistently.

Moreover, the receiver (Joan) has no actual control over gaining the rewards, since the underlying schedule on which the reinforcement is based is essentially random and therefore beyond her control.

Every addictive experience, from heroin to gambling to love relationships, is based on an intermittent reinforcement schedule. The junkie, for example, receives the "rewards" of heroin when he is able to "score," but the majority of his existence is not pleasurable. By definition, the gambler operates purely on a basis of random reward, since that is the meaning of luck paying off. If you have ever watched people lined up at slot machines in Las Vegas or Atlantic City, you have witnessed a clear demonstration of intermittent reinforcement at work. Despite the fact that most of the coins are dropped into the one-armed bandits with no resulting payout, the gambler's "big fix" comes from the periodic, random delivery of a jackpot of jingling coins and flashing lights.

Because Joan was hooked on Robert and the intermittent schedule of his love, attention, and "good behavior," she felt out of control of the very thing that made her happy or created great sadness. It was her loss of control, because Robert's behavior was not really contingent on what Joan did but rather on how he was feeling, that created the sense of helplessness and ultimately the depression from which she suffered. Because of the strength of their mutual addiction, Joan and Robert both experienced a distressful and painful loss when they tried to break up and withdraw from one another. To stop the pain of withdrawal, they returned to the relationship and Joan reaffirmed her dependence on the Big Fix.

Robert's style of relating to a woman is dangerous and emotionally abusive not because of his intent, but because of the consequences. In other words, it is not necessary to assume that Robert, or any other Big Fix, *intends* to hurt his woman. In fact, the man is likely to be quite unconscious of the motives behind his behavior, or even of the pattern itself. And it is important to note that the man who creates the addictive relationship also becomes addicted to it himself and generally becomes equally unhappy. The loss of control that he experiences from the addiction accounts, in part, for his periodic need for withdrawal and "space."

Addiction of any kind is a setup or precondition for depression. Becoming aware of how devastating inconsistent, randomly delivered rewards from a man can become to your emotional health and mood is a critical insight. Equally important is the recognition of how your own inconsistencies and capricious behavior toward a man also can create a mutually unhealthy addiction. Either way, a stable mood depends on being in emotional circumstances that on balance are far more positive than negative and that are for the most part predictable, consistent, and controllable in the sense that the love you get is more directly related to the love you give.

THE NARCISSIST

Narcissism is the name for a clinical personality disorder that has nothing to do with looking in the mirror. A narcissistic personality has a highly inflated, exaggerated sense of his own achievements, power, success, attractiveness, value, and importance. Moreover, he has grandiose and intoxicating dreams of unlimited financial success, power, and ideal romantic love.

The Narcissist lives for the attention and adoration of others. Generally, however, his relationships are impaired because of the pervasive and inescapable fact that he and only he is the center of his universe. Other people, toward whom he is incapable of genuine empathy, become like all the other objects with which he surrounds himself to create the image and persona commensurate with his blown-up self-concept.

The real trouble is that behind all the gloss and external trappings of success (Narcissists are often extremely driven, powerful, and successful) dwells a wildly and dangerously insecure human being. What he suspects or knows is that he is empty and rotten at the core. His obsession with external attainments and appearance is a defense against true self-knowledge and integrity of character.

The Narcissist vacillates between loving himself and hating himself, and his relationships with women are externalized projections of this internal dichotomy. Consequently, intimate relationships with women are marked by alternating cycles of idealization and cruel devaluation. Since true intimacy risks exposure of his fundamental self-deception and emptiness, ultimately he must protect himself from letting anyone get too close.

The Narcissist has a superb opening act in a new relationship with a woman. He does "falling in love" better than almost any other kind of man. Because he craves attention and is adept at the superficial manipulative aspects of interpersonal relationships, he showers the woman with attention and adulation. After all, when an attractive man (yes, they're also often highly attractive) can't keep his eyes off you and makes you feel high with rapturous declaration of your beauty, sexiness, and the intensity of his feelings, it is not likely that you will turn away in boredom. His strategy is successful in gaining your rapt attention back on him and inducing a wonderful mood in you. There are few mood states whose positivity, headiness, and intensity can compare with that of falling in love with such a romantic fellow.

So far, so good. But Act Two is a killer.

After you're hooked, his behavior changes. He may suddenly appear turned off, bored, preoccupied, or, worse, critical and derisive. It becomes apparent that you both are in love with the same person: him. The intoxicating ether you have been breathing (his attention, idealized concept of you, promises of unlimited love, money, and fun) is suddenly, inexplicably shut off. Predictably, your mood crashes. You become depressed. And the Narcissist—like the drug pusher—seems like the only one who can stop the pain and make you feel happy again.

At this point, like the fly with the spider you are caught in the web of his control—out of control of your own mood and utterly confused, not only about who he really is, but about who you are as well. Since you are compelled by the reflection of your self-concept in his eyes, you begin to see yourself in alternating cycles of idealization and devaluation that parallel the way he behaves toward all the people with whom he becomes identified or connected.

If you try to broach the issue of his hurtful behaviors he labels your communication "criticism" and responds with either a rageful outburst or cold indifference. Either way, your depression only deepens, as does your disillusionment, self-esteem, and sense of powerlessness to change him—which, remember, you will not and cannot do.

If you have had the misfortune of being involved with a narcissist, this brief description will seem painfully and eerily familiar. (And you thought it only happened to you.)

Eileen, at 45, had been divorced for six years when she met Richard. A stunning beauty in her youth, Eileen was still a fabulously attractive woman with a highly successful career in the fashion field. By her own admission, she had "very high standards" for falling in love, and since she was perfectly able to support herself and lead a reasonably glamorous life on her own, she required that any man she would consider marrying be no less than "fantastic in every way."

Then she found Richard. At 50, Richard was handsome, wealthy, charming and unattached. And he fell for Eileen on first sight. She in turn was similarly hit by the thunderbolt.

"Richard was the most exciting, wonderful, gorgeous man I had ever known." Eileen told me. "He was so romantic. He told me that he had waited all his life to meet someone like me, that he adored my looks, my sophistication, and my body. He was a world-class lover. After the most intense first month of any relationship I had ever had we went to Europe. We stayed in the best hotels, dined at the most elegant restaurants, and he bought me anything I wanted. He called the States every day to do business and I loved to listen to him 'wheel and deal.' Just being around Richard was thrilling for me. I've never been so sure about being in love. I was absolutely prepared to get married to him."

But sometime during their third week in Europe, at a resort in the south of France, Richard suddenly changed. It started with a display of coldness and distance. Soon thereafter, in response to what Eileen recalled as "a totally innocent question about where we were having dinner," Richard exploded in an uncontrolled rage.

"He said cruel and horrid things. I could not believe my ears. It was like he *wanted* to hurt me terribly. I was devastated. Worse than anything, I felt like a part of me had just died. It was almost like being withdrawn very abruptly from a drug euphoria. I've never crashed like that in my life. I was deeply depressed and utterly confused . . . and scared."

Following the European incident and apologies from Richard, they reconciled. The relationship resumed, but, as Eileen said, "Things were never the same again. I never felt safe. When he turned on the charm, though, I still fell in love all over again. He just turned me on so much. Inevitably, though, his temper would flare, or he would become so involved, with some new business deal that he totally ignored me for days. The depressions I experienced when I was with Richard were like none I'd ever known. They were so bleak, and the worst part of all is that he was the only one who could make me feel better. I started to need him so much that I resented him terribly."

Eventually, the relationship ended. Richard began having an affair with a much younger woman and stated that he "simply couldn't understand" why this would bother Eileen. After all, he "needed" to have the variety and couldn't be expected to stay satisfied with "a forty-five-year-old woman who is so demanding and needy."

"That remark was like a slap in the face," Eileen recalled. "I woke up to what a bastard this man really was. I never realized the extent to which I had lost my self-esteem and pride! After I recovered from the initial pain of the breakup, I wanted to call that younger woman and thank her for taking him off my back. Then, I wanted to call her and warn her to be careful. What a dangerous man!"

THE TRAGIC HERO

Just as if he were living out the script of a Shakespearean tragedy, the Tragic Hero will not permit any happy endings in his life, including a successful love relationship with a woman.

His basic problem is low self-esteem coupled with a generalized skepticism and distrust of women, love, and life itself. Since he is wedded to a view of the world in which tragic or unhappy endings are the only ones that make sense, he will act—albeit unconsciously—to sabotage a good relationship with a loving woman.

His low self-esteem makes him feel fundamentally undeserving. Consequently, he will find a way to make the woman who loves him become less desirable in his eyes. His skepticism ultimately produces the inevitable self-fulfilling prophecy, in which the relationship sours and his basic belief system is confirmed that happiness, at least for him, is impossible.

Sandra, at 37, was anxious to get married and have a family. Hal, the man with whom she was involved, was 10 years older and resistant to the idea of getting married. The reason, he told her, was that he believed "most marriages end in a bitter divorce," which he adamantly intended to avoid. Hal confessed that he wondered whether Sandra would stay attracted and faithful to him when he was in his 50s or 60s and predicted that "in the long run" she probably would leave him.

Despite Sandra's devotion and the excellent quality of their relationship, Hal would not be disabused of his belief that marriages don't work out and that she would wind up leaving him for a younger man. After failing at repeated attempts to convince him that her love was something he could trust, Sandra became frustrated, angry, and depressed. Her behavior toward Hal gradually changed and he commented that perhaps she wasn't "such a perfect mate" for him.

After two years of "getting nowhere," Sandra felt that she had no choice but to start dating other men, since her heart was set on marriage and children with "someone who believed in love." When she announced her decision to leave, prefaced by her final plea for marriage, he smugly nodded and said, "You see, I told you it would end up this way. I knew it would never last and that you'd end up leaving me."

THE AMBIVALENT STRUGGLER

In this pattern, the damage occurs because the woman becomes the ostensible object of the man's ambivalence. But the Ambivalent Struggler is undecided about many things in his life, not just his relationship with the woman. He doesn't enjoy his own indecisiveness. On the contrary, he agonizes and by so doing frequently pulls the sympathetic woman into helping him to "make up his mind" about her.

There are several ways in which this arrangement causes psychological damage to the woman. First, she buys into a view of herself that inherently involves a diminution of her self-esteem. Once she accepts the premise that she and the relationship are the source of his ambivalent feelings, she also accepts that there are aspects of her character or person and of the way she relates to him, that are not positive. Otherwise, the flawed reasoning goes, he would not be so conflicted.

The Ambivalent Struggler's indecisiveness, however, arises from unresolved issues within his own personality, about women, commitment, and intimacy. Thus, the ambivalence is *his* problem, not hers. To hear him tell it, though, the indecisiveness arises out of specific flaws, faults, or problems that he sees in the woman.

Whenever you are the object of another person's ambivalence, the damage to your self-esteem can be just about lethal. The psychological message is that his ambivalence reflects your flaws. Chronic exposure to a man's uncertainty about his feelings toward you or to the strength of his commitment to your relationship will inevitably drill a slow and painful hole through the center of your self-esteem. In addition, your inability to help or lead the Ambivalent Struggler to resolution about the relationship will compound your sense of inadequacy and loss of control. The net result: You become depressed.

Once you become depressed, the Ambivalent Struggler becomes more unsure of his feelings. After all, if this were such a good relationship, he reasons, you wouldn't be so unhappy. Or, if you were really so much in love with him, you wouldn't be criticizing him or be so negative. The ultimate guilt manipulation comes when he says that he understands how you might be sick and tired of his problems with making a commitment and wouldn't blame you if you left him for somebody better—even though he loves you a lot.

Denise and Fred had been going together for about a year when she raised the issue of commitment. Denise, 26, had been married before and wasn't necessarily particularly eager to remarry, but she did desire a committed, monogamous relationship. In her terms, she needed to know where she stood with Fred.

But Fred never stood in any one place for any length of time. He couldn't quite decide whether the relationship with Denise was right for him, or whether he could be sure that what he felt for her was truly love. Fred could admit that he cared for Denise and probably loved her, but he just wasn't convinced that he was "in love" with her. Fred said this, as do others who make this nebulous distinction, with a great deal of conviction and apparent emotional pain.

"It hurts me more to say this than it hurts you," Fred told Denise, "but I'm just not sure I'm really in love with you. You're great in a lot of ways, but there are things I worry about. I wish I could make a commitment. Why don't you just give me a little more time—we'll spend more time together—and I'll make up my mind." Denise agreed and they negotiated a deadline of Labor Day for Fred to decide yes or no on the future of the relationship.

"During those three months before Labor Day, I was a nervous wreck," Denise confessed later. "I felt like I was always on trial. I never did fully understand what it was about me that Fred was 'worried about,' but I can tell you that I started criticizing myself unmercifully. I made myself lose weight, I changed my hair, I did things with him that I don't even like to do just to show him how flexible and willing to please I was. The more I jumped through hoops to make him love me, the less I loved myself."

The punchline: Labor Day came and went but Fred's ambivalence never budged. He wasn't sure. He just didn't know. He wanted Denise's help in trying to get him to make up his mind. They bargained again, decided to extend Fred's decision period, and set a new deadline of January 1.

Denise's depression deepened. But she hung in there, this time trying to get Fred to tell her what it was about her that "was missing." He compliantly provided a short but devastating list of things that bothered him about Denise ranging from "your thighs" to "something about the way you touch me."

Denise felt helpless and hopeless. "What am I supposed to do, change everything? I don't even understand what he means about the way I touch him. He certainly never acted as though he didn't like it before. I'm so uptight around him now that I'm not even myself. No wonder he doesn't like me," she wept.

Denise went through a full year of renegotiated and repeatedly blown deadlines with Fred, until, with the assistance of therapy, she decided to resume control over her life and rehabilitate her self-esteem. The last time I spoke to Denise, she was very happily broken up with Fred. "There's nobody new yet in my life," she reported, "but I'm going out with some nice men who like me. I can't believe what I did to myself with Fred. It was sheer torture." Fred, by the way, soon was involved with another woman, but he just couldn't quite decide if she was the right partner for him.

Being involved in an intimate relationhip with any man who is like one or a combination of these dangerous types is very likely to be a major reason that you have low moods and depressions. There are no easy solutions when you find yourself in love with a man whose way of relating to you is fundamentally destructive to your happiness.

The cleanest advice is to stay as far away from dangerous partners as you can. If you're already involved, you must make some difficult choices. Perhaps, in your value system, the good things about the man and the relationship make staying in it worth the negative impact on your mood.

If you simply cannot or will not choose to end the relationship, for whatever reason, try at least to keep in mind that the basic problems arise from *his* personality. This external focus will serve as some degree of buffer on your mood. But I would be dishonest if I didn't tell you that the chances of this kind of man changing much are negligible. There may be some temporary improvements, but a personality disorder is a personality disorder—meaning that the problems run deep in the character structure and don't readily alter.

Even if substantial changes were to occur, the cost to your self-esteem and mood would be very high.

If you are involved in a relationship with a dangerous partner, you should consider seeking professional help for yourself. With the aid and support of a good therapist, you will have the opportunity to feel better about yourself and to examine your alternatives for gaining more control over your life and your moods.

Dangerous Assumptions

Now let's examine the other side of the story: your own contribution to problems in relationships that cause your depressions. Obviously, in the stories above, the women were not totally innocent or helpless victims. Each made certain decisions about the men and the relationships that made it possible for the men to behave as they did. If nothing else, each woman colluded a bit with the man's personality disorder by participating in a relationship in which he had the opportunity and target for acting out his psychological problems.

But women get depressed about men who don't fit any one of the dangerous types described previously. In many such instances, the causal attributions for these women's blues are beliefs, assumptions, and expectations that they hold about men, love, and life. These erroneous beliefs are dangerous assumptions that either produce the difficulties in the relationships over which they become depressed, or set the stage for them to interpret the meaning of a man's response in ways that lead to depressed moods. The dangerous assumptions a woman makes about men and love can also be the very reasons that she is attracted to and stays with a dangerous partner.

A first dangerous assumption is that the man in a woman's life "owns" or fully determines her self-worth. You will recognize this concept from my earlier comments on the hard feeling of rejection. In essence, the woman approaches the relationship as if it were an instrument to measure her value in life.

According to this way of looking at things, when the man displays positive feelings, attitudes, and behaviors toward the woman, she feels valuable, worthwhile, and esteemed as a human being. But if his feelings are less than positive, or he doesn't convey attitudes and behaviors indicative of love and interest in or commitment to the relationship, she experiences his responses as a repudiation of her value. In effect, the woman empowers the man with total control over her mood and the way she feels about herself.

Whenever you entitle another person to determine your self-worth, you invite depression into your life for at least three reasons: first, because you entirely abdicate control; second, because your self-worth is so tenuous that the slightest hint of rejection, such as a temporary cooling-down or backing-off by a man, can knock out its underpinnings; and third, because you make a damaging internal attribution without recognizing that a man's feelings, attitudes, and behavior are more about him than they are about you. While you are the stimulus to which he responds, his own personal history, experience, preferences in women, and a host of other factors determine whether or not he will be attracted to and want you.

If you ever have had the experience of collapsed self-esteem and a fit of depression because a man you liked didn't call you back or because he didn't feel the same way about you as you did about him, you probably made this dangerous assumption—albeit unconsciously—somewhere along the line. Otherwise, while you certainly could have felt disappointed or even wounded, your bottom-line self-esteem and sense of worth would not have been so badly affected.

Once you raise and strengthen your self-esteem and grant yourself unconditionally high value as a person, you will be far less inclined to give over the determination of your worth to another person. A wobbly self-esteem will easily tilt with the winds of a man's affections; a stronger self-esteem can withstand relationships not working out without assault to its foundation. Strong self-esteem comes from positive input and feedback from multiple sources in life—friends, family, work associates, and other contact points—not from just one man. This is true even when the one man is your husband or dearest love.

A second and perhaps more dangerous assumption is that you cannot live without a man or that you are nobody if you don't have a mate. Again, these thoughts are rarely explicit or conscious.

As I said at the outset to this chapter, I like men very much and I know that love relationships are of central importance to women. My own life is greatly enriched by the love for, and of, my husband and the soundness of my bond with him. But I do not for a moment wonder whether I would be a whole or complete person without him. In fact, our marriage works as well as it does because as individuals, we are both strong, capable, and confident.

As a psychotherapist and friend, I have watched women decompensate when their relationships with men were lost to them. They founder emotionally and struggle resentfully against the requirement that they take care of and depend on themselves. The dangerous assumption they made was that their men made them whole. Without their relationships, great and painful gaps in their self-esteem and emotional fabric became exposed.

Some women are raised to fear that if they become too self-reliant or capable of taking care of themselves, no man will ever want to marry them. This is a damaging and risky belief system, since it simply is not true in contemporary society. Furthermore, every woman should be prepared to face the real possibility that at some point in her life she may well have to stand on her own, live alone, and possibly be her own source of both financial and emotional support.

It is perfectly healthy and indeed even preferable to have a deep desire to share your life with a man and to seek a relationship that involves true interdependence. But such desires do not require you to believe that you would be less a person without a man in your life. You might, in fact, be less happy or fulfilled than you would prefer or desire, but you would still be a complete, worthwhile individual.

Making the assumption that you are not complete without a man is a prescription for getting deeply depressed if, for whatever reasons of fate or circumstance, you find yourself unattached and temporarily alone.

A third dangerous assumption is much like the belief system of the Tragic Hero. Essentially, the woman approaches the relationship and/or the man with whom she is involved with excessively low expectations. She may have endured so many hurtful experiences in the past, or have been so lonely and desirous of any man's attentions, that she is willing to settle for a level of satisfaction or happiness far lower than is healthy or protective of her mood.

The woman who assumes that she really doesn't deserve to be truly happy, satisfied, or treated as she might desire suffers from badly impaired self-esteem. Her low self-esteem allows her to justify or rationalize her acceptance of a relationship that is unsatisfactory by most others' standards.

At 29, Martha has suffered from chronic Depression for two years. Since the age of 22 Martha has been married to Jim, also 29. During the seven years of their marriage, Jim has had three extramarital affairs and once during their marriage left Martha for six weeks for another woman. In addition to his affairs, Jim treats Martha badly in other ways. He is demanding, unaffectionate, and highly critical. Though Jim has threatened Martha with divorce, Martha has remained committed and faithful to the marriage.

After seven years of demeaning experiences, Martha's self-esteem is very low. But Martha didn't have very high self-esteem before her marriage, either. Despite learning that Jim had slept with another woman just four days prior to their wedding, she begged him still to marry her. Martha claims that she understands "why Jim needs other women" and accepts that the treatment she receives from her abusive husband is all that she deserves and can expect.

It is not surprising that Martha suffers from a serious

mood problem. While Jim is clearly a dangerous partner, it is Martha's low self-esteem and assumption that she somehow deserves to be treated so badly that perpetuates the pathological relationship between them.

Finally, there is the dangerous and widespread assumption among women that they are primarily responsible for the outcomes of relationships with men. Again not completely conscious, this assumption lies behind a woman's obsessive efforts to try to change the man with whom she is involved. She struggles to find the "right" things to do that will somehow unlock his affections or flick the switch that turns on intimate behavior and commitment.

A relationship's outcome depends on the mutual and joint contribution of both partners. When you assume all or most of the blame for things going sour or downhill in a relationship, you feed your sense of inadequacy and low self-esteem. If the relationship fails or ends, your overassumption of responsibility is likely to produce intense feelings of failure, guilt, remorse, self-recrimination, and various assorted other emotions, all of which trigger depression.

While it is often the case that women take the emotional lead in relationships because they are less inhibited than men about emotional expression and generally less reticent about commitment, it does not follow that they should assume the majority of responsibility for whether the relationship ultimately "succeeds"—whether it culminates in marriage, whether it runs smoothly and satisfactorily to both partners, and so forth.

When the woman overassumes responsibility, she is quite likely to impose her own expectations for how a relationship "should" or "should not" function, or how the man "should" or "should not" behave or feel as standards for judging her own level of satisfaction or her partner's performance. In other words, if you were to assume total responsibility for the direction and outcome of your relationship, you would evaluate how you were doing, as well as how the relationship and your partner were doing, against your personal and perhaps private expectations. If those expectations were unrealistic, the risk of depression would be high indeed.

If you feel responsible for the relationship and you believe your partner *should* make a commitment to you by a given point in time and he does not, you are likely to judge yourself as having failed. This internalized blame for the disappointment breeds feelings of inadequacy and depression.

Assuming responsibility for what your partner should and should not do is also risky in that such expectations typically engender conflict, resentment, and charges of manipulation. In turn, the conflict and anger become hard feelings that trigger depression in the woman, her partner or both.

Too Much Crying— It's Not That Hard

I am sure you have heard many times that a good relationship requires lots of hard work. While the sentiment is true—in the sense that love requires attention, care, and nurturance—the so-called hard work involved in making a relationship successful should not feel like doing 10 years of hard labor. In fact, it ought to feel like the kind of hard work that you love to do.

Many women whom I have treated clinically stay in relationships in which they are brutally unhappy because they simply don't have a decision rule for when to stop trying. Because they hold on tightly to the notion of "hard work," which they confuse with suffering, these women frankly do not know when it is time to give up and get out.

I realize that these statements might sound somewhat unexpected from a psychologist, especially if you believe that psychologists are always in the business of saving relationships at whatever price. This certainly is neither my philosophy of life nor of therapy. On the contrary, I take a rather outspoken position on the issue of how many tears and how much "hard work" are healthy. A love relationship that causes more pain than pleasure is a losing investment of time, effort, and affection.

I do not mean to say that close, intimate relationships do not involve some degree of fighting, occasional hurt, and periods when bad feelings may become even more salient than love. But on balance, if a relationship makes you cry much of the time, or if the hard work constitutes grueling, one-sided laborious efforts that meet with little success, then take another close look at your choices.

A warm, stable, loving, intimate relationship is the best haven you will find against the vicissitudes of life and blues in the night. But a cold, unstable, rejecting, distant, and demeaning relationship is damaging to your emotional and physical health.

There is such a thing as too much crying and too much hard work to make a relationship worthwhile. If the cost of staying with a man is that you must endure recurrent, painful depressions, the price you are paying might just be too high.

PART FOUR

Action

19

◆

D.I.B.'S: Depression-Incompatible Behaviors

◆

Never mistake motion for action.

—ERNEST HEMINGWAY

The first set of activities you will employ to reverse your low moods are D.I.B.'s—Depression-Incompatible Behaviors.

The rationale for engaging in behaviors that are incompatible with the state of depression is the Incongruity Principle. This means that when your mood and your actions are not in sync with one another, your mind will automatically adjust to correct the incompatibility by changing one to fit the other. Thus, if your behaviors are not compatible with a mood of depression, your mind will naturally set in motion a corrective drive to change your mood so that it becomes more compatible with your actions.

D.I.B.'s can include a wide range of activities. The selection below is based on research that has shown what most depressed people tend to do (and tend not to do) and, conversely, what people who are in positive moods tend to do (and not do). By pursuing activities characteristic of positive moods, you will bring the Incongruity Principle into play and bring up your down mood so that it is more in line and compatible with your actions.

255

Physical Activity

Any kind of active physical exercise is incompatible with feeling depressed. Generally, when the activity requires concentration and strategy in addition to physical movement, the effectiveness will be even greater. But activities you do alone that don't require much concentration also are perfectly acceptable.

Solitary physical activities can include walking, jogging, working out in a gym, swimming, bicycling (stationary or moving), aerobics, dancing, jumping rope, and rebounding (miniature trampolining), as well as many others. Since depression usually involves a turning down of your internal metabolic setting, activities that generate the "aerobic effect" of accelerated heart rate and increased oxygen intake will also serve to give your metabolic rate a jump start.

Some recent nutritional research has shown that timing moderately active physical exercise, such as walking, bicycling, or swimming if you do it within 20 to 30 minutes after a meal can greatly enhance the metabolic increase effect of the exercise. This is particularly true if the meal is relatively light but composed largely of complex carbohydrates such as fruits, vegetables, bread, potatoes, and grains.

I often refer my patients to a diet book by Peter M. Miller, Ph.D., called *The Hilton Head Metabolism Diet,* specifically for the exercise program. The diet as outlined works quite successfully for weight loss. But if no weight loss is desired, the exercise program can be followed without a reduction in caloric intake just for antidepressant purposes.

Essentially, *The Hilton Head Metabolism Diet* exercise regimen calls for two 20-minute workouts per day, timed to follow two of four scheduled meals (breakfast, lunch, dinner, and snack) within 20 to 30 minutes of each meal's completion. Recommended exercises include walking, rebounding, rowing machine work, stationary or moving bicycling, swimming, or free-form dancing.

I can personally attest to the antidepressant value of this regimen, as I have followed the program myself for more than three years. The metabolic boost (Miller calls it the "thermic effect") of the exercise not only helps to keep calories consumed at an optimal level for weight control, but also gives you greater energy, helps reduce stress, and stimulates a positive mood as well.

A broad range of physical activities falls under the heading "sports and games." Some require a team, others only a partner. These kinds of activities have the added bonus of social interaction and the stimulation or arousal value of competition, plus the distraction value of concentration. Together, this combination is thoroughly incompatible with feeling depressed.

It is important that you select exercises and sports that are pleasurable for you to do. There is no sense in doing something that you don't enjoy. Try to approach whatever physical activity you select with an attitude of gaining pleasure, building skill, improving your physical health and overall well-being, and just plain having fun.

Mastery—a sense of accomplishment and special skill attainment—and *pleasure* are psychological states that are incompatible with depression. Therefore, you can combat depressive moods by learning a new physical activity or sport that requires novel skills and promises enjoyment. For example, you might take up learning tennis with a pro, or learn to ride horses, get certified to scuba dive, learn to sail, or try ice-skating or any other sport that appeals to you and is within your financial limits.

You will recall from the chapter called "Blue Alert" that your first line of defense against a prodrome or warning of the blues should be to engage in physical activity. This is equally true once you are already in a depressed mood and want to get yourself up. When you feel down, do something that involves physical activity as soon as you can.

I appreciate that you may not be able to engage in your favorite sport on a moment's notice in the middle of a workday. However, you can make plans to do so at your first opportunity. Just knowing that you have a physical activity to which you can look forward will help to counter your blues.

But there is more that you can do. If you work in any kind of private office, can easily get to a private room, or if you are at home, close the door and try running in place or doing jumping jacks for a few minutes. Don't worry about how it looks, just get your heart pumping and your activity level going. Or, leave your office or home if you can and go for a brisk walk. This action is the purest D.I.B. you can do: *Move* when you feel depressed.

One last comment about physical activity: The less you dwell on negative thoughts or worries while you exercise or play a sport, the better. If you are playing, keep your mind on the game. Suspend worries until after the game is over and they'll look different to you after you've had some fun and relaxation. If you are walking or jogging, try plugging some music or a good news or talk show into your ears with a portable radio or tape recorder. If you are exercising in a gym, count repetitions. By concentrating on counting, you will interrupt negative thoughts.

Socialize and Genuinely Listen to Others

Research on depression shows that when you are in a down mood you will be likely to withdraw from social contact, focus thoughts and attention on yourself and your problems, and become preoccupied. You probably know this about yourself and that is why you feel that you won't be "good company" if you go out when you are feeling low.

But the Incongruity Principle suggests just the opposite: When you feel down, go out and socialize. Don't permit yourself to withdraw and become isolated. Seek the company of other people, preferably others who are in good spirits and whom you typically enjoy when you are in a good mood. Do this even at work if possible. Find a reason to go talk to some colleagues about a project or set a lunch date to be with some friends or co-workers. Accept social invitations and initiate invitations on your own.

It is vitally important for you to be outgoing and interested in other people if you want to reverse your blue moods with D.I.B.'s Do *not* use your time with other people to cry to them or complain about your low mood and problems. This completely defeats the purpose of seeking the company of others at D.I.B. Instead, be a genuinely good listener. This means that you will ask questions of others and try to stay focused and concerned about their responses.

I have often noted that after spending a long day in my office seeing patients, my own mood is improved. This may seem quite surprising, since many people remark, "Being a therapist must be a real downer. You sit and listen to other people's problems all day long. You must get so depressed!"

Of course, there are days when I've heard some particularly tragic stories that make me feel sad. But on balance, the general effect of my staying involved with my patients' problems is to distract me from my own. The mood-raising effect is equally present if I spend a few hours in a meeting as a management consultant planning a training seminar or strategy for managing a corporate crisis. By caring about something other than what is going on in my own head or life, my mood is altered for the better.

The reason for this fortunate effect of my work is that talking and being with others—provided you do so with the right mindset of caring, listening, and being actively involved in what is important to them—is a D.I.B. You can practice a parallel set of D.I.B.'s by engaging in activities that are part of your work or personal life that involve reaching out to others, being among them, talking with them and being a good listener to both their problems and joys.

Altruistic D.I.B.'s

Depressed people also avoid giving assistance to others or even being friendly. By doing the opposite, you will be invoking the mood-altering effect of a D.I.B.

A number of altruistic opportunities are available to you each day. Going out of your way to assist a stranger or doing something thoughtful and considerate for a friend are examples. Joining and becoming actively involved in a charitable organization is not only altruistic, but also involves the bonus of socializing.

The truth is that doing nice things for other people makes you feel good about yourself. And feeling good about yourself is anathema to depression. Don't wait until others ask you to do a favor. Try to anticipate what somebody with whom you work, or a friend, or someone in your family might need or just really like.

It is a D.I.B. to adopt a friendly, giving, open, helpful attitude in life. You may have wondered how some people find the energy to be friendly and willing to help others. By acting in a way that is altruistic and generous, they are giving their mood states constant positive feedback. When you are nice to people, they start to do nice things back. They smile at you and begin to care about how you are doing. Feeling that others care about you is a major counteracting force on depression.

Dr. Hans Selye, the father of modern stress theory, espoused an entire philosophy of life designed to be protective against negative stress and its consequences, including depression. He called his philosophy "altruistic egoism." Selye advocated taking care of yourself in the world by doing good things for others so that you will earn their love, kindness, and hence protection in return. Ultimately, Selye maintained, the ego (self) is best served by altruistic deeds.

Be Benevolent to Yourself

In addition to being kind and giving to others, doing nice things for yourself directly is also incompatible with depression. As you have learned, when people are in low moods, they tend to be distinctly unkind to themselves. They are self-critical and derisive; they underreward themselves; they overadminister punishments; and they treat themselves as though they were thoroughly undeserving and unworthy.

Make a list of nice things you could do or say for yourself. Things to do might include buying or making yourself a gift, indulging yourself in a massage or facial, buying some fresh flowers for your home or office, getting yourself your favorite food (if weight is not a major concern), rereading your favorite book, listening to your favorite music, or anything else that is special and pleasurable to you.

Include in your list positive things that you have to say on your own behalf. If you have been doing altruistic D.I.B.'s, you will have many more good things to say about yourself as a result. You *are* a good, nice person because you have been doing nice things for others. Giving yourself praise instead of criticism is incompatible with being depressed.

Compliments, Praise, and Affection—Giving and Receiving

Of special importance in the categories of kindnesses you can give to others and to yourself are compliments, praise, and physical affection. Once again, research shows that people who are depressed are less likely not only to praise themselves but to give praise to others. And depressed people withhold compliments and physical affection. Moreover, they are particularly adept at either discouraging others from giving them compliments and affection or at discounting the value of a compliment by saying such things as "He really didn't mean that. He was just saying it because he feels sorry for me" or "I don't look good today at all. I look terrible."

It is incompatible with depression to let yourself receive and absorb compliments, praise and affection from others. If you allow such actions to have their intended positive effects, your mood will be lifted because your self-esteem will be enhanced. Try letting others praise or compliment you and responding with an appreciative "Thank you" instead of a discounting comment. It will make other people feel better, too, when you allow them to say nice things to you.

Be forthcoming with praise and verbal reward for others. In general, adults tend to be reticent about praising good behavior with one another so as not to appear "mushy" or "easy" with others. But, like children and pets, adults need to have a pat on the back and verbal praise to sustain positive behavior, too. Let people know when they have done a good job, or something nice for you, or anything else that you appreciate. Compliment honestly, but freely. Most people can sense a disingenuous compliment, but they also sense when you mean what you are saying and appreciate your attention.

When you feel down, seek and be receptive to physical affection. The best way to get affection is, of course, to give it. If the kind of affection you desire is simply not available to you (as from a man, for example), then seek a replacement like a hug from a child or cuddles from a pet. While the latter may not fill the bill completely, affection of any kind still feels good and counteracts the blues.

Pleasurable Activities

When you are depressed, your activities generally consist of a disproportionate number of things you have to do but that are not enjoyable, pleasant, or positive for you. These include household chores, errands, or perhaps work projects. This is because you feel as though you have limited energy and you had better spend what you've got on what you absolutely have to do.

In addition, since you feel undeserving and low, you won't tend to allow or permit yourself to seek out pleasurable things to do. In fact, if you get the blues a lot, you probably do not have enough sources of pleasurable activity in your current lifestyle.

Begin composing a list of positive, pleasurable activities. Some of the other D.I.B.'s mentioned above, such as physical sports or exercise, socializing, and doing nice things for yourself, may be included on your list. Write down at least 25 activities that you think would give you pleasure.

The activities need not require a great deal of time. Some items on your list, in fact, should require very little time, less than 15 minutes, to accomplish. Others might require advance planning time and several days or even weeks to accomplish, such as going on a vacation or out on the town for a series of entertaining Saturday nights in a row.

The important thing is that you (a) know what kinds of

things give you pleasure; and (b) that you do at least five pleasurable activities per week, and even more if possible.

Below is the pleasurable activities list of one of my patients. You may include many of the same activities on your own list, but be sure to personalize and tailor yours as much as possible to your tastes.

Positive Pleasurable Activities

1. Going shopping
2. Going to a movie
3. Having lunch with friends
4. Planning a trip for the summer
5. Cooking a gourmet meal
6. Painting in oils
7. Reading the comics
8. Buying some records and books
9. Signing up for a lecture series
10. Taking a tennis lesson
11. Writing notes or letters to friends
12. Buying and sending funny cards
13. Brightening my office with flowers
14. Going to Disneyland with my kids
15. Making love
16. Buying some new makeup
17. Doing a jigsaw puzzle
18. Playing cards with friends
19. Walking my dog in the park
20. Taking photographs of my kids
21. Going out to dinner with my husband
22. Planning a special evening "date" with my husband
23. Having a big family Sunday night dinner
24. Going on a Sunday picnic
25. Going to the art museum

Diversion and
Distraction Techniques

Since your natural inclination when you feel down is to begin ruminating about your problems, the prescriptive D.I.B. is to divert your attention away from rumination by engaging your mind in distracting activities. Many of the D.I.B.'s above also will function as diversionary tactics. Socializing, talking to others about them rather than about you, and physical exercise work to counteract depression in part because of their distraction value.

A number of other mental diversionary techniques can serve as behaviors incompatible with rumination and depression. Crossword puzzles, computer games or new programs, or just balancing your checkbook require a level of concentration that makes worrying about your mood or problems temporarily impossible. Other hobbies, such as gourmet cooking from relatively complicated recipes, needlepoint, knitting, sewing, and others are effective diversionary tactics for depressive rumination because of the measurement, concentration, and counting involved.

"Escape" entertainment such as movies, plays, or fast-paced books are effective mental diversions. Listening to radio or television talk shows or focusing your concentration on audiotapes of books, self-help programs, or foreign-language self-instruction are also excellent for diverting your mental energy from your own problems.

You also can project "movies" in your own mind by utilizing visual imagery techniques. To practice imagery, lie down on a couch or your bed, close your eyes, and concentrate your mental energy on a specific scene. Ask yourself to "see" someplace that makes you feel peaceful and relaxed; or ask your mind to envision the most beautiful scenery or building interior that you have ever seen; or, you may call up to your mental screen a pleasant, funny, sexy, or exciting memory. Whatever imagery you conjure up will require a sufficient concentration of mental activity to be incompatible with inward, introspective, critical, or negative thought.

Mental diversion will only serve to distract you from depressive thought for a limited period of time. That is fine for your purpose, since you are merely trying to reduce the total amount of time and energy that is channeled toward depressive rumination and worry. If you divert your concentration for only 30 minutes by completing even a mundane mental task, that is 30 minutes less that you have available to spend focusing on and fueling your low mood.

It is important that you not expect perfect performance on your diversionary D.I.B.'s. Since depression interrupts the ability to concentrate, you may find that getting your mind off your mood and onto other activities or thoughts is difficult. Do not fault yourself for this or discourage yourself from trying. The very fact that you make an effort *not* to think about yourself and your problems for a period of time will help to reverse the downward mood slide.

Look at the World Through Rose-colored Glasses

The opposite of depressed thought and perception is viewing and interpreting your experience through a positivity bias. An effective D.I.B., therefore, is to go through an entire day with the mindset that you are looking at life through rose-colored glasses. To do so means that you direct your attention toward noticing and remembering positive information or feedback, while discounting or selectively filtering out the negative.

To put on your mental rose-colored glasses, give yourself the following instructions: (1) Look for the most positive thing you can see in all the people that you observe or with whom you interact in a given day; (2) keep a written log of every compliment, pleasantry, kind word, reinforcement, or other verbal or nonverbal praise either that you generate or that others direct your way; and (3) at the close of the day, review your experiences and thoughts and write down the three best things that happened to you.

Viewing your life and the people in it with the kind of positivity filters that these instructions require will serve to distract you from selective attention to negativity and provide you with positive mental feedback that is incompatible with depression.

At first you may find the instructions quite difficult to follow, since your natural tendency when you feel low is to be down about other people as well. But as you continue to follow the rose-colored instructions, you will find that the positivity slant on your way of looking at the world becomes easier and more natural. Most important, your mood will be altered to become more compatible with the positively biased perception that your rose-colored glasses create.

Reviewing Positive Memories

Another natural reaction to being in a low mood is to become focused on negative thoughts and memories. The D.I.B. to counteract this tendency is selective exposure to material that directly stimulates positive associations. Try curling up with some old photo albums and recall the feelings associated with a fun trip or vacation, or some memorable celebration. If you keep old letters and postcards from friends or diaries from times in your life when you were happy, reading through them may help you recall positive feelings and sensations.

If you don't have tangible memories like photographs or letters, you may use your mental records through visual imagery. Select two or three very positive memories from various periods of your life. Be careful that you do not focus on thoughts about a relationship or experience that ended in a sad way, since your "happy" reminiscences may only serve to cause you pain. Just ask your mind to return to the kinds of memories that simply make you smile warmly or laugh out loud, or bask in the glow of the positive emotion that you associate with a certain period, occasion, or experience in your life.

Set aside a predetermined period for reviewing positive memories. You might give yourself an hour to look through old photo albums, or 15 minutes to conjure up visual images. The purpose is to fill a period of time with as many concentrated positive thoughts as possible to combat the flood of negativity that is so common when you feel low.

Laughter is the Best Medicine

This old adage points to one of the most effective D.I.B.'s. Anti-depressant brain biochemicals are secreted when you laugh. A real bout of belly-laughing can produce feelings of deep relaxation. And laughter is contagious. If you can get yourself laughing, other people around you at home or work will pick up on the mirth and the environment will become incompatible with staying depressed.

The trick is to get yourself chuckling when your inclination is to cry. Norman Cousins, former editor of *Saturday Review,* wrote a best-selling book, *Anatomy of an Illness,* in which he described how his own laughter therapy helped to rebuild his immune system to the point of ultimately triumphing over a near-fatal neuromuscular disease. Cousins checked himself out of the hospital where he was becoming increasingly depressed and into a hotel where he made arrangements to have a video recorder connected to his television. Every day, Cousins watched reruns of old Groucho Marx television shows and other personally selected entertainment that he knew would tickle his funny bone. And he laughed his way back to health.

Norman Cousins's cure involved some standard medical treatment as well as laughing. But his experience and philosophy of positive emotion helped launch the field of psychoneuroimmunology, which studies the relationship between positive emotions and immune response.

You can follow Cousins's lead and launch a counterattack on your own low mood. If you have a video recorder, rent some funny movies, comedy concerts, or old television shows. Practice your D.I.B. by watching the screen and giving yourself permission to forget your low mood and troubles temporarily and experience the positive sensations of smiling, giggling, and laughing out loud.

There are other ways to expose yourself to humorous stimuli designed to elicit laughter. There are records or tapes of comedic routines and always a few comedies playing at local movie theaters. Every bookstore has a humor section with joke books, cartoon anthologies, and novels or nonfiction works by noted humorists.

You also have a storehouse of personal memories associated with laughter. Again, using imagery, ask yourself to "see" a scene from your own experience in which you laughed almost hysterically or to the point where you had difficulty stopping or regaining your composure. Everyone has at least a few such memories, even if they go back to childhood or adolescence.

Approaching D.I.B.'s: Setting Your Intention

Any and all of the D.I.B.'s in this chapter, as well as any you discover on your own, will work to combat the blues provided you (a) do them, (b) believe that they will help improve your mood, and (c) intend to get out of your depression.

Without the right set of beliefs and intentions, you will act only to sabotage the effectiveness of your activity program. The paradox of activity-based treatments for low moods is that if you spontaneously felt like or had the energy for doing the activities, you wouldn't be in a low mood in the first place. So you must approach the D.I.B.'s initially with the intention of *forcing* yourself, if necessary, to get in gear and *do something active* that is incompatible with depression.

A degree of mental discipline will be necessary as well. If you go for a walk or to a party but spend the whole time internally resisting or thinking about your problems or unhappiness, the behavior will not in fact be incompatible with depression. In other words, if you socialize with other people but you keep your mind on what is making you feel blue, your actions actually are more compatible with depression than with diversion. In fact, the contrast between your thoughts and the gaiety around you might even deepen your low mood. Similarly, if you use your walking time to ruminate and obsess, the physical benefits of moving are bound to be outweighed by the dragging mental weight of depression that you bring along on your walk.

Don't forget to reward yourself for the D.I.B.'s that you perform. Give yourself appropriate verbal praise or tangible rewards. Encourage yourself to continue and try to do a few more D.I.B.'s each day. As you will discover, when you string together enough behaviors in a day that are incompatible with depression, you will be living your life in a way that is protective of you and preventative of low moods and the blues.

20

◆

Self-esteem Builders

◆

To love one's self is the beginning of a lifelong romance.
—OSCAR WILDE

Activities that build your self-esteem will raise your mood and spirits in the process.

As you have learned throughout this book, depression and low self-esteem are inextricably bound together in ways that often make cause and effect hard to disentangle. It may seem to you that the order of things is that if you just felt better about yourself, you wouldn't feel so depressed. But the causal arrow arguably points in the other direction, too. This would mean that if you could change your mood for the better, your view of yourself would improve as well.

In either event, once you develop some active means to raise your self-esteem, you will be starting a positive feedback loop between your mood and feelings about yourself, so that improvements in the one will necessarily uplift the other.

Self-Inventory and Assets Lists

The first step in self-esteem building is to do an inventory of your assets. If you have been feeling low and down on yourself, you probably have more than ample information about your liabilities or shortcomings. In fact, your depression has undoubtedly inflated your perception of your flaws out of all reasonable proportion so that you may have even forgotten that you have valuable assets at all.

Because of the negativity bias of depression, it is best to conduct your assets inventory from a perspective other than your own. Think of the person who knows you best or most intimately and who feels positively toward you. This might be your mother, a best friend, your husband or boyfriend, or even your therapist. Choose anyone who has good personal knowledge of you and your character.

Write down how that person would identify your assets or good things about you in each of the following areas:

1. Your abilities
2. Your achievements
3. The way you treat other people
4. The attitudes you have about other people and life in general
5. Your special talents
6. Your inner thoughts and feelings
7. Your dreams, aspirations, and goals
8. Your physical appearance and characteristics
9. Your interests and activities
10. Your family, education, and other relevant background data
11. Other personality traits and aspects of your disposition

Try to identify at least three to five assets in each category. By assuming the perspective of another person who is not negatively biased by your low mood, you may find it easier to access thoughts about your assets. Of course, you may add to the list any additional assets *you* know about yourself but of which the person who knows you best may not be aware.

Read over your inventory of assets. Select the 10 assets on which you place the highest value. Try to put them in rank order from the one you personally value the most to the one you value the least on this list.

Keep your assets list close at hand and read it over whenever your self-esteem begins to droop. As you go through each day, try to be conscious of opportunities to show yourself and other people the 10 things about yourself that you value the most.

Shaping Yourself
in Your Ideal Image

The closer you can bring your current self-concept to the way you would most like to be, the higher your self-esteem will become. Begin by completing the following sentence *five times:*

"I would like myself much better if I were *more* . . ." Now complete this sentence *five times:*

"I would like myself much better if I were *less* . . ."

You now have 10 specific elements of your ideal self-concept. Your goal is to move your current view of yourself closer to the ideal. Notice that I did not tell you to move all the way there, only somewhat closer.

Improving your self-esteem is not an overnight process. It is a gradual, cumulative process that represents evolutionary changes in the way you see yourself. Expecting yourself to be ideal or perfect is a setup for failure. But expecting yourself to be better is a motivation for self-improvement.

The method for moving yourself closer to your ideal self is called the "act as if" approach. The most direct way to change your personality is to *act as if* you were the way you want to be. In relatively short order, your mind will follow your behavior.

Let's assume that you would feel much better about yourself if you were more confident. The first step is to break the concept of "more confident" down into quantitative, measurable, and concrete behavioral terms.

In building self-esteem, it is vitally important to ensure success. Therefore, *set your goals at attainable, realistic levels.* Start by imagining how you would be different if you were 10 percent more confident tomorrow than you are today.

How would you act differently? What kinds of behaviors, including verbal behaviors, would you do if you were 10 percent more confident? It is essential that you specify your goal in action terms.

Assume that you have answered the question this way: "If I were ten percent more confident I would have better posture, stand up taller and hold my head up with pride, and I would go up to a person whom I didn't know at a cocktail party and introduce myself."

The next step is to *act as if* you were more confident. You only have to act 10 percent more confident to be successful, and since you have specified your role in concrete terms, you know exactly what to do: Stand up straight, hold your head up with pride, and introduce yourself to one new person at a cocktail party. That's it. You don't have to do anything more to act 10 percent more confident than you are right now. Note carefully that your success in completing your "act as if" directions is in no way contingent on whether the other person likes you or even responds to you. Don't make the mistake of measuring your behavior according to how another person chooses to respond.

Continue to target four more opportunities, and the specifics of each that would mean you were 10 percent more confident, and put yourself into action. *Act as if* you are more confident. After you have completed your four "act as if" exercises, you will have taken concrete steps toward moving closer to your ideal self. And you will be ready to move 10 percent closer still.

Continue your "act as if" technique over the course of a few weeks. Remind yourself of how far along the road to becoming "more confident" you are moving.

The same technique can be applied to changing something about yourself in the other direction. For example, if you would feel a lot better about yourself if you were less sensitive to criticism, *act as if* you were. Specify how you could tell from self-observation that you had changed in the direction of becoming less sensitive. What behaviors would you see? Indicate precisely what behaviors or actions would mean that you were 10 percent less sensitive to others' criticisms; then, the next chance you get, *act as if* you are less sensitive.

Developing Mastery

Having a sense of accomplishment and doing things well are self-esteem builders. Instead of focusing on your short-comings, identify a list of four things that you do very well. These do not have to be complex or difficult things. They may be things you do every day and completely take for granted because they have become such a normal part of your daily routine. Or they may be special talents or abilities that you have not used for a long time and have partially forgotten.

After you have composed your list, put it in rank order with Number One being the least difficult and Number Four being the hardest. Every day for the next week, try to do at least one thing on the list, starting with the easiest. By including things you do very well in your daily regimen of actions to counteract depression, you are guaranteeing a defense against the criticisms and insults you hurl at yourself when you feel down, such as "I never do anything right!" or "I don't accomplish anything."

At the end of the week, give yourself a report card on your accomplishments. Use traditional A–F grades to evaluate your mastery of the four items on your list. If there are any that you grade below a B, keep them at the top of the list for the next week. Add some new things to next week's list or keep the same items from your original list. Continue to perform the things you do very well and aim for straight A's. Since this is a customized list loaded with your aptitudes, a straight-A report card is not an inflated expectation. But remember, I said "A," not "A + ."

The "What I Did" List

Just about every woman I know is so busy that she con-structs "to do" lists an arm long. Naturally, since no one human being could reasonably expect to complete everything on a Herculean "to do" list, she winds up focusing on what she didn't get done and feeling disappointed with herself.

If this sounds familiar, start keeping a "what I did" list right next to your "to do" list. Remember to include on your list all the things you do every day that you never bother to write down because they get done automatically. Compiling a daily list of what you accomplished will generate an impressive "what I did this week" list as long as your arm after seven days.

By reviewing your accomplishments, your self-esteem will be enhanced. After you give yourself due credit for all things you did get done, you may be less critical of yourself for what you never got around to doing.

Points of Pride and Sources of Distinctiveness

When you feel proud of yourself and reassured that you are a special kind of person, your self-esteem is enhanced enormously.

Instead of throwing mental darts at your self-esteem, try tossing rose petals by giving yourself reasons to feel proud and a basis for feeling distinctive. The depressed feelings of shame, guilt, and worthlessness are debilitating to self-esteem. They will be counteracted by behaviors that generate pride and a sense that you are not only worthwhile but special among women as well.

Start by reflecting back over your life during the last month. See if you can identify at least one thing you did or thought or feeling you had of which you are proud. Just getting in touch with the sense of pride in yourself is enhancing to self-esteem. As you think about a reason to feel proud of yourself, focus on the way pride operates internally. Using visual imagery, picture the pride flowing through your body, strengthening your spine, and filling your chest. Let yourself puff up. You deserve it.

Now reflect on at least one thing you did or on an aspect of your character or personality that is distinctive and special.

275

Don't make the mistake of believing that the things you do well or the ways you behave toward other people are necessarily done by everyone. Feeling special doesn't have to mean being unique; it is sufficient if you have one quality or trait that is not shared with the majority of women. Just as you did with pride, take a few moments to experience the feeling of being special. When you have something special, it is wise to treat it carefully and gently. Focus on how it feels to treat yourself carefully and gently, since you now know that you do have something special—*you.*

Doing the Most With What You've Got

In women, physical appearance and self-esteem go hand in hand. When you feel unattractive or overweight, you don't feel good about yourself. Your confidence and actual performance in many areas of life are tied to your self-image.

One of the best self-esteem builders you can do is what I call "re-foxing"—making yourself look and feel as attractive as possible. Just spending time and money on yourself is curative of the blues and low self-esteem. Moreover, doing so makes a statement that you place a high value on yourself and on your physical appearance.

There are lots of ways to improve your appearance. In the short term, you can have your hair restyled, have a facial, get a manicure and pedicure, or have your makeup done by a professional who can show you how to make the most of what you've got. And of course, you can buy yourself some sharp new clothes or just some special, indulgent accessories.

In the longer term, you can go on a diet to lose some weight (or gain some if you are too thin), and get yourself on a good exercise program for firming and toning muscles and/or reshaping your figure. You might even look into plastic surgery to correct facial features, body areas, or skin lines and wrinkles that bother you and lessen your attractiveness in your mind. Similarly, new techniques in dentistry such as bonding or "invisible" braces might correct a minor or major flaw in your appearance about which you are self-conscious.

Your primary objective is to look your best, *not* for the sake of other people, but rather to enhance the image you hold of yourself. When you feel that you have done the most with yourself and for yourself, your self-esteem will rise and remain high.

Becoming More Interesting by Being More Interested

A major blow to self-esteem is the perception that you are a dull, boring, or uninteresting person. If you worry that you don't have enough to say, the problem may well be that you are not interested in enough things.

The cure for this problem is straightforward and effective: Get interested—in people, places, and things. A wealth of information on a varied number of subjects is available to you via television, radio, lectures, newspapers, magazines, books, and films but it is up to you to avail yourself of the opportunities to learn. When you feed your mind, you will feel not only more interested and more interesting, but also stimulated, distracted from self-centered negative thinking, and probably even excited.

There are groups and social events based around common interests. Book clubs or discussion groups, political organizations, or travel clubs are just a few examples. Joining or participating in interest-based activities helps improve your self-esteem and overall mood by combining new opportunities for personal growth and learning with socializing and the support of like-minded people. If you are single, the chances of meeting a man and liking him as well are increased if you share a common interest.

The Positive Feedback Loop

Self-esteem and mood are connected in such a way that suppression of one generally leads to suppression of the other and vice versa. Taking action directly to build your self-esteem is, therefore, equivalent to acting to restore a more positive mood state. And if your mood is already good, self-esteem builders will serve to protect and maintain it.

21

◆

Worry Regulators

◆

Only one type of worry is correct: to worry because you worry too much.

—JEWISH PROVERB

To master your blue moods, you must stop worrying so much.

Worry, rumination, and obsessive negative thinking are the hallmarks of depression. Now that you have discovered so much new information about the reasons women get depressed, your natural temptation will be to do a lot of thinking. That is fine, provided that your thought content is positive, constructive, and nonrepetitive. If you let your mind wander uncontrolled, dwelling on the dark side of your problems, on self-blaming attributions, and negative predictions and memories, your mood will only grow dimmer.

Managing the blues means managing worry. The key is mental discipline and learning effective methods for regulating what you think about, how long you focus on why you feel depressed, how to stop certain thought patterns, and how to replace counterproductive worries with constructive, pleasurable thought.

Thought Stopping:
The "Stop Sign" Technique

I know just what you're thinking: "I'd love to stop worrying but I can't. It's not possible for me to stop thinking about the problems that get me down."

But it is possible to interrupt conscious thought, through a straightforward behavior modification technique called *thought stopping*. There are several different methods to accomplish thought stopping, but the one I recommend is called the STOP sign technique.

Let me tell you how I developed this method. I once treated an eight-year-old girl whose mother had left for cigarettes one evening and never returned home, leaving her and her two brothers to live with their busy, workaholic father.

The little girl was depressed and intensely worried. She told me that the reason she couldn't concentrate in school was that her mind was totally preoccupied with thoughts of whether her mother would ever come back, what would happen to her father, and with whom, ultimately, the children would live.

I told the girl that while I understood her concerns, these were not the kinds of things that eight-year-olds needed to worry about. Then I asked her if she would like to learn some secrets for how to stop worrying so much.

She insisted that she wanted nothing else more. I gave the girl some paper and crayons, and told her to draw a picture of a traffic Stop sign. She was an astute observer and a good artist, and after about 20 minutes of white-knuckled crayoning, she had a picture that was readily recognizable as a street sign.

I told her to take the picture, fold it up, and carry it with her everywhere. Then, when she started to worry, she was to take out the Stop sign and stare at the word "Stop" until her mind came to a halt.

The second secret was called "the worry box." This exercise required that her father purchase a small lock-box or miniature trunk with a key.

She came back the next week with the box. I took a three-by-five-inch pad of paper and asked her to write down one worry on each piece of paper, until she had exhausted her thoughts. The girl produced about 10 pieces of paper, each with a separate concern.

Then I asked her to select one worry to talk about and to put all the rest inside the box and to lock it. We spent about 10 minutes discussing her worry, at which point she volunteered, "I think I want my Stop sign now." And she took her neatly folded (and by now somewhat tattered) picture out of her little purse, opened it up, looked at it, closed her eyes, and then smiled up at me and said brightly, "Okay, let's talk about school!"

I have used the Stop sign technique ever since with both children and adults.

Instead of carrying around a picture of a Stop sign, you will learn to visualize a Stop sign very clearly in your mind. Try it right now: Close your eyes until you have a very clear image of a bright-red, eight-sided Stop sign with white letters that say "stop." Keep working at refining your visual image until you have it sharply in focus. Imagine the sign getting larger as if you were moving closer to it; now imagine the sign and the word, "stop," getting smaller as you distance yourself from it. Now, move it back again to a comfortable distance where you can see the whole sign and the letters clearly.

You have just stopped thinking about anything other than the Stop sign. Your mind simply cannot work effectively at developing and focusing on a visual image while continuing to worry about something else at the same time.

The next time you want to stop a thought, close your eyes and visualize a Stop sign. Do the focusing exercise, and adjust the perspective by moving closer and farther away from your visual image. Stay centered on your image for at least 30 seconds and say to yourself, "I am stopping this thought." If the worry returns, visualize the Stop sign again until the thought ceases.

The Worry Box
and Worry Time

One of the most annoying aspects of down moods and the obsessive thoughts that accompany them is that intrusive worries interfere with your concentration and completion of work throughout the day. Like my young patient, you need a worry box. And you need to set aside a predetermined period of time, preferably in the early evening, when you can worry to your heart's content.

Throughout the day, keep a pad of paper and pencil close by and simply jot down each worrisome thought that intrudes on your mind. After you write a quick note on the thought so that you can recall it later, put the piece of paper, folded up, inside a little box or container of some kind. Any kind of container will do, but I recommend that you buy yourself a special little box for this purpose. If you can get one with a lock, that's ideal.

Each time you put a worry inside the box, tell yourself that you can't deal with it now because it isn't time to worry. Your heavy worrying can only be done during a period of no more than one hour that you reserve for this purpose in the early evening. If you don't have time every evening to worry, that's just fine. Put it off to the next night's worry period. Trust me, the problems will hold.

During your assigned worry period, open your worry box and sort out your problems into piles. Why piles? Because if you are a first-class worrier, then you will no doubt have repetitive statements of the same problem in your box. Sort the obsessive, redundant worries into piles. Then throw away all but one piece of paper from each pile. You really don't need all the repetitions to crowd your mind—do you?

Okay. Now worry away. Except, you're going to have to worry slightly differently than you probably have before.

The Worry Journal

Instead of just keeping the worries inside your own head, you will be writing down all of your thoughts—uncensored—

in a journal. Write the general problem from your worry box collection on the top of the page. Then, let your mind just stream ahead and transcribe its contents onto paper.

It is up to you how many different worries you want to address during a particular worry period. If you have 10 concerns in your worry box, you probably won't have time for all of them during one worry period. Simply put them back for the next evening. Decide at the beginning of the hour how many minutes you will allocate to worrying about each issue or problem. *Then follow your schedule.*

One more thing: Don't write down the same thought in your journal more than three times. Worries, as you will soon see, are obsessional, circular, and as repetitive as a broken record. To break the habit of obsessing, simply replace writing out a repetitive thought—once you have reached your limit of three—with a big X mark on the page. Make an X mark for every recurrent, repetitive thought to indicate when you have had that same thought more than three times during one worry period.

Reducing Worrying Time

One hour is the outside limit for constructive worry. There is value to a certain amount of worry, provided the thoughts are directed toward constructive problem solving and don't involve repetitive, circular replays of negativity.

You will soon find that one hour is probably too much time for your worry period. This will happen as you automatically reduce repetitive thinking by becoming conscious of it and using X's to replace redundant thoughts. Further, over the course of even a few days, you will tire of writing down the same problems or worries over and over again. This means that you are making progress.

Once you feel that 60 minutes is too long, reduce your worry period by five minutes per day. You can start the reduction on Day Two if you like, or on the second week if that feels more comfortable. In any event, you should start reducing the length of your worry period by the fifteenth consecutive day. Then continue to subtract five minutes each day.

Most of my patients are able to reduce their constructive worry time down to five or 10 minutes total within 10 to 12 days. All of them report improvements in their mood as their worry time decreases.

The Pie-Chart
Principle of Worrying

Most worriers experience their own mind as a burden. "I just wish I could stop worrying so much about what others think of me," one patient says. "I'd love to stop worrying about money all the time. If I spent more time working and less time worrying, I'd probably be rich," quips another. "My mother-in-law drives me so crazy," still another complains, "she'd be thrilled if she only knew how much of my precious time I spend worrying about her antics."

The common theme of all these complaints is that the amount or extent of worrying is too great. Nobody is actually saying that they would like to stop worrying altogether. In fact, were I to respond with flip answers such as "Don't think about money" or "Just ignore other people" or "Forget your mother-in-law," my advice would likely be rejected out of hand as unrealistic and even undesirable.

A certain amount of worrying can be productive and appropriate. Appropriate worry about money, for example, might involve sound financial planning or setting budgetary guidelines. Similarly, some amount of concern or worrying about other people, including mothers-in-law, seems inevitable and probably adaptive if it helps you to discover social behaviors that effectively gain what you want while avoiding or minimizing criticism.

The real issue is: How much worry about a particular subject is enough? And how much is too much?

You will be able to limit your worrying time and contain your obsessive ruminative thinking once you adopt the "pie-chart principle" of worrying. This technique has been one of the most effective ways for my patients to reverse and control thought habits that were considered by them to be virtually uncontrollable prior to practicing the method.

The first step in the pie-chart exercise is to identify a particular subject of your worrying. It might, for example, be money, or your relationship, or something about your job, or maybe it's the very fact of your depressed moods you are worrying about. The selection of a subject area should be constrained only by the requirement that it feels to you like something you are worrying about excessively.

Having identified the topic, the next question is: What *percentage* of your time do you currently spend worrying about this issue? This estimate need not be based on an actual calculation of hours. Merely make a judgment of how much of your total waking time during a typical day is currently spent consumed with worries about the subject in question. Is it 50 percent of your time? Do you worry as much as 75 percent? Only 10? Whatever feels like the most accurate percentage is the baseline from which you will measure improvement.

The next question is: What percentage of your time would you *like* to dedicate to worrying about this subject? Given that a certain amount of worrying is natural and probably useful, decide on the *maximum* amount of time in a typical day—again as a percentage—that you consider appropriate. Perhaps you would like to cut your worry time in half. Then your answer to this question will be one half of the percentage that you estimated you are currently spending on the subject. Maybe you would like to cut down worrying on this issue to as little as possible—2 percent, or 5. Again, whatever you elect to be the amount of time you find acceptable or desirable to worry is fine, as long as it is *less* than what you currently are doing.

You now have two numbers, one representing the percentage of your time that you currently are worrying (which you believe represents too much time), and the other, the percentage of time to which you would like to reduce your worrying.

The next step is to draw two pie-chart diagrams that show each percentage graphically as a portion of a whole circle or "pie." Color the portion of each circle that represents the worrying time in a dark color, preferably black or dark gray; color the remainder of the two pies in a bright sunny color such as yellow.

Now take a good long look at the two pie charts. In particular, compare the amount of "bright" unworried time that is available in the second chart (depicting the reduced amount of worrying) with that available in the first. Underneath each pie chart, write the percentage of worrying that the chart represents.

Here is a set of pie charts from one of my patients who wanted to cut back her worrying time about finances from a baseline level of 40 percent to a desirable but still realistic level of 10 percent:

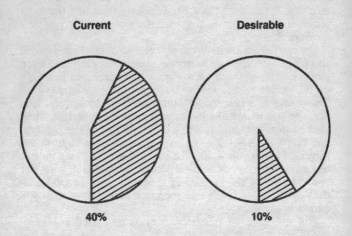

Current **Desirable**

40% 10%

Pie Chart Worry Reduction Technique

You now can use the pie charts as a graphic standard or criterion against which you can judge quickly and easily whether your worrying time on any given day has exceeded or is within the acceptable limits of your allocations. My patients make several copies of their charts and keep them in locations in which they are apt to start worrying. For example, the patient whose pie charts are illustrated here keeps one set taped to the dashboard of her car, since her mind wanders to worries while she is commuting to and from work. Another one is taped to her bathroom mirror, and she keeps one by each telephone (including in her office), since as she says, she worries "out loud to my friends."

"By keeping the charts in places where I can easily look at them," she explained, "I am very conscious of whether or not my worrying time is within the ten-percent acceptable limit. When I sense that I've spent my maximum for the day, I just cut it off. It's actually easy. I turn on the radio, take a look at the old chart and remind myself what a total waste of time it was to worry about money forty percent of my waking hours. I look at the ten-percent pie chart and smile at all the open space I have in the circle to spend thinking about more pleasant things."

Incidentally, the pie charts do not require any labels beyond the percentages, since they will be perfectly understandable to you. This is an advantage if you don't want their meaning to be clear to others.

Replacement Thoughts

When you have succeeded in reducing your worrying periods and the percentage of time you allocate for worrying about a particularly troublesome issue in your life, you will have freed up more time for thinking about something other than negative concerns and worries.

For hard-core worriers, though, worry is such a deeply ingrained habit that they do not immediately know what else to think about if not of their troubles. To help you develop a repertoire of replacement thoughts to fill in the time previously spent on worrying, write 10 completions of the following statement: "Instead of worrying, I'd rather think about . . ."

The replacement thoughts that you produce with this exercise should be about ideas, plans, memories, or fantasies that make you feel happy, interested, excited, or otherwise pleasantly engaged or aroused. The next time you hit your limit on worrying time, take out your list of replacement thoughts and pick one of them to think about instead of your worries.

The Worry Implosion-Replacement Thought Tape

The final technique for worry regulation involves making an audiocassette tape. Ideally, if you spend a significant amount of time driving, your tape should be the type that can be played in your car if it is equipped with a tape deck. In any event, use whatever equipment you have to record a tape of 30 minutes' duration on each side.

Side One of your custom-made worry-regulation tape will consist of a monologue of worries straight from your journal. Simply dictate onto tape, with as much tension, concern, anxiety, and feeling in your voice as you can muster, the worries that you wrote down during a series of nightly worry periods. When you come across an X on the page, signifying that you have had a repetitive thought, repeat on the tape any one of the redundant worries on the page. In other words, for these purposes, make the tape as redundant, repetitive, and obsessional as possible.

Continue your monologue until you have recorded at least 20 and as much as 30 minutes of uninterrupted worries.

On Side Two of the tape, you will record a running monologue of pleasant replacement thoughts. This time you may need to write out a script from your list of replacement thoughts before you actually dictate. If you are comfortable dictating your free associations, using the list only as a prompter, then the written script will not be necessary. The objective is to fill the 30 minutes of Side Two with a stream of pleasant thoughts, using a vocal tone and quality that is consistent with the content of your replacement thoughts.

The concept of worry implosion means that by listening to the first side of your tape, you will be virtually assaulting yourself with anxieties and worries, imploding your psyche with highly uncomfortable stimuli. But don't worry. As you will rapidly discover, listening to Side One of the tape will become a boring rather than agitating experience. Most of my patients say that they can't stand to listen to themselves worrying for longer than about three minutes. Their explanation for turning off the tape is not that the worries make them feel nervous or upset, but, instead, that they can't bear listening to themselves whining and complaining. The implosion technique operates, paradoxically, to desensitize you to the content of the tape and thus to take the psychological "upset value" out of your worries.

The second side, not surprisingly, will be much more enjoyable to hear. Many of my patients prefer to turn on the replacement-thought tape in their cars instead of music. When they do turn it off, it is generally because they want to continue thinking about a particular idea on the tape rather than go on to the next recorded replacement thought.

The tape will aid you in making a critical *choice* about whether or not you really want to worry. When you find yourself engaging in ruminative, negative thoughts, ask yourself if this is really what you want to be doing. To remind yourself of the choice you have, listen to Side One of your tape. Say to yourself, "This is what I sound like when I worry." After you listen for as long as you can tolerate it, stop the tape and ask yourself, "Would I rather worry or think about more pleasant things?" Now play Side Two and say to yourself, "This is what I can choose to think about and this is how I sound when I don't choose to worry."

Worry is a bad habit. But with determination and the right techniques, bad habits can be broken. The choice is up to you.

22

◆

Active Problem Solving

◆

I always view problems as opportunities in work clothes.

—HENRY KAISER

If your worries are over some thorny dilemmas, part of your activity program should include problem solving.

Chances are that your depressed mood has made you feel debilitated or inadequate in the face of difficult decisions or life problems. To overcome your tendency to give up or become overwhelmed by the seeming complexities of your particular issues, you will need a directive, step-by-step approach to decision making and problem solving. If you follow the steps outlined in this chapter, you may be assured of making a high-quality decision. This is not to say that you will be guaranteed of finding a perfect solution or of becoming invincible in terms of making mistakes. But I can promise that the technique of active problem solving will ensure that you make a careful, intentional, and thoughtful search for solutions and that you make the most well-advised choice of the possible alternatives with as full anticipation of their consequences as you can realistically expect without a crystal ball.

290

The Seven-Step Method

The first step is to define your problem. Specifically, your definition should be cast as a question of what to do in regard to a certain problematical situation, dilemma, conflict, or source of unhappiness.

Step Two requires that you open your mind to all possible—however improbable—alternative solutions. You will recall from our earlier discussion of the cognitive effects of stress and depression that your tendency when confronted with a difficult decision will be to stop prematurely in your search for alternative solutions, before you have thoroughly exhausted all possibilities. To counteract the tendency toward premature closure, brainstorm for answers in the most free, unconstrained, and creative way possible. You may do this alone or with the help of a friend, family member, or therapist.

In your brainstorming, remember to include "Do nothing" and/or "Keep on doing the same thing that I'm doing now" as possible alternatives, because choosing to do nothing still constitutes a choice. Don't exclude any alternatives from your list, no matter how unlikely or undesirable they may seem at first glance. Sometimes the best solutions are the ones that first appear improbable. When you have written down every possible alternative solution or decision option that you can think of, take a break for at least 15 minutes. When you return, try to come up with at least one more idea. Really push your limits so you feel confident that, as far as you can tell, all alternative solutions are represented.

At this point you have already brought your problem within manageable proportions because you have identified the parameters of its solutions. Focus on the fact that you have choices—even though no particular alternative holds the promise of being a panacea.

Armed with your list of alternative solutions, you are ready for the third step. You must now set about collecting as much information as possible concerning your various options. Perhaps some formal research is required; you might need to ask someone for input about his or her feelings and reactions to your proposed solutions. The concept of making an informed choice means that you need data or input to inform yourself.

The third step of information gathering is both critically important to the outcome of your problem solving and potentially disruptive at the same time. Many people become unrealistic or overly compulsive about collecting data so that the process becomes a form of procrastination instead of a method to facilitate decision making. This is a version of "analysis paralysis."

To guard against procrastination, keep in mind that there will always be some things that you simply cannot know, such as what will happen in the future. Moreover, there are categories or types of information that, while they would be desirable, are simply too difficult, costly, or time-consuming to obtain.

A good way to structure your information gathering is to formulate two or three main questions regarding each alternative, the answers to which would help inform your selection of a solution. Then make a plan for collecting the necessary information. You might, for example, believe that a given alternative or option would be too expensive to do. But in the absence of actual cost information your evaluation might be flawed. So Step Three would include collecting relevant price or cost information.

Inevitably, time is an important factor in problem solving. A "pressing" problem is one that requires a relatively fast response. Sometimes time constraints are placed externally on your data-gathering phase. Your boss, for example, might require your answer or decision by a particular date. When external time limits do not exist, it is wise to impose some constraints yourself. If you don't establish a cutoff point for your data gathering, you run the risk of procrastinating and even of confusing the issue with too much information.

Finally, if you feel pressured about making a decision, remember that gathering relevant, useful information about various alternatives is part of the decision-making and problem-solving process. Reassure yourself that you are in the process of making a decision when you are collecting the input you need.

Step Four is to assimilate the information from the third step and to write down the arguments in favor and against each alternative. Assign a weight of -1 to -10 to the "cons" of each option that reflects an overall subjective rating of how "bad" the downsides of that particular option, collectively considered, would actually be to you and/or others who might be affected. Give a score of -1 to arguments against an alternative solution that are only slightly bad or even neutral; score as -10 "cons" of a given option that represent dire consequences. Scores from -1 to -9 would reflect consequences of intermediate weight.

Similarly, give a weight to the relative "goodness" or positivity of the "pro" arguments of each option. Considered together, assess how good the consequences for each option would be to you. Score $+1$ this time if the consequences would be only marginally positive or almost neutral; score up to $+10$ for "pros" that represent consequences that would be terrific.

Now you have a weighting for how relatively good or bad, desirable or undesirable, each of your alternative solutions or decision options is.

The fifth step is to select the best alternative. Bear in mind that sometimes the "best" might actually mean "the least undesirable" option. Often, life problems are stressful precisely because there really is no good or right thing to do. In other cases, the best solution might be the one with the highest "good" ratings and the lowest overall "bad" ratings.

The Japanese have an ancient proverb that says, "To know and not to act is not to know at all." Step Six requires that you implement your selected solution. In most cases, you will already have obtained the necessary implementation information during the third step, since knowing exactly (or as exactly as you can) what is entailed in putting a solution into action is vital input to your evaluation and selection process.

Although you have selected and implemented an alternative, your problem solving is not yet complete. The final step is to reevaluate your decision on the basis of new information that comes as a result of the implementation phase.

You may be thoroughly satisfied that you have made a sound, effective choice. On the other hand, you might discover that what looked like a good idea on paper became a bad idea in fact. Most likely, you will see ways in which your solution requires some refinement.

Generally, especially with complex, ongoing issues in life, your final step will lead you right back to the first step again. Now, your new problem or decision will concern how to adjust and refine the implementation of the last solution so that it works even better.

To recap, the seven-step problem-solving method to ensure high-quality decisions is:

1. Define the problem as a decision to be made.
2. Brainstorm alternative solutions.
3. Collect relevant information.
4. Weigh the pros and cons of each alternative.
5. Select the best (or least undesirable) alternative.
6. Implement your decision.
7. Reevaluate and identify new problems.

The ongoing process of problem solving is really what is meant by good coping. Think of it not as a series of problems but rather as a series of solutions.

23

◆

Order on Chaos: Regaining a Sense of Control

◆

If you sweep the whole house, you will find everything.

—JEWISH PROVERB

Activities that help you to gain a sense of control—even if only illusory—also will help to reduce anxiety and improve your overall mood.

As you will see, these activities are not directly targeted at your mood or emotions. Rather, they are designed to impose order and cleanliness on what may seem to be a chaotic, disorganized, or messy environment; to regulate your eating, exercise, and personal health habits; and to structure and schedule your time and activities. While none of the activities is aimed directly at your low mood, the cumulative effect of doing them will be to make you feel much better.

These activities serve to enhance your sense or illusion of control in a number of ways. First, by ordering what has been previously chaotic in your environment, your internal sense of order will be positively affected. Second, getting things organized reduces the hassle factor of misplaced items or the loss of time involved in not being able to place your hands on something important that you may need. Next, activities that regulate personal health habits are just plain good for you. Moreover, taking care of yourself improves self-esteem and personal appearance. Better time management reduces stress and also improves self-esteem by increasing your sense of accomplishment. Finally, getting yourself and your environment neat, clean, well organized, and smooth-functioning can even provide you with a reassuring feeling of "righteousness."

Organizing and Cleaning Your Environment

One of the great advantages of activities that involve cleaning and organizing things when you feel down is that they generally require little in the way of mental horsepower. Consequently, they will serve you well during those inevitable bouts of low mental energy or motivation, when you simply can't get yourself cranked up to do more intellectually taxing or creative work. Nevertheless, organizational "no-brainer" activities do require enough moderate attention and concentration to divert your mind from worrisome ruminations.

Here is a sample list of activities that will help you to organize and clean your environment and, in the process, enhance your overall sense of control. Feel free to add whatever else might work for you.

1. Straightening up your home or office
2. Seriously cleaning (e.g., washing floors, woodwork, carpets, etc.)
3. Organizing your desk
4. Reorganizing files
5. Cleaning out drawers or closets
6. Sewing or mending articles of clothing
7. Repairing broken objects

8. Balancing your checkbook
9. Gardening
10. Cleaning, feeding, pruning houseplants
11. Organizing tapes, records, or books
12. Updating address books or Rolodex files
13. Buying and installing drawer, cabinet, or closet organizers
14. Sharpening pencils; throwing out old pens and pencils
15. Painting home or office walls
16. Refinishing or polishing furniture
17. Washing and/or waxing your car and cleaning the interior
18. Throwing out old magazines
19. Organizing and arranging photograph albums
20. Inventorying and restocking household goods and pantry items

There are many more activities of this kind. The important thing is to do two or three of the activities listed or ones of your own choosing when you feel down. You will get the biggest relief value from doing something that has been hanging over your head and bothering you for a long time. When you complete your work, take a step back, admire how neat, clean, and organized things look, and give yourself a reward for your hard efforts.

Regulating Diet and Exercise

Even if you are satisfied with your current weight, there is a value to going on an eating and exercise regimen geared toward optimal nutrition and fitness. If you do need or want to lose or gain weight, you have more good reason to follow a prescribed, nutritionally sound diet.

Most nutritionists agree that it is important to eat three meals a day with an added light fourth meal or snack. Keeping your eating within this kind of regular schedule, while avoiding in-between meal snacking or skipping meals, will regulate your metabolism for the best caloric burn and keep you feeling satisfied. If you don't know the fundamentals of nutrition, calories, the carbohydrate/protein/fat composition of foods, and methods of low-fat cooking, I suggest you visit your local bookstore and pick up a few guides.

With a demanding lifestyle and schedule, integrating exercise into your daily regimen may be more difficult than regular, healthy eating. But no excuses are acceptable here. Nobody is too busy to do what is good for her, and if you can't find the time to do 30 minutes of moderate exercise per day (at least five days a week), then you are indeed way too busy and should take immediate steps to reduce some of your other activities.

For the present purpose of regaining your sense of control, you should try to schedule your exercise at regular times each day. Wake up a little earlier in the morning if necessary and make your exercise period the top of your day. Or stop at the gym on your way home in the evening or go for a walk after dinner. The important thing is for you to develop a consistent regimen and stick to it. Not only will you enjoy all the antidepressant and figure-toning and -shaping benefits of exercise, but your sense of control will be greatly enhanced as will your overall energy level and sense of well-being.

Minding Your Health

How about that habit that you've been thinking about breaking for a long time now? Quitting smoking, stopping or lowering caffeine consumption, stopping or reducing alcohol consumption, or doing exercises for stretching your lower back are perfect examples of activities you could do now that would give you a much better sense of control. There is nothing like kicking an addiction or burdensome habit to make you feel as though you are back in charge of your own life.

Of course there are other things that you probably should do for your health but forget or just avoid doing. Do you floss your teeth every night? When was the last time you drank six glasses of water in a day? How about giving up those salty foods or at least cutting back substantially on sodium intake? There must be at least one positive health habit—and probably more—that you can incorporate into your daily practice. Doing so will not only improve your health but also, by increasing your sense of control, improve your mood as well.

Time Management

Clocks and timekeeping are universal methods for imposing structure on what would otherwise be only broadly demarcated phases of daytime and nighttime. You may want to impose even more order on your use of time through effective management techniques.

There are a number of good books and a host of magazine articles on time-management methods. One I recommend to patients is *How to Get Control of Your Time and Your Life* by Alan Lakein. Most of these guides emphasize the value of scheduling your projects, meetings, and work so that your time is used most efficiently and productively and so that you have the time to do the pleasurable activities you want to do, not just the things you have to do. Time management is designed to increase the amount of work you can accomplish while building in periods for necessary rest, relaxation, and exercise.

To gain better control of your allocations of time, it will be useful for you to keep a record of exactly how long you currently spend on the various things that you do throughout the day. You will probably discover that one source of your feeling that there is never enough time for all you have to do is that you are underestimating—probably by a significant factor—the time actually required to complete a given task. As a consequence, you overbook your time and wind up feeling that you haven't accomplished enough.

Using your Daily Mood Rating and Diary from Chapter 4, analyze how your energy level fluctuates at various times of the day. Most people have more energy to do creative or demanding work in the morning; most hit a slump in energy and motivation in the late afternoon. Knowing your mood and energy patterns will help you to schedule your time in ways that maximize your strengths while minimizing the impact of low points.

The most important point, for the purposes of this discussion, is not exactly how you manage your time, but rather that you manage it all. When you choose to structure your time more carefully and intentionally, you are gaining control of a precious resource. And you will be imposing a greater sense of order, which in turn will lead to a greater sense of internalized control.

24

◆

Controlling Crying

◆

*It is as much intemperance to weep too much as to
laugh too much.*

—THOMAS FULLER

While a good cry under the right circumstances can be an
enormously relieving and even pleasurable experience, crying under the wrong circumstances can be embarrassing,
frustrating, and downright undermining of your position and
intended message.

Clearly, women are far more prone to cry than most men,
at least under anything other than the most private circumstances. Even then, the difference probably still holds.

Since the basic physiological mechanism of crying
operates the same way in both sexes, the most likely explanation for the difference has to do with psychological and
cultural conditioning. Male infants and little boys cry every
bit as much as girls. But as early as age five or six, boys start
to get the message that it is not acceptable for males to
exhibit tears, at least not publicly, and certainly not in response to anything other than extremely emotional events
and/or great mental or physical pain.

But girls simply don't get the same message. It is acceptable—even expected—for girls to cry. Consequently, adult
women operate at a distinct disadvantage when it comes to

being able to control their overflowing tear ducts in situations where crying is considered inappropriate.

Most women cry in response to a great many more feelings than merely sadness. Indeed, if female tears corresponded only to sadness or pain, the dilemma would be far less troublesome. But women cry in response to frustration, anger, helplessness, rage, fear, anguish, anxiety, depression, and other emotions besides these, including, of course, great joy and happiness.

And to make matters worse, women cry in response to the very fact that they *are* crying in situations where they know their tears will only reinforce the worst stereotypes about females' undercontrolled emotions.

Inadequate Tear Control: A Sexual Analogue

For a number of years I have been working with women patients to develop behavioral methods to enhance control of involuntary crying. My approach, surprisingly, is based on the methods used for treating male sexual dysfunction—specifically, premature ejaculation.

The relationship between crying when you don't want or intend to and ejaculating too quickly is not as farfetched as you might think. In fact, the crying and ejaculation responses are, in my view, closely allied in the following ways: Both are involuntary reflexes that need to be brought under better voluntary control; both occur in response to a level of excitement or stimulation (positive for ejaculation and frequently negative for crying); in both cases, a willing subject can learn to become aware of the sensations that lead up to the response; and, finally, both involuntary crying and premature ejaculation are mediated by anxiety.

In other words, the common experience that gets in the way of controlling both reflexes is feeling highly anxious.

There are, to be sure, major differences between the two, which require no exposition. Nevertheless, I have applied behavioral techniques analogous to those used for treating

premature ejaculators—with some obvious modifications—
to help women retrain themselves to achieve far better voluntary regulation of their crying response.

NOTE: The best time for you to practice the exercises that
follow is when your mood is neutral or positive. Don't try to
do them when you are feeling low.

Describing the Sensations
That Occur Right Before Crying

The first step is to refine your awareness of what you are
experiencing, in terms of your internal bodily sensations,
when the crying response is triggered. Many women, for
example, describe a sense of heat rising to their face and a
pressure behind their eyes. Others describe how their facial
muscles first tighten in an attempt to fight back the tears and
then loosen as the crying begins.

Once your chin is trembling and your eyes are filled with
water, you have already begun crying. Your goal is to become
acutely sensitive to your internal cues right *before* this happens. A good way to do this is to understand the kinds of
feelings and/or situations that are associated with crying for
you—especially where you would rather not shed tears.

If, for example, you tend to cry when you feel enraged, try
to describe the physiological sensations that accompany anger. If you cry when you feel humiliated, embarrassed, or
insulted, try to describe in physical terms the internal sensations that correspond to these emotions.

The purpose of this exercise is to make you aware of
exactly how you feel when you are *about* to cry. By becoming
aware of these sensations, your voluntary control will be
enhanced, and you will be able to practice the following
control techniques, which require that you try to bring yourself right to the brink of actually crying without crossing over
the line into full-blown tearfulness or weeping.

Making Yourself Cry:
Sensory and Emotional Memory Methods

The first thing you need to do to practice the control exercises is learn how to make yourself cry. This is probably not something you are at all accustomed to doing, especially if your main focus has been on trying to stop yourself from shedding tears. But by learning how to induce crying on command you will be greatly increasing your voluntary control over the response.

"But this is acting!" you say. That is precisely what it is. And the best exercise for inducing crying is my adaptation of the techniques taught by the Method school of acting. Did you ever wonder how actresses are able to make themselves cry in a scene when the emotions that are represented in the script aren't their own?

What many of them do is call upon some very personal memory that makes them feel like crying. They try to feel as they were actually feeling in the situation they conjure up from their memories. And they try literally to "feel" the experience in a sensory way as well—how the fabric covering on a chair on which they were sitting felt, or the warmth of a person's touch to their skin, or the heat or cold of the climate in which they found themselves. So while they are speaking their lines from the script, the actresses also are internally *feeling*—both in emotion and sensation—exactly how they felt when they were in a scene from their personal history that made them overwhelmingly sad and tearful.

Now think back over your own life experience. Select a memory that evokes a great deal of emotion. For the present purpose, the scene from your memory should be one in which you cried. As you bring the scene from your memory clearly to mind, let yourself experience the emotions you experienced back then. Be very conscious of the internal sensations the emotions elicit. Focus on various parts of your body as you let yourself feel the sadness (or any other emotion that made you cry): How does your stomach feel? Your chest? Let yourself experience the emotion flowing throughout your body.

304

Visualize yourself in the scene from your memory. Can you recall what you were wearing? Think about the furniture around you or, if you were outside, the setting. Now, try to let yourself experience the sensations associated with the scene. Actually feel the touch of your clothing, or the wind, or the warmth or coldness of the air. See if you can trigger your sensory memory of the smells you associate with the scene.

By using emotional and sensory memories, your goal is to "be" in the scene from your memory. As you reexperience the feelings, you should also be aware that you are about to start crying. Stay with the sensations and emotions until you really begin to cry.

Obviously, you don't need to weep uncontrollably. Rather, I want you to learn what a powerful tool your own mind is and how much control you actually have over the crying response—at least to get it started.

If you weren't successful on your first try, don't worry. Either select a different memory, or try again to stimulate your emotional and sensory recall and let yourself become emotional. You don't have to do an award-winning performance. Your purpose here is to identify a personal memory that will serve as a reliable stimulus for crying so that you can practice the control teachniques below.

The Facial-Squeeze Technique

Now that you have become aware of the way you feel right before you start crying, you probably have identified the fact that your facial muscles tighten, your brow furrows, your eyes may close or squint, and you feel a buildup of pressure seeking the release that crying brings. Take a look at a baby's face right before a crying fit begins and you'll see what I mean.

Acting coaches whose purpose is to instruct students in how to release and express emotions often point to the facial muscular tightening as a reflexive way of holding back the tears. Therefore, they teach would-be actors and actresses who are working on an emotional scene that requires crying to relax the facial muscles in order to release the flood of tears.

Your purpose now is to do just the opposite. Remember, you are trying to become highly aware of the degree to which you can voluntarily control your tears. So instead of letting go, you will be doing just the opposite. As you feel the impulse to cry build, pinch your nose closed and intentionally squeeze your facial muscles as tightly as you can. While you are squeezing, place your tongue on the roof of your mouth and direct your breath back toward your ears as you would to clear your sinus passages when you are in a plane that is landing or when you are diving. Hold the squeeze for a count of five seconds, then let go. Do you still feel like crying?

Crying is an expulsive response. It represents a letting go of pent-up feeling. By doing the opposite of letting go—the facial squeeze—you are counteracting the crying response.

The Stop-Start Exercise

The stop-start technique combines the emotional and sensory memory methods of eliciting the crying response with the facial-squeeze technique in a repetitive exercise. To begin, recall the memory that makes you feel like crying. Right before you actually start to cry, make yourself stop by doing the facial squeeze for five seconds. Then take a few deep breaths and repeat the sequence. Bring yourself almost to the point of crying; then stop the response with the facial squeeze. Repeat the sequence four times, ending with breathing and cessation of crying. When you have completed the exercise successfully, you have proved to yourself that, at least in an exercise outside of an actual situation, you *can* interrupt and control your crying response. You have developed an important degree of voluntary control over crying that you never before believed you had.

Obviously, the facial-squeeze and stop-start techniques will not serve you in an actual face-to-face situation. The exercises are designed to teach you more awareness and control of the response outside the context of a stressful or upsetting situation. The challenge now is to control your tears in an actual interpersonal setting.

Emotional and Sensory
Memories Incompatible with Crying

The next step is to identify a particular feeling that for you is *incompatible with crying*. Ask yourself what feeling or set of feelings would be highly unlikely to cause you to start to cry.

Because women cry at so many different emotional cues, this may not be an easy question for you. Some of my patients have identified feeling strong, indifferent, detached, in charge, elated, brave, or cold as emotions they explicitly associate with *not* wanting or having the impulse to cry. You may use one of these or any other feeling that has personal meaning to you.

Again, you will use the emotional and sensory memory method to recall an experience in which you felt either strong or brave or however you have defined your emotional cue for *not* crying. Once again, visualize the scene and get in touch with the physical sensations associated with it. Keep the sensory and emotional memories salient in your mind until you actually feel as you did then—until you are feeling strong, or in charge, or indifferent. If you are doing the exercise correctly and have selected a good emotional memory for these purposes, you should *not* feel like crying.

Desensitizing Yourself to
the Situation That Elicits Crying

The next step is to address an actual situation—preferably something that you may face in the near future—about which you feel concerned that you might cry. Perhaps you envision a confrontation at work, or a discussion about your relationship with a man, or having to deal with a person who enrages or even tries to humiliate you. Obviously, these situations are inherently stressful. Moreover, the fear that you might cry when you least want to heightens the anxiety that anticipation of the situation arouses.

Assume a very relaxed posture, either lying down on your bed or couch, or comfortably reclining in a chair. Close your eyes and inhale deeply through your nose, while exhaling through your mouth. Try to inhale slowly to the count of seven; hold your breath for a moment and exhale slowly, again to the count of seven. Do this for a minute or two until you feel pretty relaxed.

Now, while maintaining your relaxed feelings as much as possible, visualize the stressful situation. Try to be very detailed in your imagery. Actually see what you are wearing and how you are sitting or standing. Visualize the other person in as much detail as you possibly can.

If your anxiety about crying is triggered by the possibility of an undesirable outcome, try to develop a "worst-case" scenario in your mind. If, for example, the stressful scene you envision concerns an impending salary or performance review in which you anticipate needing to challenge your boss or supervisor, let yourself imagine the worst thing that might happen or an occurrence that makes you think you might cry. Is he or she angry with you? Highly critical? Whatever you anticipate, visualize the scene.

As soon as you feel yourself tightening up and becoming anxious, open your eyes, count to 10, do some deep breathing and get relaxed again. Then, when you are comfortable, return to the visualization. Repeat this exercise until you are able to imagine the stressful scene while maintaining at least partial relaxation.

So far, you have used a potent behavior-modification technique designed to desensitize yourself, or lower your anxiety response to a fearful or stressful situation. The technique works by combining visual imagery with the physiological cues of relaxation. Next, you will combine the sensory memory of a feeling incompatible with crying and visual imagery.

Assume your relaxed position. This time, visualize yourself alone about 10 minutes before the anticipated meeting or situation. Perhaps you are in your office at work, or at home in your bedroom. What I want you to see in your mind's eye is yourself assuming the emotional state that you have identified as being incompatible with crying. You will visualize yourself becoming strong or brave or whatever your particular tearproof emotion is.

Now imagine yourself maintaining the selected emotional state while you enter the anticipated stressful scene. Actually see yourself in the meeting or confrontation armed with the protection of your tearproof feeling. If your situation, for example, is a confrontation with a work associate where you fear that you might cry, see yourself interacting with the person while behaving as though you were feeling strong, brave, in charge, or your own personally selected emotion that is incompatible with crying.

The most important part of this phase of the exercise is to *visualize* yourself handling the situation—no matter how stressful—without becoming emotionally unglued. See yourself dealing with the other person in a way that makes you feel proud. Focus on the fact that you have conquered the impulse to cry.

Putting the Techniques into Practice in Real Life

Finally, you will apply everything you have learned to the task of controlling involuntary crying in real life. The next time you face a situation that you anticipate may become upsetting to you, plan to spend at least five minutes by yourself prior to the occasion itself. Naturally, there are some events for which you are given no forewarning. But here you will be planning ahead for an anticipated stressful or upsetting experience.

To get five minutes alone, you may have to retreat to the women's bathroom, or perhaps you can go outside and find a place to be by yourself. When you are alone, begin your preparation by instructing yourself that you *are* able to bring your impulse to cry under control. You have done it repeatedly with the facial-squeeze and stop-start techniques that you have mastered.

Next, use your sensory and emotional memory method to induce the feeling that you associate with *not* crying. Since you have practiced at home and even visualized yourself successfully doing this, it should not be too difficult. Spend a minute or so becoming very focused on your protective emotion.

Now, you are ready to *act as if* you are internally braced so that it is impossible for you to cry. You should envision yourself surrounded by an invisible protective shield that represents your protective emotion. Instruct yourself as to how you want to behave in the situation you are about to face. Remind yourself again how much control you have over crying. Notice that your preparation exercises have dramatically lowered your anxiety.

The rest is up to you. I can assure you that I have taught these methods to a large number of patients who have put them into practice with great success. You will find, as have my patients, that once you have your first successful experience controlling crying in an actual situation, your confidence in your ability to resist tears when they are not wanted will increase greatly. With continued practice, you will be able to use the self-instructions and emotional memory methods spontaneously when you find yourself in a stressful situation for which you haven't planned or prepared.

Once you have learned that you can control your impulse to cry, your overall sense of being in control of your emotions will increase and your mood will improve as well.

25

◆

Conditioning Sensory Pleasures

◆

*People earnestly seek what they do not want, while
they neglect the real blessings in their possession—
I mean the innocent gratification of their senses,
which is all we can properly call our own.*

—MARY WORTLEY MONTAGU

When you feel down nothing seems as pleasurable to you as
when you are in a good mood. Food doesn't taste quite as
good, for example, and your tendency toward preoccupation
and rumination distracts you from really even seeing or hearing things that you might otherwise notice with satisfaction
and appreciation.

Activities that directly stimulate the five senses in pleasurable ways operate to restore more positive feelings.

Sensory Exercises

This chapter will provide you with a sample of exercises
that are targeted toward stimulating each, and a combination,
of the five senses. You may add any other sensory exercises
you wish, since the most important thing about the activities

is not what you do, but rather maintaining the proper mindset while you are doing them.

It is vital, therefore, that you concentrate your mental energy on the sense or senses being stimulated by the exercise. Since personal preferences in what constitutes pleasurable sensations must be considered, select only those activities that appeal to you. Don't try to force yourself to do something because it is "supposed" to be pleasurable when you know it to be uncomfortable or unpleasurable for you.

Concentrate on the sensory experience; don't allow distracting worries or intrusive thoughts to take hold of your mind. Simply let the thoughts occur if they happen, all the while trying to keep yourself focused on the pleasurable sensations that you are experiencing.

SIGHT

1. Take yourself to a beautiful natural setting such as a park, the beach, a lake, a river, or mountains. Focus your eyes on the beauty around you. Pay attention to the array of colors in nature. Take photographs if you like.

2. Visit a public garden. Let your eyes roam over the flowers and exotic plants. Go up very close to the flowers and examine the petals and leaves. Look for the intricacy of design which is the hallmark of nature's work.

3. Go to an art gallery or museum. Allow your eyes to rest on the paintings, sculpture, or other works of art that you admire most.

4. Buy a photography book—not a "how to" guide but a collection of works by a famous photographer. Direct your eyes to focus on the subtle nuances and shadings, especially in black-and-white photography.

5. Go to a movie or rent a video that has been praised for its cinematography. Pay particular attention to the scenery, the costumes, and the technical mastery of the film.

6. Go to a tropical-fish store or a public aquarium. Feast your eyes, particularly with saltwater fish, on the incredible delicacy of design and marvel at nature's palette of colors.

7. Go to a park, playground, or zoo and watch little children and/or animals. Think about how pleasurable it is to look at them play or take care of each other.

HEARING

1. Go to a concert of your favorite music. Close your eyes and marvel at the blending of sounds and rhythms.

2. Buy some new tapes or records. Try to listen to them with stereo earphones or a Walkman. Close your eyes and listen to the music inside your head.

3. Go to a beautiful natural setting and listen to the sounds of nature. Pay attention to every sound you hear, even if it is the hush of quiet or the rustle of wind in the trees.

4. Buy an audiocassette of a novel or works of poetry recorded by an actor or actress whom you know to have a mellifluous or lovely, resonant voice that you particularly like. As you hear the words, listen to the voice itself as a kind of music to your ears.

5. Watch a television program of a virtuoso performance by a musician or singer. As you watch, focus on what you are hearing and remark on the person's innate ability to generate such inspiring sounds.

6. If you live near an ocean or lake, go to the beach. Lie down on the sand, close your eyes, and listen to the sound of waves rushing to the shore and back again, or at a lake, the gentle sound of water lapping onto the shore.

TOUCH

1. Go to a fabric store and explore the different textures of a variety of textiles. Close your eyes as you run your fingers over the cloth.

2. Get a massage from a skilled masseuse. Feel the strength in her hands and the tension releasing from your muscles as your body is massaged.

3. Get a facial. Close your eyes and feel the pleasurable sensation of the steam, the massage of your face, the lotions and treatments as each is applied. When you are finished, close your eyes and feel your own face. Notice how soft and smooth your skin feels.

4. Make love with your partner, paying close attention to all the tactile sensations of his body and yours. Keep the lights off or low so that your sense of touch is heightened.

5. Pet and cuddle a puppy, kitten, dog, or cat (but only if you're a true animal lover). Feel the softness of its fur, the coldness of its nose, and the gentle folds of its skin.

6. Give a baby a bath or just hold a baby and feel the smoothness of his or her skin.

7. Buy an automatic foot soaker/massager. Feel the warmth on your tired feet and concentrate on how relaxed the massage action makes you feel all over.

SMELL

1. Bake some cookies or bread and enjoy the wonderful aroma that permeates your kitchen and the rest of your house.

2. Visit a bakery early in the morning and inhale through your nose. (Buy something at the same time so the baker doesn't think you are strange.)

3. Go to a perfume counter in a department store and indulge your olfactory sense with your favorite scents.

4. If you love Italian food, cook something delicious or go out to your favorite restaurant and indulge yourself in the aromas of garlic, tomato, onion, and whatever else is in the kitchen.

5. If you love coffee, go to a coffee store or your grocery where they have bins of whole beans. Open four or five (or sniff the outside of the individual bags) and focus on the richness and complexity of the various aromas.

6. If you love wine, go to a wine tasting or buy some special red and white wines for you and some friends. Try to refine your sense of smell enough to identify a particular varietal grape or even a specific label. As you check the "nose" on various wines, learn what is meant by the various terms that wine experts use, such as "fruity," "like vanilla," "oakey," and so forth.

7. Hold a baby and get a whiff of how good he or she smells. (Be sure to choose the *right* time.) Or hold a puppy (if you like them) and enjoy its distinctive aroma.

TASTE

1. Arrange a taste table of foods that runs the gamut of textures, temperatures, crunchiness, richness, saltiness, sweetness, sourness. Close your eyes and let your taste buds take control.

2. If you bought the wine and went to the wine tasting, sip the selection and learn what is meant by the different taste descriptors that wine experts use, such as "buttery," "dry," "full-bodied."

3. Cook a wonderful dinner, if you're a good cook, or go out to your favorite restaurant and try to savor each biteful of food. Eat very slowly and think about the unique tastes you are experiencing with each bite.

4. Think of a candy that you loved as a child. Treat yourself to some and focus on the taste and on the memories the taste conjures up.

5. Go to an ice cream store, if you love ice cream, and try a new flavor on a cone. As you lick the ice cream slowly, focus on the sensations of coldness, smoothness, sweetness, and richness that you are experiencing.

6. Set up a cheese tasting table (maybe with the wine) to enjoy with friends. Get a wide array of cheese (if you love cheese) along with different types of crackers, bread, and fruit. As you try various combinations, focus on the richness, fullness, and complexity of tastes and flavors in your mouth.

7. Have a beef or chicken fondue dinner, or a curry dinner, or a fajitas dinner (meat or chicken grilled with green peppers and onions inside a flour or corn tortilla). These offer the opportunity to create your own variety of tastes by using different sauces or condiments. Focus on the unusual and pleasurable taste sensations you are experiencing.

COMBINING SENSORY PLEASURES

1. Take a soothing bath by candlelight. Bring in a portable radio or tape player and play your favorite music softly. Perfume the bathwater with warm, scented bath oil or bubblebath. As you immerse yourself, focus on the pleasurable sensations you are experiencing.

2. Go on a picnic in a beautiful park—alone or with someone whose company you enjoy. Bring an array of different tastes, textures, and flavors in your picnic basket. If you have a portable cassette player or radio, turn on some of your favorite music (classical makes a picnic seem elegant). Try sitting on the grass and feel the blades of grass with your bare toes. Watch the dogs and kids and look up at the sky.

3. Go snorkeling—if you like the water, beautiful fish, and can get away to a resort that offers some choice spots. As you snorkel, be conscious of the sun, the sparkling clarity of the water, the beauty of the life below the surface of the water, and the sensation of being immersed in another world.

4. Soak in a spa or hot tub with a tape deck or radio nearby. Tune in your favorite music, listen to the bubbling water, and feel the heat unwind your tense muscles.

5. Do any one of your favorite sports, especially one that involves a pretty setting such as skiing, sailing, horseback riding on pretty trails, or scuba diving. As you engage in the physical activity, pay special attention to the sensory experiences that are involved. Be conscious of every sense—sight, hearing, taste, smell, and touch.

Don't Wait Until You're in the Mood

Until now, you've probably ordered your life so that you avail yourself of the opportunities to experience sensory pleasures when you are already in a pretty good mood. Naturally, to do so enhances your already positive state and protects your mood from slipping.

Now, however, I am telling you to stimulate your sensory pathways precisely when you are *not* necessarily in the mood—when you are feeling down. You must rely on the fact that by putting the behavior first, your mind and your mood will follow.

26

◆

Fine-tuning Your Mood

◆

Man is the artificer of his own happiness.

—HENRY DAVID THOREAU

In the chapter "How Black Are Your Blues?" you were asked to evaluate the three dimensions of your mood state: pleasure, activity or alertness, and sense of control.

Now that you have learned most of the activities that will help you to restore a more positive mood, you can actually fine-tune your mood state so that it comes as close as possible to the optimal profile. You will recall from Chapter 4 that the most desirable mood state is one that has the scores of 8 to 9 on the pleasure dimension, 4 to 6 on activity/ alertness, and 7 to 8 on your sense of control. This would mean that your mood would feel very or extremely pleasant to you; that your arousal level was "up" enough to feel energized, but not so overrevved that you would feel hyper, manic, or agitated; and that you would feel very much, though not totally or compulsively, in control.

Take the measure of your own mood state right now, using the scales on page 55. If your scores are in the ideal range you are in an optimal mood state. The activities you have been learning should be used to maintain your positive mood and protect it against slipping.

But if your mood scores on any or all of the three dimensions are outside of the optimal range, as they surely will be when you feel down, agitated or lacking in energy, and not very much in control, you can select activities with an almost surgical precision and with the specific intention of moving your score higher or lower on each dimension until it is closer to your optimal desired range.

Adjusting the Pleasure Dimension

The only direction in which to move your score on the dimension of how pleasant or unpleasant you feel is up. Even if you are in a good mood, remember that you should take responsibility for mood protection and maintenance.

If your mood score on the first dimension is lower than 8, focus your activities around pleasurable D.I.B.'s, including games or sports you enjoy, being with people whom you like, engaging in pleasurable activities, and laughter.

In addition, you should be sure to include at least three activities from the sensory pleasures lists in Chapter 25.

These activities are most closely related to your brain's pleasure centers and are designed to have the most direct impact on the pleasant-unpleasant dimension of your mood.

I know that when you are feeling down you don't much want to do the kinds of things that you would naturally think about doing if you were in a better state of mind. But that is no excuse. In fact, it is the best reason for *forcing yourself* to do one or two of the pleasurable activities, in spite of how you are feeling. You will be surprised to learn how effectively pleasure stimulates the desire for more good feelings. Once you get yourself going, your motivation will take care of itself as long as you stay committed to the program.

Adjusting the Activity-Alertness Dimension

It feels best to be right in the midrange on this dimension. Therefore, if your score is too high—7 or more—you will need to do activities that produce a sense of relaxation and result in slowing you down a bit; if your score is too low—3 or less—you are underactive, low on energy, or mentally sluggish, and you will need to do activities designed to "rev" you up, stimulate you mentally, and energize you physically.

If you are too high on this dimension, try doing some aerobic exercise for 20 to 30 minutes (assuming you are in shape to do so, less time if you are not), so that you work up a good sweat and burn up some of your excess nervous energy. You might also try some pleasurable relaxing activities such as soaking in a spa or hot tub; taking a bath by candlelight; taking a walk in a park, by the beach, or in another pretty setting; getting a massage; listening to calming music; or practicing mental minivacations.

One of the best relaxation exercises is progressive muscle tensing and releasing. To do this, lie down on a bed or couch and regulate your breathing by inhaling through your nose to the count of seven, holding your breath for a second or so, and then exhaling slowly through your mouth, also to the count of seven. Try to picture waves rolling to and from the shore and keep your breathing as rhythmic as the ocean.

Now, focus your concentration on your right hand. Close your fist in a tight ball, hold it for five seconds, then release your hand slowly. Repeat the tensing and releasing three times. Next concentrate on the muscles of your right arm: tense and release, three times.

Continue the sequence of tense-release, channeling your concentration up your right arm; then from your left hand up your left arm; right foot, knee, and whole leg; left foot, knee, and leg; stomach, buttocks, and facial muscles. The entire sequence shouldn't take you much longer than about 10 to 20 minutes and will help to release the tension stored in your body.

Feeling hyperalert may result from being mentally over-stimulated. The distraction and diversion D.I.B.'s and the laughter D.I.B.'s are effective adjustment exercises. If you are worrying obsessively about an unresolved problem, you might try the worry regulators in Chapter 21 as well as the active problem-solving technique in Chapter 22. And if your mood is overactive from trying to be everything to everybody, you may need some of the other Type E stress-management methods in Chapter 16.

If, on the other hand, you are too low on energy, you will need to activate yourself. Physical activity is what you need, even though you feel inclined to collapse and pull the covers over your head. The best activities for stimulation are games or sports, but any kind of movement that raises your heart rate and boosts your metabolism will suffice.

The sensory pleasure exercises are designed to awaken your senses and will therefore awaken you as well. Focus in particular on sensory exercises that are *active,* since you don't need to get yourself any more relaxed than you already are.

A number of sources of mental stimulation are available that also will serve to build self-esteem by raising your mastery and accomplishment levels while increasing your alertness. Many people find controversial talk shows or political discussion shows stimulating. Try watching a television quiz show, preferably one that allows you to match wits with the contestants. Exciting books or movies also can energize you when you are underalert.

If you are a sports fan, watching a televised game or, better yet, attending as a spectator can get your blood going and wake you up. Playing a competitive card or board game might help, as will listening to upbeat popular music with a strong rhythm or an exuberant classical piece or symphony.

Finally, if you are too low on energy, it is possible that you are sleeping too much. Yes, I said "too much." Contrary to popular myths, most healthy adults can function quite well on less than eight hours of sleep. In fact, patients with major clinical Depression have been treated successfully by lowering their sleep time. Try cutting back by 30 minutes for a few nights and see how you feel. Then try staying up or waking earlier by another 30 minutes. Many of my patients have reported feeling energized on six hours of sleep, whereas they were chronically tired on eight or nine. Be sure as well that your diet is nutritionally balanced and that you are getting an adequate supply of daily vitamins.

Adjusting the Control Dimension

Your optimal mood state should be one in which you feel that you are mostly in control. However, you do not want to become compulsive about order or about maintaining control of yourself as well as everybody around you. Obviously, if you are 9-plus on the third dimension, you need to lighten up. Try some relaxation methods and go back and reread Chapter 9 on accepting what you can't change or control.

For the most part, though, your low moods are likely to reflect feeling less in control than you would like. In Chapter 23 there are numerous suggestions for activities that will indirectly or directly raise your score on this dimension. Practicing the crying exercises, provided your mood is not already very sad or low, will also augment your sense of control. The Type E exercises are designed to help you regain control over the demands of your time and energy and should help to raise your control score.

Active problem solving also will help you to feel more in control by bringing your alternatives into focus and making you feel that you are doing something constructive about a problem or decision that has felt overwhelming to you. Anything new that you learn or can do to improve on the skills and talents you already have will enhance your sense of mastery and control, as well as build your self-esteem.

Aim for Improvement, Not Perfection

Shooting for scores in the optimal ranges on the three mood dimensions is neither unrealistic nor perfectionistic. Score yourself the next time you feel as though you are in a very good mood, and you should find that your ratings fall right in the optimal range.

When you are feeling very low, however, your scores are likely to be quite far from the desirable points. The purpose of your activities is to repair your mood so that it feels *better*—not necessarily great and certainly not perfect. Your goal should be improvement, however gradual, so that your scores move in the right direction. Don't set yourself up for failure or give yourself rationalizations for quitting the program by expecting a few activities fully to repair a very low mood immediately. That would be self-sabotaging and self defeating.

Ask Yourself What You Need

As you become more and more adept at mood management, you will be able to recognize when your mood is "off" and to identify quickly which dimension or dimensions need repair and which need protective maintenance. And you will know exactly what to do to feel better.

Trust your inner adviser to know what is best for you. Ask your "best self" this question: "What do I need today?" You have the tools, techniques, and methods now to give yourself exactly what you need in order to restore a more positive mood.

27

◆

The Importance of
Scheduling Activities

◆

Each morning sees some task begun,
Each evening sees its close.
Something attempted, something done,
Has earned a night's repose.

—HENRY WADSWORTH LONGFELLOW

In order to make the activity step of the Triple A Program work for you, it is essential that you prepare personal activity schedules for each day. Planning ahead will ensure that you have set aside the time to do what you need to and will also help improve your mood by giving you lots of fun things to anticipate.

All behavioral approaches to treating mood problems emphasize the importance of making and keeping to schedules. It is widely believed among psychologists that the act of scheduling, in and of itself, is therapeutic. Looking back over your completed activity schedules after a week or two also will give you an important sense of accomplishment.

Make Mood Management a Priority

Scheduling activities that are designed to improve your mood demands that you make the program a priority. If you believe that other things are more important than improving your mood and self-esteem, you are making a serious mistake. The quality of your performance at work, your relationships, and your health are all negatively affected when you feel down. It is in everybody's best interests, therefore, for you to keep your mood as stable and positive as possible.

Making mood management a priority is not selfish. It is self-protective. Scheduling selected activities from the program, as well as those that you have added to your individualized activity regimen, guarantees that you *will* keep your priorities straight.

Maintaining Psychological Fitness

People who are committed to physical fitness not only make exercise a priority, but are proud to announce that fact to others. "Needing" to work out or go to an exercise class is widely accepted as a valid explanation for adjusting or canceling appointments and dates.

Your psychological fitness should be every bit as important as a physically sound body. Indeed, as I have emphasized throughout this book, the two are intimately related. You won't find it as difficult to modify your customary daily regimen to accommodate mood-management activities once you adopt the proper attitude.

How to Schedule Activities

In starting the mood-management program, try to accomplish three to five activities per day. Naturally, some will take only minutes to accomplish, whereas one or two might require more time and effort. Don't overschedule your time, but on the other hand, don't be so easy on yourself that you revert back into old habits of staying passive, inactive, and ruminative.

Many of the D.I.B.'s are actions looking for opportunities. In other words, being sociable, giving praise, looking for the best in people, or listening and helping others require that you set your intention in the morning by adopting the attitude that, given a suitable opportunity (some of which you can of course create), you will perform a D.I.B. These kinds of activities merely need to be scheduled by way of notation at the beginning of your day such as "Look for ways to be helpful to others," "Remember to compliment and praise people honestly for what they do well," or "Put on 'rose-colored' glasses."

Other activities, however, require more precise scheduling. If you are learning a new sport, you will probably need to arrange lessons by appointment with an instructor. Some of your pleasurable activities will require advance planning and even may involve traveling. It is a good idea to try to balance your activities between those that necessitate precise scheduling and those that can be fit into "open" times that you keep blocked out during the day for a self-esteem builder or similar exercise.

Be conscious of your limitations as you prepare your schedules. Do not, for example, expect yourself to do three mentally demanding activities after a particularly heavy day. While it is vitally important that you keep to your schedules, it is also important to maintain a flexible attitude in case some rescheduling becomes necessary.

Do Activities in
Graded Order of Difficulty

When you are feeling down, some of the activities may seem too difficult or demanding. As you become familiar with the majority of activities in the program, you will have a clearer idea of exactly how much effort each will require.

On the basis of your reading, however, you can probably estimate with reasonable accuracy how difficult each recommended activity might be. Start with the easiest ones initially. Try your best to do three activities on the first day of the program. Remember that you will have to force yourself somewhat into an active mode if you have been down and low on energy for a while. Stay at the same level of difficulty and time expenditure for a few days with either the same or different but equivalent activities. Then add one or two activities to your schedule that seem to require slightly more effort or appear somewhat more difficult.

This method of scheduling is called *graded task difficulty* and ensures that you will have success experiences from the beginning of the program. Your motivation will improve as you gradually but successfully increase your quantity of activities as well as their difficulty or time requirements.

Keep Your Daily Mood
Ratings and Diary

Use the Daily Mood Rating Form and Diary on page 55 throughout your mood-management program. Each day, evaluate your mood. Review your schedules and mood ratings after each week. Be particularly attentive to the relationship between doing positive, pleasurable activities and improvements in your mood ratings. This self-monitoring will be the best reinforcement for your efforts.

Don't worry about normal mood fluctuations. Everyone's mood goes through ups and downs over the course of a week's time. You are looking for overall trends for the better and should not be disturbed by slight slips that may simply be due to hormonal factors or external events.

Mood-Maintenance
Activities as a Way of Life

Once you learn how to get yourself up when you are feeling down, you won't spend nearly as much time as you have in the past suffering from the blues and being in the doldrums. Downturns in mood are inevitable, but your ability to bound back will become stronger and more like second nature.

The activities outlined in this section can and should become part of your normal way of life. It is your responsibility to do what you can to keep yourself happy, productive, and positive about life.

PART FIVE

Conclusion

28

◆

The Triple A Program: Putting It All Together

◆

Fortune helps them who help themselves.

—ENGLISH PROVERB

When new patients ask me how long I think their total course of psychotherapy will last, I generally reply that it is largely up to them. "The best day for me," I usually tell them, "is the day that we shake hands, say farewell, and I wish you good luck in taking full charge of your own life."

You and I have almost reached the best point. My job in teaching you the attitudes, techniques, skills, and information necessary for you to become a highly effective manager of your low moods is just about complete. The measure of *your* success, however, will be whether or not you commit to putting what you have learned into practice as part of your everyday life. If and when you do, I know that the quality of your life will improve as the blue moods and depressions of which you once were a passive victim become subject to your capable control.

But before we conclude, let's start from the top and review exactly how to follow the Triple A Program the very next time you feel even a little bit low.

By learning about mood management, you are now far more sensitive and aware of your blue moods and their warning signs than you ever have been before. So the next time your mood starts to slip, you will immediately recognize the prodromes or warnings of the early stage of depression. Hopefully, your emotional barometer will become so sensitive that you will detect when a change in your mood state is imminent even before the blues actually hit.

What do you do first? As soon as possible after you recognize a prodrome, you will want to distract your attention from your inner emotions by diverting your mind elsewhere. Ideally, you also will engage in some form of physical activity. Sometimes, as you know, your shift in mood may be truly transitory so that becoming overly focused on it may only have counterproductive consequences. Since you are in the "Blue Alert" mode, you will be appropriately suspicious that your thinking may be negatively biased and distorted.

After an hour or so, you will check with yourself again as to the state of your mood. If your mood has recovered to a normal or even positive level after a temporary downswing, then you need to do nothing more. You will have successfully averted a bout of depression.

On the other hand, if your recheck indicates that you still feel down, or perhaps that your mood has sunk even lower, you will immediately move forward to Step One: *Accept that you are feeling depressed.*

In accepting that you have a mood problem that needs repair work, you will maintain a confident attitude of *control*. You feel down but you know that there are things that you can do to make yourself feel much better. Knowing that you are in control, you will grant yourself unconditional, nonjudgmental permission to feel blue, although you will decline giving in to the depression. You will not engage in any futile resistance thinking. Remember that *you* are not depressed— your mood and feelings are.

To get a better grasp of your mood problem, you will quickly assess its three dimensions: how pleasant or unpleasant it feels; how physically active or mentally alert you feel; and how much in or out of control you feel.

Since you will not fall into the trap of obsessing over trying to change things that are not within your control to change, your energy will be properly channeled toward those things that are yours to alter.

The entire first step of the program will only require a matter of minutes to complete. Then you will move directly forward to Step Two: *Attribute your depressed mood to its proper cause.*

First you will locate the causal source of your low mood— is it primarily Event-Centered, Thought-Centered, or Feeling-Centered? You will use your knowledge about cognitive errors, self-blame, and negative thinking to make corrective reattributions about the reasons that you feel depressed. You also will do a quick mental survey of some of the common causes for low moods such as too much stress, a problem with a man, a date on the calendar, or another unresolved problem in order to determine what might be causing your drooping spirits.

But all the while that you are seeking to find the reason behind your down-turned mood, you will be careful *not* to slip into rumination, self-criticism, or repetitive worry. And you will use the proper means to counter any of these natural depressive tendencies should they arise.

The second step also should be relatively short in duration. If the cause or reason for your low mood is not apparent to you within half a hour or so, you will know that the wise thing to do is to let go of the search for a while and move on to the next step. After your mood is improved through positive action, its causes are likely to become clearer to you. While attaining full understanding of your low mood will be important and desirable, you will be very conscious of the risks involved in using the search for "why" as a form of procrastination. Moreover, as a skilled mood manager, you will know that the best thing you now can do is Step Three: *Act to restore a positive mood.*

Your repertoire of activities already will have been developed from your work in learning the third program step. Now you will select the D.I.B.'s that work best for you and that can be done immediately. In addition to behaviors that are incompatible with feeling down, you will tailor your other activities to the particular nature of your mood. If you are agitated, you will do things that calm you down or help you to actively solve your problems. If you are too lethargic, you will seek stimulating activities.

Fine-tuning your mood by engaging in behaviors that increase the organization of your environment and your self-discipline will also move your sense of control toward the higher end of the scale. If your mood feels decidedly unpleasurable, you will force yourself to do activities that will enhance your pleasure level, even though you may not be "in the mood" to do them. You will now have the insight to understand that in mood management, the rule is to do the behavior first, and let your mind follow.

The activity step has no beginning or end, since you will have integrated many of its aspects into your daily routine. Because you will be repairing your low mood, however, you will be increasing your level of activity and targeting problem areas with a precise focus. Your expectations for feeling better will be realistic, and you will give yourself credit for following the program, recognizing that, depending on how low your mood had fallen, improvement may be gradual, though eventually complete.

As your positive mood is restored, your self-esteem and commitment to the Triple A Program similarly will rise. You will notice that your fearfulness about becoming depressed again in the future has abated. And you will understand your responsibility to play an active role in protecting and maintaining the good mood you now will have regained.

Finally, congratulations. You have completed a thorough self-study course in mood management. You now know what you need in order to take charge of your own emotional life. You have learned the secrets to getting up when you are feeling down.

So, on that upbeat note, I wish you good luck and farewell.

About the Author

◆

DR. HARRIET BRAIKER is a practicing clinical psychologist in Los Angeles, where she has helped hundreds of patients conquer low moods, the blues, and common feelings of depression. Her groundbreaking book, *The Type E Woman*, which originated the concept of Type E stress, was met with international acclaim. As director of The Praxis Training Group, a management consulting firm, she conducts seminars and workshops on stress and mood management for corporations, hospitals, and health centers throughout North America. A highly sought-after speaker, Dr. Braiker also is a contributing editor to *Working Woman* magazine.